GRAZIOSO CECCHETTI

COMPLETE MANUAL OF CLASSICAL DANCE

ENRICO CECCHETTI METHOD

Volume 1

With the author's own drawings

Edited by
Flavia Pappacena

Translated by
Ann Franklin

GREMESE

Originally published in Italian as
Manuale completo di danza classica

Drawings:
Grazioso Cecchetti

Photocomposition and Photolithography:
Graffiti - Rome

Cover:
Fabrizio Patucchi

Printed and bound by:
SO.GRA.TE. - Città di Castello (Italy)

We would like to thank the Bernardini family
for their kind permission to publish the Manual.
Special thanks also to Livia Brillarelli
to whom we owe the rediscovery of the book.

ISBN 88-7301-072-5

CONTENTS

Part Two: Port de Bras

Part Three: Exercises in the centre

BOOK THREE

Part One: Poses

Part Two: Adagio Movements

Part Three: The Adagi

PREFACE

The rediscovery of the work of Grazioso Cecchetti, son of the great Italian Maestro, is of particular importance. It is the only direct testament to the profession, mentality and culture handed down from generation to generation of the Cecchetti family and which made the method of great Italian maestro Enrico Cecchetti so famous.

The text was conceived in the Italian tradition of practical-theoretical treatises. It follows a rigorous academic structure, and is characterized by detailed theoretical and methodological analysis and a clear didactic program. This illustrates not only the principles and rules (i.e. the theory), but also the correct execution and use (i.e. the practice) of each movement, step, pose, exercise and combination. The author goes beyond a schematic description – thorough and detailed though this is – to more deeply explore the aesthetic, scientific and didactic principles behind the method, even revealing some "family secrets." This offers subsequent teachers the logical and methodological means by which to penetrate the artistic and technical essence of dance and with which to train the pupil in critical analysis – "mental gymnastics." This is considered just as fundamental to the pupil's intellectual and artistic accomplishment as is a high level of general culture in the fields of literature, music and the fine arts (painting and drawing).

Grazioso Cecchetti was a true Cecchetti in every sense. He was born in St. Petersburg in 1892 and was still very young when he studied under his father's method at Enrico's private school in St. Petersburg, alongside his mother Giuseppina De Maria. He then carried on the family tradition as a choreographer (also in collaboration with his uncle Giuseppe) and a director of dance schools. After an interval due to financial difficulties and the events of World War I, his father helped him to open a photographic studio (after the birth in 1925 of his second son from his marriage to Rina Diberti). Ten years later, in 1935, he founded his dance school in Turin, at Via Lagrange 29: the Classical Dance Academy Scuola E. Cecchetti. This was destroyed in an air-raid in 1943. At the end of the war, during which he had been deported to Germany for a year, he was engaged by the Ente Autonomo Lirica e Concerti di Torino (later the Ente Autonomo del Teatro Regio) as director and ballet master of the ballet school, a post he held from 1945 to 1951. At the end of his appointment he opened a school in Paris: the Académie Enrico Cecchetti. About two years later he transferred the school to Turin, where he died in 1965.

During his years as director of the ballet school of the Turin theatre (to which he dedicates the first part of the text regarding the organization of a dance school and its courses) Grazioso worked on the material which, in agreement with his father, he had gathered with a view to publication.

The text, entitled Trattato generale teorico-pratico della danza classica [General treatise on the theory and practice of classical dance], *had a long period of gestation. It was typewritten in three successive versions, dating from 1946 to 1956, and was intended for worldwide publication. The first contract was made in 1954 with the Parisian publisher Richard-Masse for a French edition under the title,* Traité générale théorique et pratique de danse académique. *This work, whose translation was entrusted to Ferdinando Reyna, was to appear in two volumes with around four hundred illustrations and completed by a third volume containing the musical scores for all the exercises. In 1959, after several revisions, the contract was annulled and, despite the amount of advance publicity the publisher had given the book, Grazioso Cecchetti's work was not published. Indeed, it appears from the correspondence regarding the work that it had been the focus of a great deal of international interest.*

Except for a few small alterations made to the text and the title (chosen for editorial reasons), in this edition we present the work of Grazioso Cecchetti in its original form. As in the original, the text is divided into two volumes, the first of which covers theory (Book One); barre exercises, ports de bras, exercises in the centre (Book Two); poses, adagio movements, adagi (Book Three). The second volume deals with allegro exercises, pointe work and turns, exercises in turns, enchaînements, variations (Book Four); the programs and a glossary of dance terms (Book Five). The musical score referred to in the text and which was to have formed the third volume, will be published separately.

The drawings used here are the original sketches that Grazioso Cecchetti himself made in 1956 to be used as a basis for the illustrations in the French version of the book; we have also reproduced his graphic scheme for the exercises in the second volume. Also copied faithfully from the original is the terminology which, in the Italian tradition, is a complex and eclectic language resulting from the overlaying of French academic terminology of the eighteenth and nineteenth centuries, with traditional Italian expressions and more modern definitions which arise principally from the Paris Opéra.

With regard to the translation of the Italian terms so widely employed by the author, we have adopted the following criteria: a) terms derived from the academic Italian terminology of past centuries have been translated into the traditional French equivalent (therefore tempo *becomes* temps, filato *becomes* filé, col di piede *becomes* cou de pied, arabesca *becomes* arabesque, mezza piegata *becomes* demi-plié, appiombo *becomes* aplomb, mezza altezza *becomes* demi-hauteur *and so on); b) those expressions specific to the Italian school, such as* legati, *have been translated into the equivalent historical term (therefore* legati *becomes* enchaînements – *not* liaison *as cited elsewhere by Grazioso and Enrico;* sciogliere *becomes* dégager*); c) the terms which appear in both the French and Italian variants have been standardized according to the French version as defined by Grazioso himself in the glossary at the end of the second volume (e.g.* arabesca aperta *becomes* arabesque ouverte*).*

The resulting vocabulary may seem somewhat inconsistent, at times even contradictory (for example, the synonyms effacé *and* ouvert *are both found, the former picked up by Enrico Cecchetti in Russia, the latter used in the old French tradition). However, it is precisely this aspect that renders the terminology so interesting. Alongside the eclectic and expressive phraseology of the Italian tradition, we find a rigid and scientific approach to structure and basic methodological principles typical of the nineteenth-century Italian methods, which is nevertheless alive and in constant evolution, as shown by Grazioso's record of his father's theory, and by Enrico himself in his own writings (currently being published in the Italian magazine* Chorégraphie*).*

Rome, April 1997

Flavia Pappacena

ORGANIZATION OF A CLASSICAL DANCE SCHOOL

The classical dance school, like all other academic schools, requires organization and planning to make it technically balanced and compatible. Everything proceeds with mathematical precision; every movement having a precise purpose.

From the choosing of the aspiring young dancer to the full-fledged graduate, the instruction follows through systematically and methodically.

General rules

The enrolment procedure is quite simple and logical, the requirements being:

1. entrance form completed and signed by the parents or guardian;
2. birth certificate of the candidate;
3. medical certificate of health and fitness.

The examining board will first assess the candidate's physique, to determine his (or her) suitablity for training in dance.

On admission to the school, the candidate provides the special shoes and uniform required. The timetable must be strictly adhered to and the pupil willingly and enthusiastically puts his trust in the teaching of the maestro.

For the first two years only the teacher decides who is disqualified or who passes to a higher level.

At the end of three years, selection will be by a board of examiners. At this time those elements who have been seen to be unresponsive to the teaching will be eliminated; this has the dual purpose of:

1. giving these youngsters the possibility of taking up other work or a profession to which they are more suited;
2. not creating inferior artists who must always struggle to find work, degrading the art, contributing to its decadence.

For the remainder of the courses, the final exams at the end of the year are presided over by the same board of examiners.

At the end of the intermediate course, when the pupil has passed the necessary exams, he is given a certificate by the school stating which studies have been completed. From that moment on, the pupil is sufficiently trained to dance in the corps de ballet with honor and decorum.

At the end of the final year the pupil is licensed and receives the regular Diploma of the solo dancer; he can certainly be proud of his school.

The final judgement of the board of examiners allows the (female) pupils with the highest marks to be named: First Pupil and Second Pupll.

If they continue their studies with a year of "perfection," they will certainly be given the title: Prima Ballerina.

With hard work and enthusiasm throughout their training and careers, they can even achieve the coveted goal, Prima Ballerina êtoile, enjoying the fame and glory of great artists. This is the reward for sacrifice, tenacity and hard work.

The period of the scholastic year is the same for all schools, from September/October until the following June.

Complementary to the study of dance

The study of classical dance is one of the obvious academic premises of this art. However, a true artist should have a good, solid cultural base including studies in literature, the fine arts and music.

The brain must be trained as well as the legs. The essence of dance can never be understood or performed by a strictly technical dancer.

A dancer with a deficient culture will never be able to give an intelligent, lively interpretation or have enough warmth of feeling to be convincing and charming. The execution of movements, poses and virtuosity may well appear to be technically perfect but they will be lifeless and colorless, dry and mechanical; in other words, meaningless and therefore completely uninteresting.

For this reason we believe that a training in dance should be accompanied, wherever possible, by a suitable literary course. The most important of all is the study of fine arts, especially drawing and painting; particular reference to be made to the historical development of the usage and customs of people, as well as the history of dance throughout the ages. Added to this, it is important that the pupil applies himself to studying music and its history.

Dance and music from time immemorial, have walked hand in hand, developing at the same time. If music can do without dance, dance certainly cannot do without music.

A dancer who has an excellent general cultural education, especially in music, will possess sensitivity, a refined feeling and spiritual elevation which will be communicated to the audience.

School premises and equipment

The premises of a classical dance school should be large, airy and well illuminated; decorated with moderation and be well equipped.

It must have a room adapted for use as a studio with special requirements and characteristics; there is a common room, secretary's office, at least two changing rooms, one for male and one for female pupils equipped with lavatories, wash basins and showers.

The common room is furnished simply with good taste. In the secretary's office: a writing desk, filing cabinet, small bookcase, typewriter and a telephone will be sufficient.

Along the walls of the changing rooms are benches and chairs, a sufficient number of pegs, a small table with drawers and several mirrors.

The studio, which is the most important area, is quite large with an area of at least 15x10 yards (15x10 meters); big windows allow it to be inundated with light and be well aired.

A bright, pleasant and inviting studio encourages the scholars to face the challenges of training with pleasure and delight.

The floor is constructed with wooden planks and acts as a spring-board. It is even better if, in imitation of the theatre stage, it has a rake of 3.5-4%; as well as working on a raked surface right from the beginning, the greater difficulties occurred while finding his balance obliges the pupil to exercise the muscles of the lumbar region, reinforcing and strengthening them.

The studio must never be over-heated; at most the temperature is around 56° F (14°C). It is fitted with the characteristic equipment of a dance studio, that is: on the side and back walls, horizontally and parallel, there are two rows of round wooden barres set away from the walls and held in position by suitable brackets.

One barre has a diameter of 1¼ inches (3 cm) and is about 2 feet 8 inches (80 cm) above the floor, and set about 3¼ inches (8 cm) from the wall. This barre is for the smallest pupils to hold. The second barre has a diameter of 1½-2 inches (4-4½ cm) and is about 3 feet (93 cm) from the floor, set about 4 -4½ inches (10-12 cm) from the wall. This barre is for the older pupils.

A large mirror covers the front wall. This is indispensable as it gives the pupils the possibility of seeing themselves in the mirror during the exercises and of understanding the remarks and corrections of the teacher more easily, training the eye for the correct poses and movements.

A clock is useful for the Maestro to control the length of the exercises and the lesson.

A piano is indispensable for the accompaniment and the musicality of the exercises.

A timetable with a daily program is necessary; also a watering-can to water the floor, with moderation, as it always needs to be fairly damp to avoid slipping. A box of rosin which is used by the pupil in his shoes also prevents him from slipping.

Finally, pictures showing representative poses and classical dance positions provide teaching material.

Academie de Danse
des Professeurs G. & E. Cecchetti

Certificat

Corri Cecilia

Londres le 1er Décembre 1924

Corri

Madame Cecilia

... ce dit certificat est adjugé à la dite personne pour son mérite acquis plus lui donne l'autorisation d'intituler son cours de danse Méthode Prof. Cecchetti.

Signé Prof. Enrico Cecchetti

Diploma of the Scuola E.-G. Cecchetti presented to the graduates of the full eight-year course, also authorizing them as teachers of the Cecchetti method.

Dance courses

The most advisable age to commence studying classical dance is from eight to maximum eleven years; apart from exceptionally rare cases of children with great natural ability, it is difficult to mold and correct defects after this age. The complete course of dance lasts for eight years plus one year of perfection and is divided thus:

1. Elementary course: three preparatory years
2. Intermediate course: three years
3. Advanced course: two years
4. Perfection course: one year

Teaching must be gradual and constant, without haste and without unnecessarily tiring the pupil physically.

Particular care is taken during the preparatory course, as the successful outcome of a pupil depends in great part on this.

Lessons are given every day of the week throughout the whole period of the school year. On Sundays there is a much needed weekly rest.

It is a good idea to pass the summer vacation resting, preparing the body to be in good form for the new year.

A dance lesson comprises:

1. exercises at the barre
2. exercises in the centre
3. temps d'adage
4. temps d'allegro (temps simple, sprung, turned, on pointe, compound temps)

The length of a daily dance class is one hour, divided more or less in the following way:

15 minutes of exercises at the barre
12 minutes of exercises in the centre
15 minutes of adagio
18 minutes of allegro

To begin with, lessons for beginners are shorter, gradually lengthening without haste or impatience, to one hour.

The advanced classes, on the other hand, can be lengthened throughout the week with wider programs. This all depends on the decision of the teacher.

It is unadvisable to continue beyond the fixed time every day because this places the body under excessive stress; rather than achieving any major benefit it has the reverse affect, tiring and weakening the student. Every extreme force is harmful, so we insist on keeping to the prescribed hour since, through experience, we know that this length of time is more than sufficient to achieve the necessary progress if the lesson is followed willingly and enthusiastically.

Paraphrasing an old adage, we repeat that it is not the quantity but the quality of the exercises from which the most benefit is gained if executed rationally and in correct measure.

On the other hand, under no circumstances should the continuity of the lessons be interrupted (except in cases of illness or for other serious reasons) because it is only through continual, methodical daily exercise that slowly and surely, without excessive force or strain, the body is made supple, loose and more agile. Through constructing and creating slowly, progress is mathematically secure and surprising.

Missing lessons from time to time causes serious, almost irremediable harm; a few days' laziness is enough to demolish what has been gained by weeks and months of unyielding perseverance.

The pupil who abandons himself frequently to this deplorable habit, will never achieve anything at all and would do better to leave dance training because he is obviously without vocation. Much better to take another road.

BOOK ONE

PART ONE
THEORY

General Information

As the art of dance is essentially decorative and aesthetic, the dancer should try to mold his body into vigorously artistic forms; this gives the poses, even transiently, all that grace and artistic beauty that never grates upon the eye of the audience. A dancer who gives expression to all his movements never tires the spectator, he captivates him, leaving for a long time in his mind a gentle and enduring, dreamlike vision.

Therefore, the study of dance brings with it a continual participation of all parts of the whole body which is completely trained, each part being in coordination with the other parts.

Therefore, the movements of the body, head and arms, cannot be left uncontrolled, without any sense or aesthetics. They must be disciplined and regulated according to precise rules whose theories form the basic canons from which all the movements come and, together with the exercises, shape the dancer as an artist.

Having said this, it is obvious that before he can begin learning the dance exercises, the pupil must be thoroughly grounded in the principals on which the whole structure and method of the school is based. He can therefore, in the course of the lesson understand the Maestro in the language particular to the study of dance.

In this section of the manual, with a technical study, we specify the rules which prepare each individual part of the body in different positions.

THE HAND

We know how much importance painters and sculptors give to studying this part of the body. A badly drawn hand in the wrong position completly ruins the harmony of a painting.

The hand has its own profound and particular way of expressing emotion: agitation, fear or coldness, etc. In dance, where there is a continuous search for grace and softness, the rules which govern the use of the hand are very definite. These must be strictly observed by the pupils in order to avoid forming bad habits and irreparable faults.

In this section we learn the exact academic rules regarding the position of the hand during the various exercises.

Study of the Hand

The three principal positions of the hand are:

1. The manner of holding the hand during the exercises at the barre and in the centre.

The fingers are together, as demonstrated in figure 1. The first and the fourth fingers are straight, the second and third fingers are slightly curved.

The thumb is extended and rests on the first joint (between the 1st and 2nd bones) of the middle finger which, in its turn, rests on the second bone of the ring finger.

The hand, turned at the wrist, curves slightly forward.

Pupils must hold their hands in the manner described above during the first years; in this way, they become used to holding the fingers rounded and together in the correct position and refrain from pointing stiffly in all directions; this very bad habit

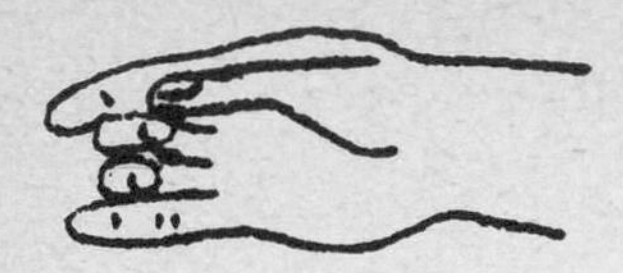

Fig. 1 Hand in training position

frequently occurs during moments of tension and is extremely difficult to eliminate completely.

2. The manner of holding the hand during the adage and the allegro.

This position is more or less the same as before except that the fingers, still together, are more extended and the thumb, well down, no longer rests on the middle finger (fig. 2).

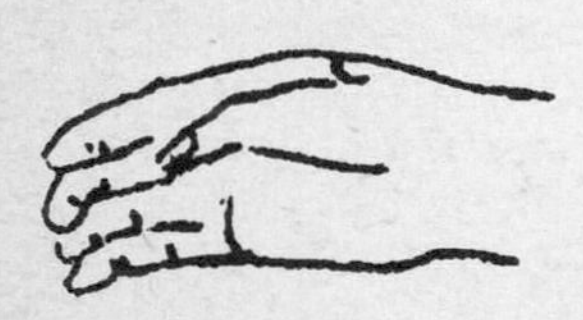

Fig. 2 Hand in normal position

3. The manner of holding the hand in arabesque

The hand is held in exactly the same position as before (fig. 2) except that the palm faces down (fig. 3).

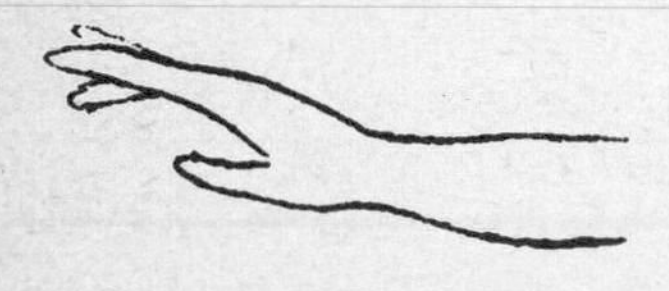

Fig. 3 Hand in arabesque position

The hand in arabesque should be turned slightly outwards and upwards from the wrist (never downwards and inwards) or, better still, almost straight, in a horizontal line to the arm.

4. The manner of holding the hand in attitude.

In attitude, the hand of the arm in demi-seconde is the same as the hand in arabesque (fig. 3); slightly turned up from the wrist.

The hand of the raised arm can be held in the following two ways:

1. in the normal way (fig. 2), with the wrist curved inwards (fig. 4).
2. in a straight line with the forearm and the wrist curved inwards. In this case the fingers are not held too closely together; the index finger is straight, the other fingers are curved, each one a little more, one over the other, one joint at a time. The little finger almost rests on the palm of the hand (fig. 5).

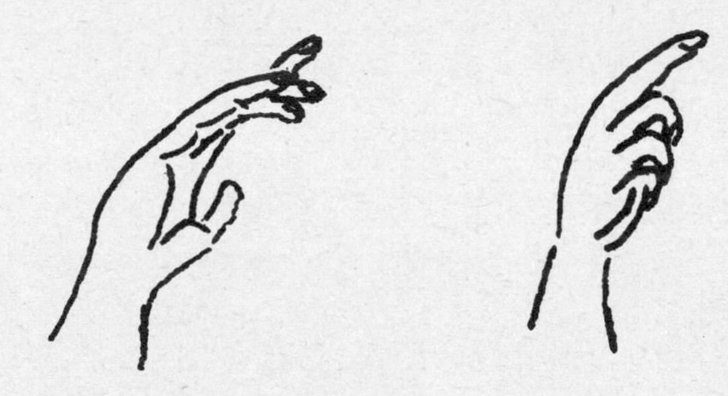

Figs. 4 and 5 Hands in attitude position

THE ARMS

The positions, the oppositions and particularly the movements or carriage of the arms, are probably the most difficult part of dancing and require a great deal of study and attention.

Opposition is a natural law of balance in which, if the right leg is brought forward, the left arm is taken back in order to balance the downward line from the centre of gravity; this makes the dancer appear much more graceful because it is a means of avoiding uniformity of line, as advocated in the art of painting.

When lowering the arms from a raised position, the wrists and the elbows indicate the movement, holding back just a little (with the palms of the hands facing the floor), so that when the arms lower completely, the elbows extend and the wrists and hands go into line with the arms.

On raising the arms, the procedure is the same: first the upper arms arrive, then the forearms and finally the wrists and hands. This play of movements gives a soft, light quality to the arms.

The arms are always held rounded so that the points of the elbows are invisible; otherwise they form angles which detract from the graceful, smooth contours that the upper limbs must always present.

As the arms move, the shoulders should be kept in a normal lowered position and without movement.

The wrists must be held without being too curved, otherwise they will appear to be broken.

The movements of the arms must not be exaggerated or jerky.

Positions of the Arms

The arms have fixed, precise rules so that they can move correctly and in harmony with the other parts of the body.

The arm movements are arranged into five basic positions plus the position de repos. All the arm movements are contained in this group.

Every position has its own number with which it is identified. This classification was originally devised by Beauchamps and passed on by the great teachers of the past. Experience has shown this idea to be perfectly logical for its rationale and its clear and simple technique which is ideal for this purpose. We believe that every new change in this area only causes confusion without providing any useful or serious benefit.

The principal positions of the arms are five plus the position de repos:

0. position de repos (fig. 6)
1. first position (fig. 8)
2. second position (fig. 10)
3. third position (figs. 13 and 14)
4. fourth position (fig. 16)
5. fifth position (fig. 18)

0. Position de repos

This position is numbered 0, for two important reasons:

The first is of a physical nature. When the arms are held for a lengthy period in one of the other positions, they become tired and ache; they need to be lowered so that they can rest and the blood can resume normal circulation.

The second reason is technical. This is the classical position in which the arms commence and to which they return.

Description of the position

Still keeping them rounded, hold the arms as low as possible in front of the body, slightly away from it with the hands about 4 inches distance from each other; palms turned and facing each other (fig. 6).

Open position de repos

Remaining in the previous position, open the arms so that the space between the hands is the same as the width of the body (fig. 7).

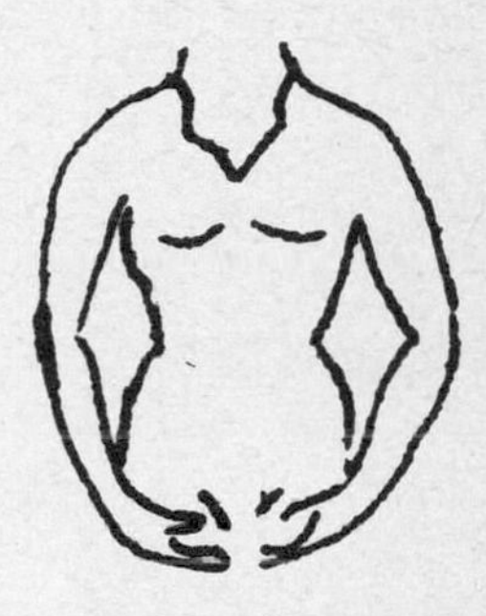

Fig. 6 Normal position de repos

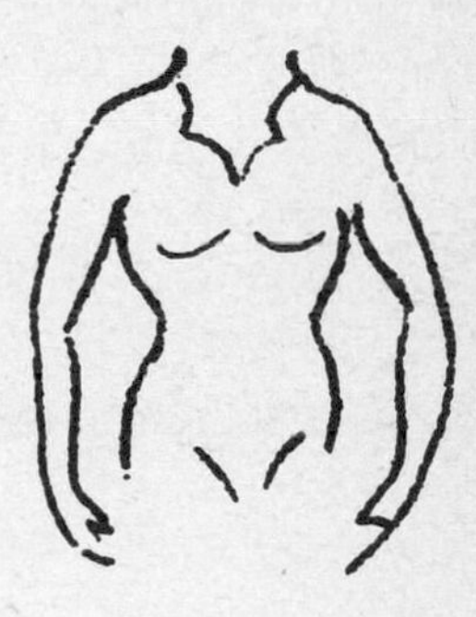

Fig. 7 Wide position de repos

1. First position

The arms are still rounded (but extended as much as possible); raise them, from position de repos in front of the body almost to shoulder height, keeping the space between the hands to around 4 inches (10 cm) (figs. 8 and 9).

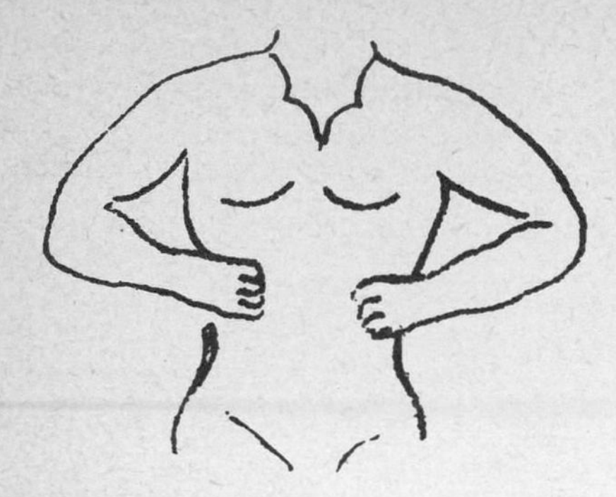

Fig. 8 First position

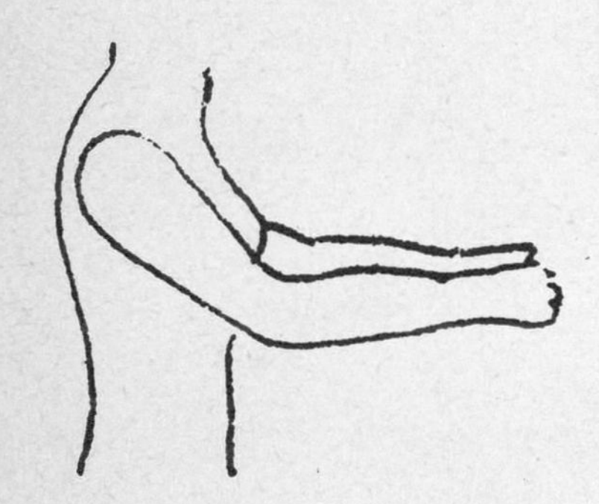

Fig. 9 First position

Wide first position

Remaining in the previous position, the arms open; the space between the hands is the same as the width of the body.

N.B. The first position is of particular importance because in order to go to any other position, the arms must pass through first; this way the movement is technically and rhythmically correct.

2. Second position

Without bending the elbows, open the arms from first position, until they extend almost at shoulder height.

The palms of the hands face front (fig. 10).

Demi-seconde (half second position)

The arms lower from the previous position to 3/4 height, slightly rounded; palms of the hands facing down (fig. 11).

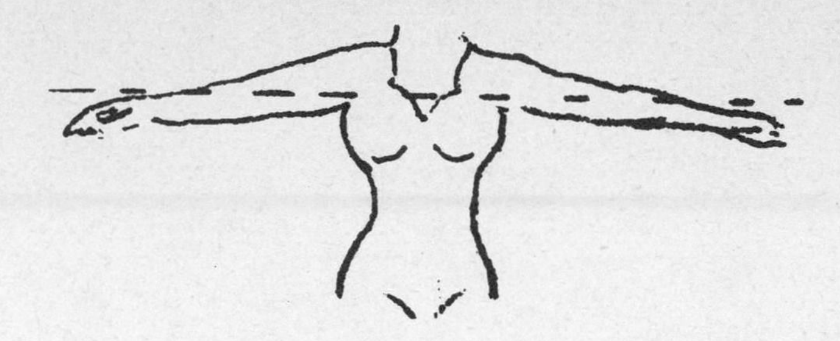

Fig. 10 Correct second position

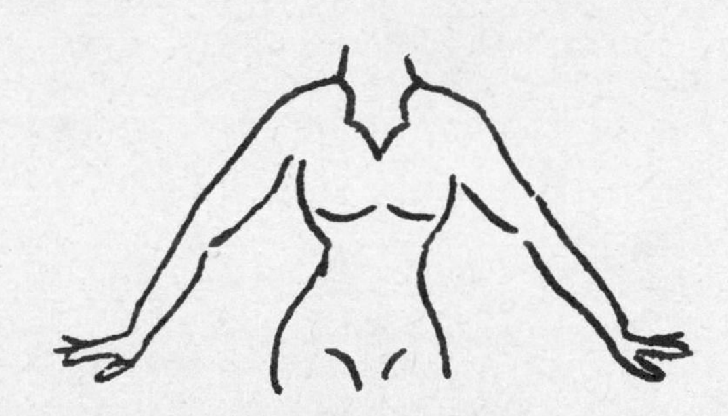

Fig. 11 Demi-seconde (half second position)

Fig. 12 Incorrect second position

Figure 12 shows second position with faulty arms which must be avoided.

3. Third position

From second position, raise the right arm, rounded, directly over the head, palm of the hand turned inward; the position is third right (fig. 13).

Reverse the positions of the arms; the arms are now third left (fig. 14).

Fig. 13 Third right

Fig. 14 Third left

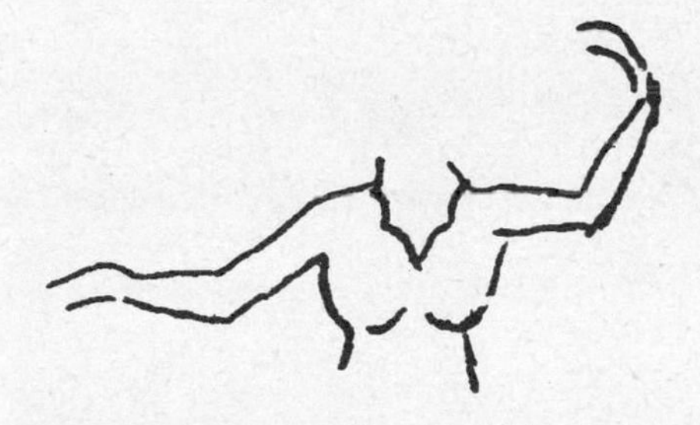

Fig. 15 Incorrect third

Figure 15 shows third position with faulty arms.

4. Fourth position

In fourth position, one arm is raised to fifth, as we shall see presently; the other arm is taken to first, increasing the bend of the elbow; this brings the forearm close to the breast. In this position the lower arm is no longer in first but in that position peculiar to the fourth.

From third position right, the right arm remains high; the left arm is taken to a much more rounded first position with the palm of the hand facing the breast (fourth right).

Reversing the positions, the arms are in fourth left (fig. 16).

Fig. 16 Fourth left

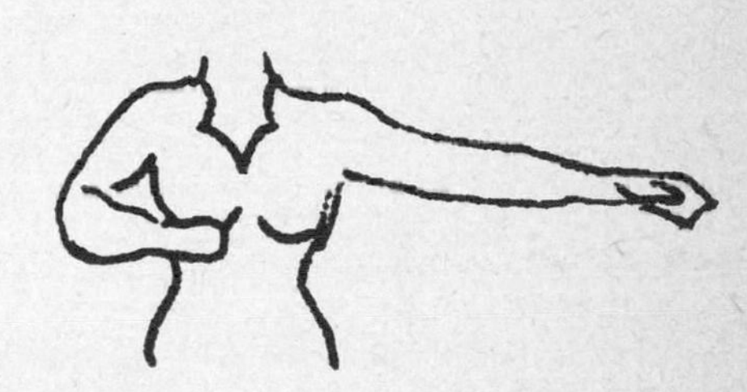

Fig. 17 Low fourth left

Low fourth

This important position does not have a name of its own as it derives directly from the fourth. One arm is taken to first in the characteristic position peculiar to the fourth. The "low" refers to the other arm which, instead of being in fifth, is in second position:

Remaining in position fourth right, lower the right arm to second (low fourth right).

By reversing the position, the arms are in low fourth left (fig. 17).

5. Fifth position

The arms are raised over the head, from first position, rounded and extended with the shoulders down; the space between the hands is about 4 inches; the palms face in. This is a very difficult position and

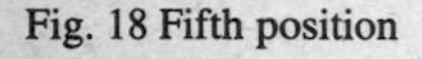

Fig. 18 Fifth position

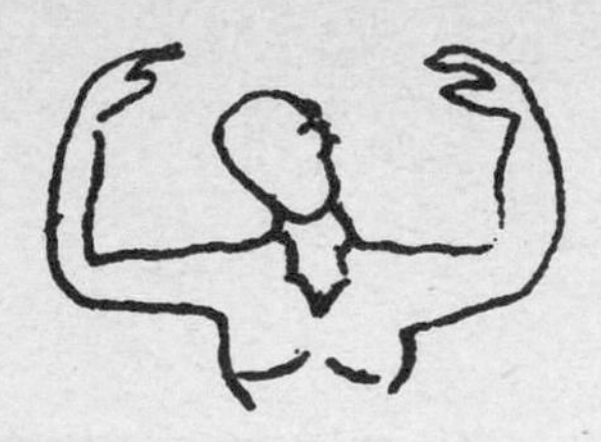

Fig. 19 Incorrect fifth

particular attention should be given to its execution (fig. 18).

Figure 19 shows an incorrect fifth position; this must be avoided.

As we have said before, in dance all the movements of the arms are contained in these five basic positions, plus position de repos.

The exceptions to this rule are arabesque and attitude. In these cases, the arms conform to the rules which pertain to these very important poses.

For the moment we are interested only in the arm positions of these poses; we deal more fully with the poses themselves in a chapter of Book Three, Part One.

There are two basic positions of the arms in arabesque. The attitude has one position only.

6. Arms in arabesque

a) Arabesque with arms in opposition

Extend the right arm forward, slightly above shoulder height, perfectly straight with the hand in line with the arm and the palm turned down. Take the left arm back, slightly below shoulder level, well extended in line with the right arm; the hand is in line with the arm; the palm faces down.

It is particularly important for the shoulders to remain square and perpendicular to the arms; they do not turn, following the direction of the arms (fig. 20).

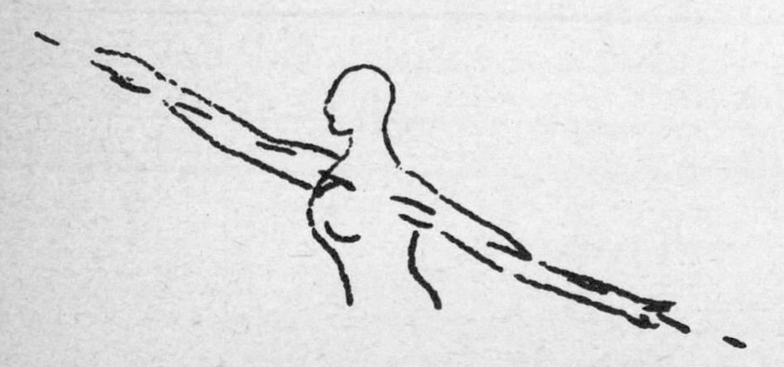

Fig. 20 Arms in opposition

b) Arabesque with both arms forward

Extend the right arm forward, slightly above shoulder height with the hand in line with the arm and the palm turned down. The left arm, extended and slightly rounded, is taken forward, about 8 inches below and parallel to the right arm; the hand is in line with the arm and the palm turned down (fig. 21).

7. Arms in attitude

Take the right arm to fifth position slightly forward, the palm turned inwards. The left arm moves to demi-seconde, slightly back, palm facing down (fig. 22).

Fig. 21 Parallel arms

Fig. 22 Arms in attitude right

N.B. We have only described the position of the right arm. To obtain the same position on the left, just reverse the arms.

Theory of port de bras

The arms move continuously in dancing, always in coordination with the rest of the body, particularly with the legs.

These movements cannot be left uncontrolled; they follow precise rules which are in harmony with the elementary laws of artistic symmetry.

By carefully studying the theory of port de bras, we learn the way in which the arms move when they are in opposition.

The movements of the arms in dance are just as important as the movements of the legs, so it is easy to understand how much care and attention must be given to practicing the arm movements.

The theory of port de bras can be understood best by a geometric diagram which gives a clear and mathematically precise explanation.

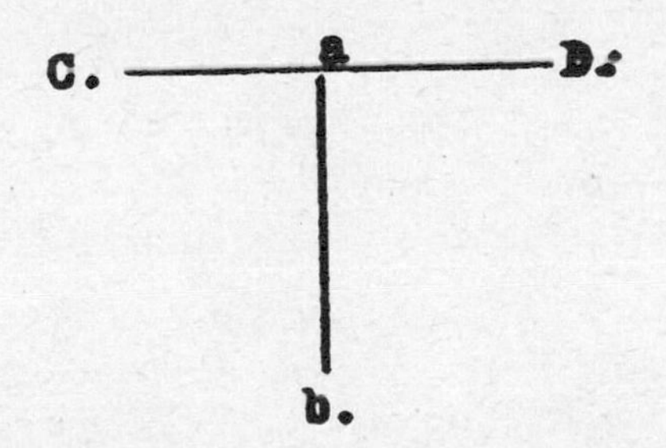

Fig. 23

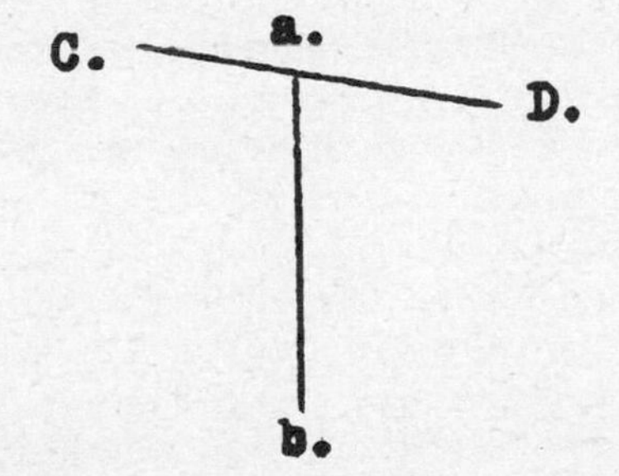

Fig. 24

Demonstration

The body is represented by the vertical straight line *ab*. The arms are represented by another horizontal straight line *CD*. *CD* crosses the vertical straight line *ab* at point *a* which acts as a pivot.

Raising or lowering the horizontal line *Ca*, causes the line *aD* to lower or raise in equal measure.

In conclusion: when moving in opposition, the arms must always be in the same straight line (figs. 23 and 24).

THE HEAD

In dance, as well as in painting or sculpture, the head and face give the most life to a person's expression.

A head which properly inclines, turns, lowers or is raised, in other words, moves in an artistically correct manner and is always in harmony with the rest of the body, gives the dancer an exquisite grace and fascination and brings out the best qualities in his dancing, completing the fluidity of all his movements.

A head which is stiff like a puppet's, moves in an unbecoming way and is always an unpleasant sight. It has the same effect on the eyes as a consistently flat note in a harmonic chord on the ears.

As in other art forms, when training to dance, nothing is left to the free will of the dancer. The movements of the head, like those of the other parts of the body, are regulated and disciplined by precise rules which are strictly observed.

The principal positions and movements of the head relate to the movements of the other parts of the body.

Positions of the head

There are five principal positions of the head:

1. Head erect (fig. 25)
2. Head raised (fig. 26)
3. Head lowered (fig. 27)
4. Head inclined to one side (fig. 28)
5. Head turned to one side (fig. 29)

Movements of the Head

There are seven basic movements of the head. These are controlled in strict agreement with the movements or actions of the other parts of the body:

1. Walking normally, hold the head erect.
2. If, in advancing, the movement commences with the right foot, the head inclines slightly over the right shoulder and vice-versa.

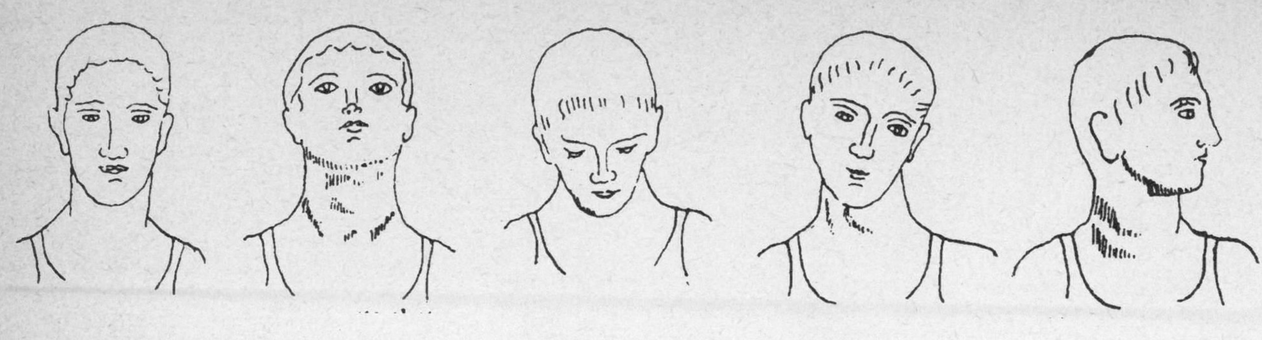

Fig. 25 Head erect

Fig. 26 Head raised

Fig. 27 Head lowered

Fig. 28 Head inclined to one side

Fig. 29 Head turned to one side

3. However, if in retiring, the movement commences with the right foot, the head inclines slightly over the left shoulder and vice-versa.
4. Executing grand rond de jambe à terre en dehors (the foot describes a semi-circle on the floor from fourth front to fourth back) the head commences turned to the side of the working foot; during grand rond de jambe, the head gradually turns until, at the end of the movement, it is turned to the opposite side (figs. 30 and 31).
5. Executing grand rond de jambe à terre en dedans (the foot describes a semi-circle on the floor, from fourth back to fourth front) the head commences inclined away from the side of the working foot; during the rond de jambe, the head gradually turns until, at the end of the movement it inclines to the same side as the leg extended to fourth (figs. 31 and 30).

Fig. 30 Right leg fourth front, head right

Fig. 31 Right leg fourth front, head left

6. In turning movements, the head turns to the side of the turn.
7. During a pirouette, at the beginning of the turn, the head is the last to leave; at the end, it is the first to arrive back to the audience.

THE FACE

The face is the mirror of the state of one's soul. The dancer uses his face to give life and expression to his dancing.

Generally, dance is the demonstration of a happy disposition, exuberant, full of vitality, healthy; so a pleasant face with an intelligent expression gives life and energy to the dancer's interpretation. A radiant face and smiling mouth make it easier to disguise hard work and fatigue; this presents an agreeable impression of health and exceptional stamina which surprises an admiring audience.

Right at the beginning of dance training, the pupil must be made aware, during the exercises, of keeping his face alert, eyes alive and his mouth agreeably smiling. This is in order to avoid the bad habits which could cause the irreparable defect of making ugly grimaces or showing suffering in moments of great tension and worry about the execution of a step; or even worse, falling into the habit of dancing mechanically with a bored, absent, cold and in any case, an inexpressive face.

The artist must study and understand the subject of the dance, interpret it with intelligent passion, infusing it with life and soul and he must succeed in eliciting enthusiasm in the spectator.

THE BODY

The body is the centre of equilibrium and the place where all the limbs assemble. This is why it must be exercised to strengthen the lumbar region and acquire complete flexibility to combine force with smoothness.

The body must be erect and well poised over the legs. The exceptions are in arabesque, when it may incline slightly forwards; in attitude when it may incline slightly forwards and backwards, altering balance.

The chest is out and the abdomen pulled in; the back must be slightly arched and the lumbar region tensed (fig. 32).

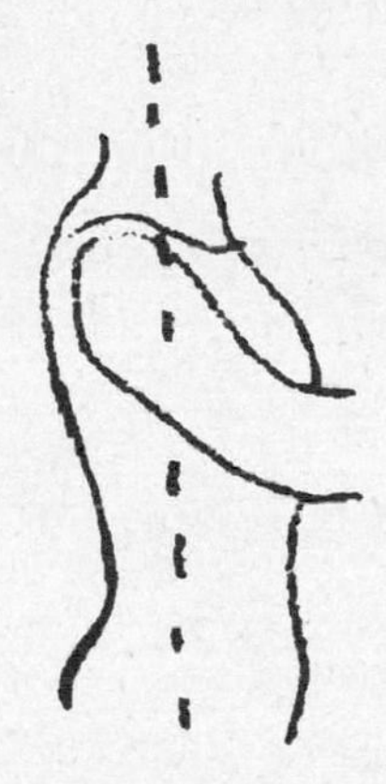

Fig. 32 Back slightly arched and the lumbar region tensed

It is a serious mistake, however, to lift the chest pushing out the abdomen at the same time, or to pull it in, pushing out the behind.

The whole balance depends on the strength of the lumbar region.

Some fortunate subjects are naturally gifted, but in general these qualities are acquired at a good school which understands the importance of dedicating attention and constant care to this part of the body where all the secrets of balance lie.

The body must always be erect and perpendicular in order to remain perfectly balanced. The line of balance begins from the sternum and passes between the two ankle bones. When standing on one leg, the weight is over the centre of gravity of the supporting leg. When the body is away from the line of balance, a certain amount of natural or casual weight is transferred from the opposite side, balancing eventual displacement from the centre of gravity at the base of the supporting foot.

In certain attitudes and arabesques unnatural to normal equilibrium, the dancer has to find his own balance.

The dancer's balance is the basic principal of his stability and strength; it is of equal value whether the weight is on both legs or on one leg only.

The qualities of this "equilibrium" depend on the flexibility of the back, the aplomb and the centre of gravity.

THE LEGS

A dancer's legs are as important as a pianist's hands. Therefore, if other parts of the body, which only complete a step or position, are important enough to be studied intensely, the training of the legs is essential. The legs perform every technical skill and, with good schooling, they become wonderfully supple, light, steel-like levers, shaped into elegant and marvellous pieces of workmanship.

Whoever aspires to this art must have long, straight legs, open in the hips, with knees and feet turned out.

These qualities certainly facilitate a pupil's training, ensuring success.

In spite of the most persistent training, a person who is naturally "turned-in" will never achieve his desire. The feet may turn out, the pointes arch strongly, but his hips and knees will always remain turned-in.

The arqué (fig. 33) and the jarreté (fig. 34) are most certainly excluded from the art of dance.

All the movements of the legs in dance are executed in a series limited to three basic positions. Every position has three more positions which derive naturally from these. These positions of the legs are entirely

Fig. 33 Arqué (or "bow-legs") Fig. 34 Jarreté (or "knock-knees")

based on the positions of the feet, as we will see in the following chapter.

The cou de pied

The part of the foot called the cou de pied is found between the ankle and the base of the calf.

N.B. Every time the leg is raised, and whichever position it takes, the pointe of the foot is always fully forced downwards.

Fig. 35 Second pointe on the floor

Positions of the legs

1. *Second position:*
   second pointe on the floor
   second at half height
   high second [at full height]

2. *Fourth position front:*
   fourth front pointe on the floor
   fourth front at half height
   high fourth front [at full height]

3. *Fourth position back:*
   fourth back pointe on the floor
   fourth back at half height
   high fourth back [at full height]

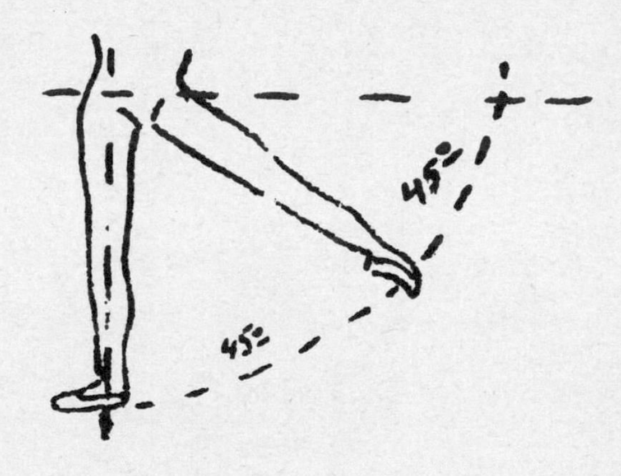

Fig. 36 Second at half height

1. Second position of the legs

a) Second pointe on the floor

With the feet in second position, adjust the weight onto one leg only; the heel of the other foot is raised and the toe remains pointed on the floor. The knees are straight (fig. 35).

b) Second at half height

From second, pointe on the floor, raise the leg to half way between the floor and the hip around 20 inches (50 cm) from the floor; the knees are straight (fig. 36).

c) High second

From second at half height, raise the leg, fully stretched, to the height of the hip. The horizontal line of the leg forms a right angle with the vertical line of the body and supporting leg (fig. 37).

2. Fourth position front of the legs

a) Fourth front, pointe on the floor

The feet are in fourth; adjust the weight backwards onto the back leg and raise the heel of the front foot. The toe remains pointed on the floor (fig. 38).

b) Fourth front at half height

From fourth front, toe on the floor, raise the leg about 20 inches (50 cm); the knees are straight (fig. 39).

c) High fourth front

From fourth front at half height, raise the leg to the height of the hip; the knees are straight (fig. 40).

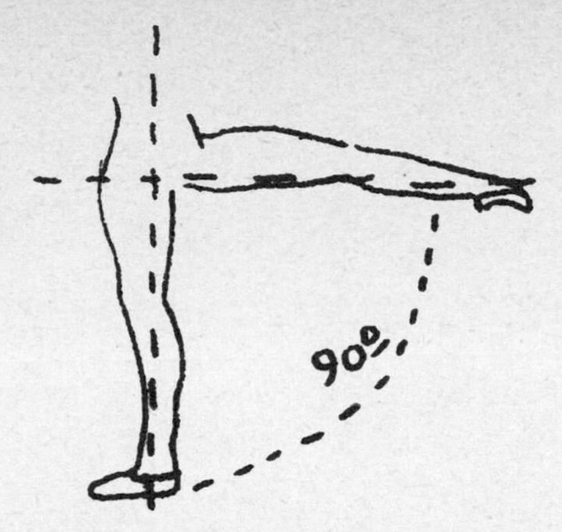

Fig. 37 High second

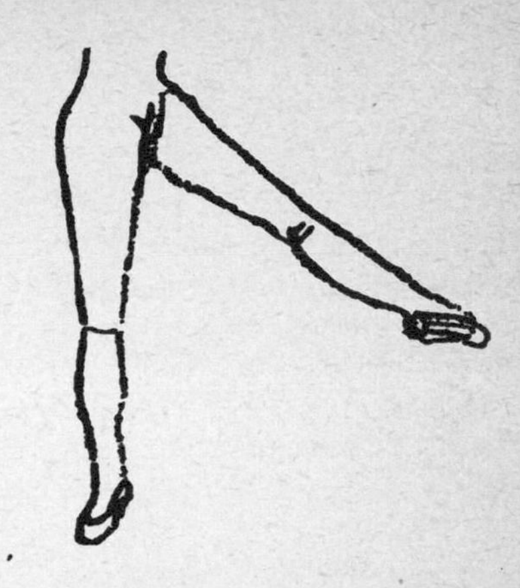

Fig. 39 Fourth front at half height

Fig. 38 Fourth front pointe on the floor

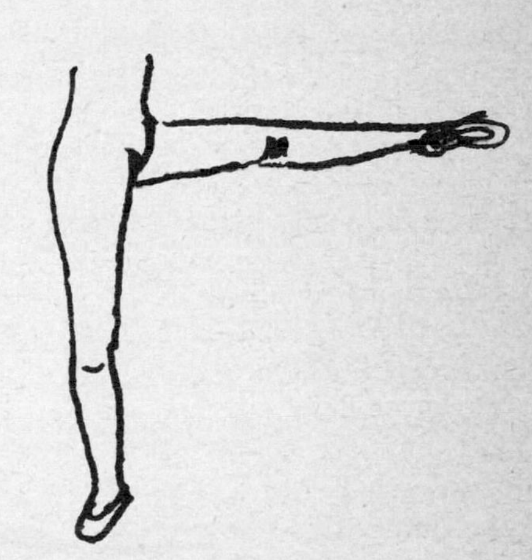

Fig. 40 High fourth front

Fig. 41 Fourth back pointe on the floor

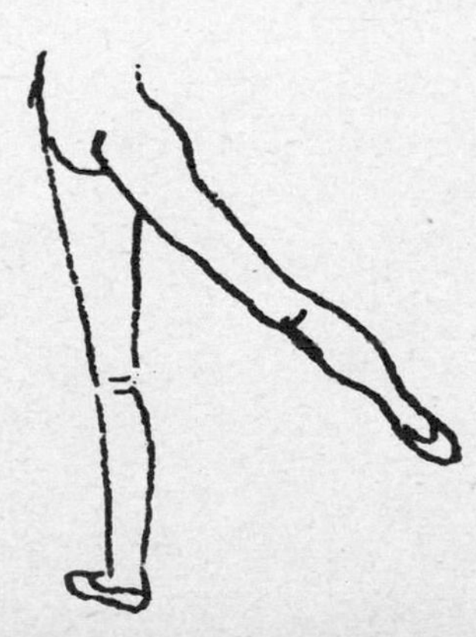

Fig. 42 Fourth back at half height

Fig. 43 High fourth back

3. Fourth position back of the legs

a) Fourth back pointe on the floor

The feet are in fourth; transfer the weight slightly forward onto the front foot, raising the heel of the back foot. The toe remains pointed on the floor; the knees are straight (fig. 41).

b) Fourth back at half height

From fourth back on the floor, raise the leg about 20 inches (50 cm); the knees are straight (fig. 42).

c) High fourth back

The leg is raised from fourth back at half height to hip level; the knees are straight (fig. 43).

N.B. In the drawings, it can be clearly seen that the legs are always well turned out whatever the position; particular emphasis is on the knees and feet.

THE FEET

The feet and legs are the invaluable instruments of the skillful dancer when performing his technical feats.

Unfortunately, not everyone has feet which are suitable for dancing. Practicing appropriate exercises every day can be very beneficial but this cannot change the structure of defective feet or those otherwise unsuitable for dancing.

A good foot should have a strong cou de pied and be well arched; it should turn out easily and be able to sustain the weight of the dancer when rising onto pointe. Its movement should be easy and natural giving it speed, agility and suppleness for dancing.

One of the most important movements of the instep is raising and lowering the toes, because then it must support and balance the full weight of the body. A strong instep can be compared to a powerful, steel lever which throws the dancer into the air then, acting as a shock absorber, allows him to alight gently and smoothly, through the whole foot sur la demi-pointe.

In the action of springing, the movement of the knee and the instep are inseparable. The movement of the knee is different from the movement of the instep because it is only perfect when the leg is stretched.

The hip joint moves first, leading the movements of the feet and knees.

The positions of the feet were cleverly evolved and handed down by the famous choreographer Beauchamps; this theory has become as important in dance as the notes in music.

Five basic positions are used as the feet move through the various dance steps; seven poses control the way they are placed in the various movements.

Positions of the feet

There are five basic positions of the feet and they form the rock foundation of all dance movements:

1. first position (closed and in line)
2. second position (open and in line)
3. third position (closed and crossed)
4. fourth position (open and crossed)
5. fifth position (closed and crossed)

1. First position

Both feet are together; holding the heels together, pivot on the heels and turn the points of the feet outwards. The feet are in line with each other, the knees are straight, parallel to the shoulders (fig. 44).

2. Second position

Slide the pointe of the foot to the side from first position maintaining the line and sliding the pointe along the floor as gradually the heel is raised. When it is about 14 inches (35 cm), from the other foot, lower the heel. The weight is equally balanced on both legs. The toes and the knees, straight, must always be parallel to the shoulders.

The feet are now in second position (fig. 45).

3. Third position

Raise the heel in second position; slide the pointe along the floor, drawing in the foot and gradually lowering the heel; the working foot crosses half way in front of the other. The ankles are held well together, legs still fully stretched and turned out (fig. 46).

4. Fourth position

Slide the pointe of the foot forward gradually raising the heel. Lower the heel at about 14 inches (35 cm)

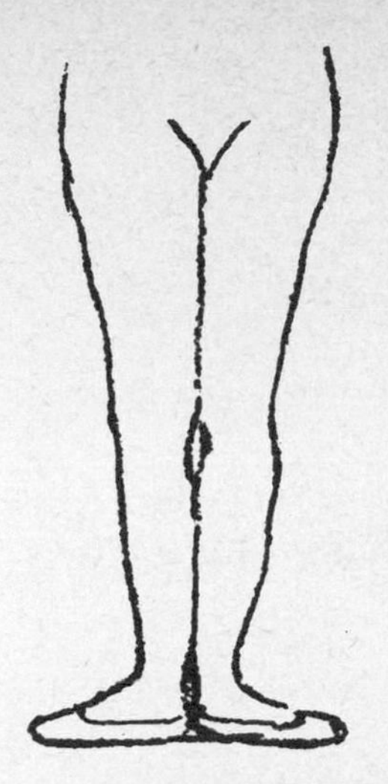

Fig. 44 Fifth position

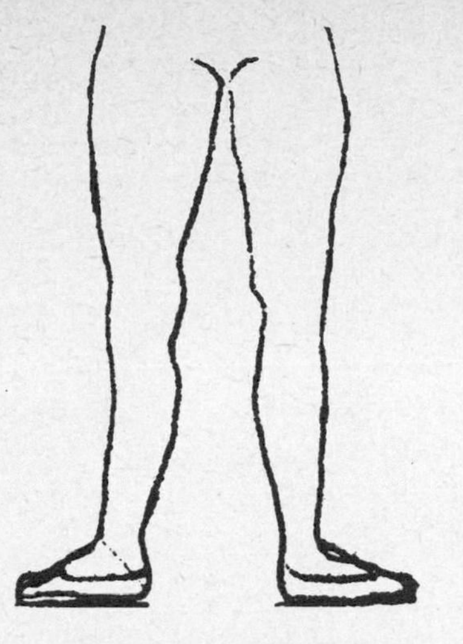

Fig. 45 Second position

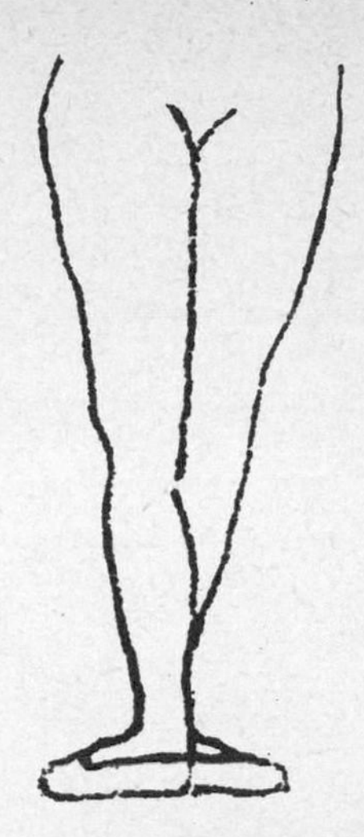

Fig. 46 Third position

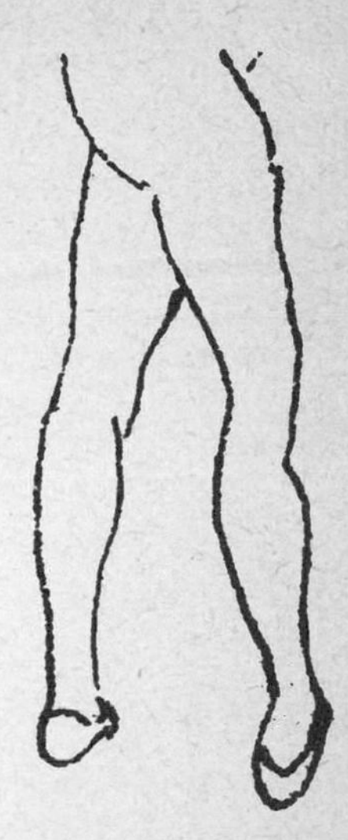

Fig. 47 Fourth position

distance from the other foot; the feet are well turned out and parallel, one crossed in front of the other, as much as in third position. The weight is equally balanced over both legs, the knees are straight and turned outwards (fig. 47).

5. Fifth position

Raise the heel in fourth position; slide the pointe along the floor towards the other foot, gradually lowering the heel; close the foot crossing it in front of the other. Unlike third position, the feet are completely crossed; only the first joint of the big toe protrudes beyond the heels (fig. 48).

An over-crossed foot would create a faulty fifth; this must be avoided (fig. 49).

In each of the positions described, the soles of the feet are wholly in contact with the floor.

Make sure that the pupil, who at first finds it difficult to hold the feet turned out, does not allow the feet to "roll" forward, dangerously weakening them.

In all of the positions of the feet, the body is equally placed on both legs.

First, third and fifth are closed positions.

Second and fourth are open positions; the positions of the legs derive from these.

Third, fourth and fifth are crossed positions.

In first and second positions the feet are in line with each other.

In spite of the variety and quantity of combinations of steps, it can be seen that the legs can only make two movements: close and open.

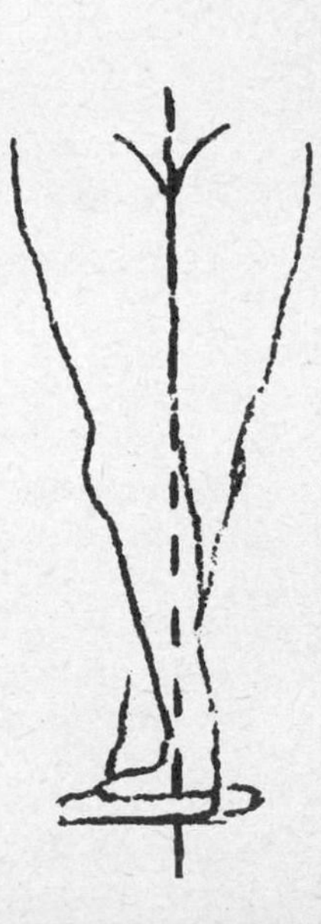

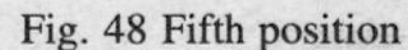

Fig. 48 Fifth position

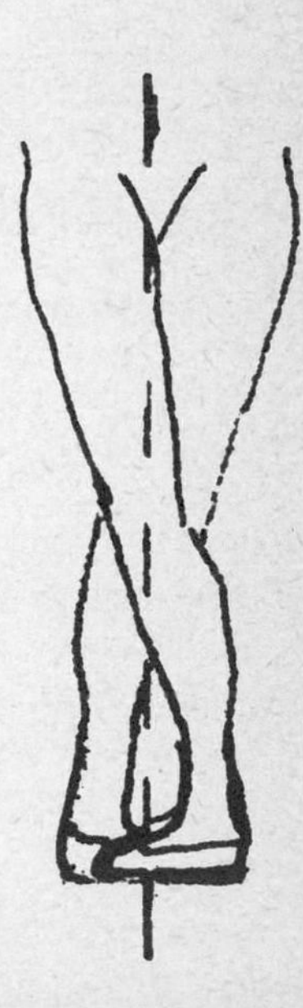

Fig. 49 Incorrect fifth

The movements of the foot and its positions

The seven basic movements of the foot are regulated by seven fundamental poses:

1. *Pied à terre*: foot flat on the ground (fig. 50).
2. *Pied à quart*: the heel is slightly raised from the ground (fig. 51).
3. *Pied sur la demi-pointe*: the heel is raised much higher from the ground (fig. 52).

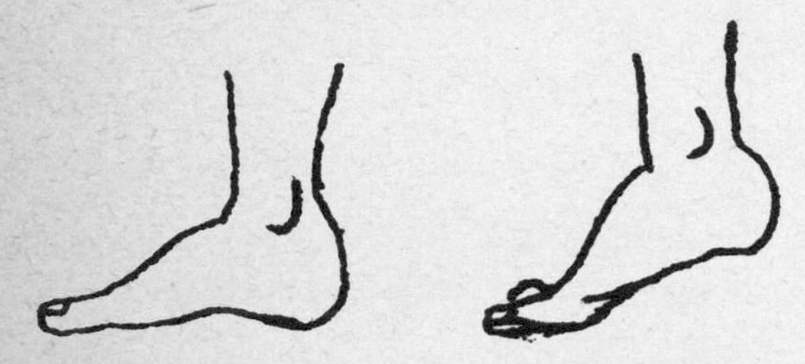

Fig. 50 Pied à terre

Fig. 51 Pied à quart

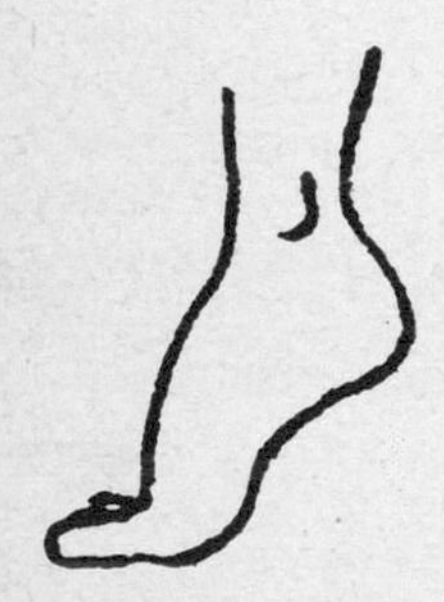

Fig. 52 Pied sur la demi-pointe

4. *Pied à trois quarts*: the heel is raised considerably from the ground (fig. 53).
5. *Pied sur la pointe*: the foot is supported on the extremity of the toes (fig. 54).
6. *Fully arched foot*: (for movements in second) the foot is raised in the air and extended as much as possible; instep forced well out, toe well down (fig. 55)
7. *Fully arched foot*: (for movements in fourth); the foot is turned out as much as possible; toe forced down and back so that the heel is brought well forward (fig. 56).

Fig. 53 Pied à trois quarts

Fig. 54 Pied sur la pointe

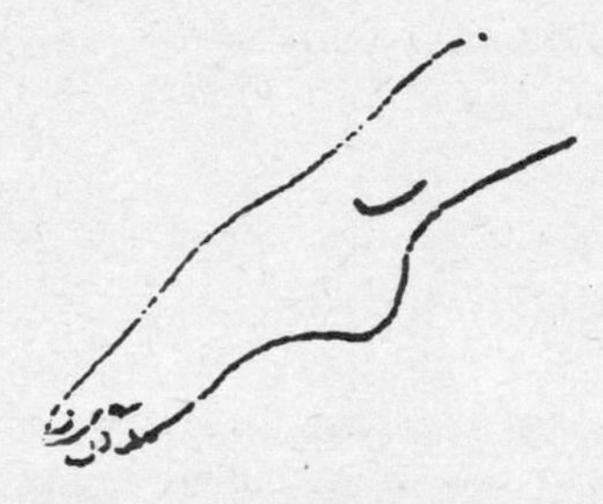

Fig. 55 Position of foot in second (fully arched foot)

Fig. 56 Position of foot in fourth (fully arched foot)

Errors

a) Curling the toes instead of forcing the pointe downwards, and the instep turned out as in figure 55 (fig. 57).
b) Forcing the pointe forward with the heel remaining behind (sickle), instead of forcing the pointe outwards, bringing the heel well forward as in figure 56 (fig. 58).
c) The turned up foot is used only in some character dances; it is not acceptable in classical dance (fig. 59).

Fig. 57 Toes curled under

Fig. 58 Pointe forced forward (sickle)

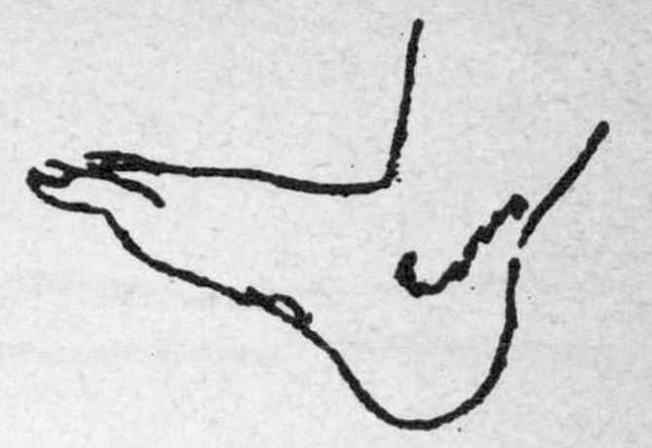

Fig. 59 Turned up foot

N.B. For a closer study of the positions of feet when on pointe, see: section two of Part One, Book Four, which deals extensively with the movements on pointe (see Volume 2 of this work).

MOVEMENTS IN DANCING

All dance steps are made up of a few basic movements, divided into groups according to their particular characteristics. The relationship between the various steps depends on the group to which they belong.

There are seven basic movements and they form the dynamic part of dancing:

1. Plier
2. Étendre
3. Relever
4. Glisser
5. Sauter
6. Élancer
7. Tourner

Directions of the body

The dancer changes directions in order to highlight and enhance the various artistic poses. Even these are controlled by basic rules which restrict the number of directions to eight:

1. En croisé en avant (fig. 60)
2. À la quatrième en avant (fig. 61)
3. Écarté (fig. 62)
4. Effacé (fig. 63)
5. À la seconde (fig.64)
6. Épaulé (fig. 65)
7. À la quatrième en arrière (fig. 66)
8. En croisé en arrière (fig. 67)

As these eight basic directions are very important in dancing, we thought that they would be more clearly illustrated using drawings.

Divisions of dance movements according to musical divisions

A "dance" is the amalgamation of many movements made up from the action of the legs and the feet into a variety of combinations. Gradually, the simple movements become more complex until they develop their own characteristics. These, in turn link together until they form a "dance."

The *temps* (Italian "tempo") is the simplest movement of the legs. It is part of a "pas" (step); but it can also have a meaning of its own. "Temps" is simple or compound depending on whether there are one or more movements of the legs and feet (e.g. Temps levé).

The *dance movement* is an action of the legs made up of one or more parts, but without having any specific quality. A movement is generally performed slowly.

The *dance step* is a complete action of the legs made up of one or more temps and movements; it has a precise quality.

The step is the most complete basic element in dancing.

The "pas" is the base from which the whole dynamics of dance are derived.

An *enchaînement* is a small, and the most simple group of steps and movements linked together and forming a complete phrase of dance; it is usually arranged in eight bars of music.

Fig. 61 À la quatrième en avant

Fig. 60 En croisé en avant

Fig. 62 Écarté

Fig. 63 Effacé

Fig. 64 À la seconde

Fig. 66 À la quatrième en arrière

Fig. 65 Épaulé

Fig. 67 En croisé en arrière

The *variation* is the combination of many phrases of dance joined together to form a sentence of dance; this is more complete and usually arranged to a length of music of 16 or 32 bars at most.

Dance is the combination of many sentences of dance; they are joined together, with a higher ideal, to form a dance poem which has a complete meaning, defined and arranged to a complete piece of music.

PART TWO
RATIONAL BREATHING AND PHYSICAL HEALTH IN DANCE TRAINING

Rational breathing

Breathing is extremely important whenever the body has to make a particularly strenuous physical effort. Breathing incorrectly can make even the least demanding movement more tiring and in consequence, as the years go by, can cause damage to the internal organs, especially the heart, considerably decreasing the stamina of a dancer.

When learning to dance, the basic rules of healthy breathing should be strictly observed.

These are not always considered a priority in many schools and only rarely are pupils given the necessary advice or counsel.

By breathing rationally at the right moment and in accordance with the development of the movements in the lessons, the pupil will gain stamina right from the start. As well as being an undeniable advantage for his health this also allows him, with training, to be able to execute very difficult, tiring dances and end without showing the least sign of fatigue. Instead of offering the very unattractive spectacle of heavy breathing accompanied by strong and damaging heart-beats, the pupil presents a natural vigor causing the amazed admiration and spontaneous enthusiasm of the audience.

If he is well trained, the professional dancer can continue his career for much longer since unfortunately, as is well known, a career in dance is usually highly ephemeral.

After a particularly heavy exercise the lungs need more oxygen so it is necessary to breathe more deeply in order to regain strength and energy. If breathing is always correct and rational, a few deep breaths during and immediately after strenuous exertion will be enough to change the air in the lungs and calm the racing heart so that breathing can be reduced to a slow, even rhythm. On the other hand if, after such great efforts these rules are not observed, the dancer will be out of breath and obliged to open the mouth in order to take in more air.

If the Maestro carefully sees that the pupil breathes sensibly and suitably in every single exercise, the lesson can proceed without causing stress to the body which could damage the body as well as affect the progress of training.

Exercise combined with correct breathing trains the body to be able to withstand the greatest physical efforts as easily as the usual daily exercises. The pupil's health, training and career benefit greatly.

The manner and timing of inhaling and exhaling are relative to each individual movement.

Based on past experience, the most suitable way of breathing during basic training exercises will be explained in relation to the movements which make up that exercise.

Inhaling and exhaling naturally through the nasal cavities must become a habit, for hygienic and artistic reasons.

Physical health in dance training

Through daily exercise the muscles are trained so that the joints and ligaments are stretched and made mobile. This training must be maintained on a regular basis as otherwise these are the parts that suffer the most through lack of work.

Breathing coordinates with the movements.

If these rules are observed, the immediate result is energy and a feeling of well-being which gives the pupil encouragement as well as keeping the professional artist in condition.

Dance exercises must be designed so that they avoid useless and dangerous over-exertion which can cause stress to the heart; this is the most sensitive organ of the human body, even in the least robust subjects.

This type of daily activity gradually produces harmonious muscular development and a strong, healthy physical appearance; combined with suppleness, lightness and swiftness of movement, it creates the excellence of the artistic dancer.

After a class it is a very healthy habit, as well as refreshing and pleasant, to take a long, relaxing shower; it must never be too cold, however.

It is also important not to let perspiration dry on the body when resting after a strenuous lesson; apart from being unhygienic, it is always dangerous as colds and pneumonia frequently begin in this way.

At the end of a lesson and before taking a shower it is advisable to wait until the heart returns to its normal rhythm; however, a few deep breaths should be sufficient.

BOOK TWO

PART ONE
EXERCISES AT THE BARRE

Observations

The positions and movements at the barre are indivisible and are the simplest elements in dance; they form the basic "cell" of technique. Combined in various ways, they become complete steps in themselves. These in turn, when repeated in regular succession or in alternated groups to a set musical rhythm, in set figures, form the dance proper; depending on the composition of the types of steps and figures, they have different names, characteristic features and distinctly different identities.

In order to become part of the harmonious art of dance, every movement is controlled by the precise rules and disciplines of classical dance technique.

The following exercises represent the simplest and most elementary dance movements. They have the two-fold purpose of teaching the pupil to recognize these movements and how to train muscles to execute them correctly. It would be wrong to think of these exercises only as gymnastics, or only as technical exercises because they are both one and the other, each one closely linked to dance training.

Right from the start, the pupil learns to fully and clearly understand the use and particular purpose of each of these exercises and practice them until they can be executed with complete ease.

Dance is art, not athletic games. Perfect technique can only be acquired gradually in stages, as the fruit of patient and sensible exercise. Only in this way are the muscles of each participating limb able to move smoothly, with the graceful quality, lightness and elegance which make dance an art.

The pupil with a good foundation in the basic theories of dance is ready to begin learning the exercises at the barre and able to understand and follow the Maestro through his progressive teaching.

All the exercises at the barre are listed in the order and rhythm in which they are executed. The order of the exercises follows established technical requirements in which one exercise is always a preparation for the next. It is this principle, followed throughout the whole course of study, which makes the method unique.

In the following chapter, each exercise will be treated individually and illustrated as clearly as possible.

TABLE OF EXERCISES AT THE BARRE

1. *Pliés* (in the five positions of the feet)
   2 in each position

2. *Grands battements*
   8 to fourth front
   8 to second
   8 to fourth back
   8 to second

3. *Battements tendus et dégagés*
   16 battements tendus in second
   16 battements dégagés
   4 battements relevés (with movement of pointe)

4. *Ronds de jambe à terre et rond de jambe soulevé*
   8 ronds de jambe à terre en dehors
   8 ronds de jambe à terre en dedans
   8 ronds de jambe soulevés en dehors
   8 ronds de jambe soulevés en dedans

5. *Battements frappés et avec petits battements sur le cou de pied*
   16 battements frappés
   16 battements frappés avec petits battements sur le cou de pied

6. *Rond de jambe en l'air et rond de jambe fondu avec grand battement*
   8 ronds de jambe en l'air en dehors
   8 ronds de jambe en l'air en dedans
   8 ronds de jambe en l'air fondu en dehors et en dedans

7. *Petits battements sur le cou de pied et frappés en avant*
   16 petits battements sur le cou de pied
   16 petits battements sur le cou de pied on full pointe
   32 petits battements frappés en avant

8. and 9. *Grand battement arrondi et battement à cloche*
   4 grands battements arrondis en dehors
   8 grands battements à cloche

10. *Grand rond de jambe développé*
    4 grands ronds de jambe développé en dehors
    4 grands ronds de jambe développé en dedans

11. *Grand battement fondu avec plié*
    2 grands battements fondus to fourth front
    2 grands battements fondus to second
    2 grands battements fondus to fourth back
    2 grands battements fondus to second

12. *Détirés*
    2 détirés

13. *La pointe à la barre*

14. *Backbends*

Position for commencing the exercises at the barre

All the exercises at the barre commence in the same position with the exceptions of exercises 13 and 14.

Although each of these exercises has a different quality and purpose, they all have a common goal. They train, limber and prepare the legs and feet in every way for the movements required in dancing; they develop the muscles and keep them in practice. For this reason there is only one initial position for all the exercises.

Explanation

Stand sideways to the barre with the left hand resting lightly on the barre; the arm is well stretched, the back of the hand is up, the thumb is down.

The torso is held upright in a gymnastic manner; the shoulders are held naturally down and open; the head is erect.

The legs are well turned-out in fifth position, right foot front, knees fully stretched.

The free right arm is rounded in position de repos (fig. 68).

During the exercises, the body, which is the centre of balance, remains perfectly still as the head, the free arm, the legs and the feet move.

At the end of the exercise everything returns to the initial position of departure.

In exercises 13 and 14, the initial and ending positions are different because both hands are on the barre.

The pupil stands facing the wall clasping the barre with both hands; the arms are extended, the backs of the hands turned up and the thumbs down.

The erect torso is in a gymnastic position with the shoulders held naturally, down and open; the head is upright. The feet are closed in fifth position, knees fully stretched.

In these exercises, a position is right or left depending on which foot is front in the fifth position (fig. 69).

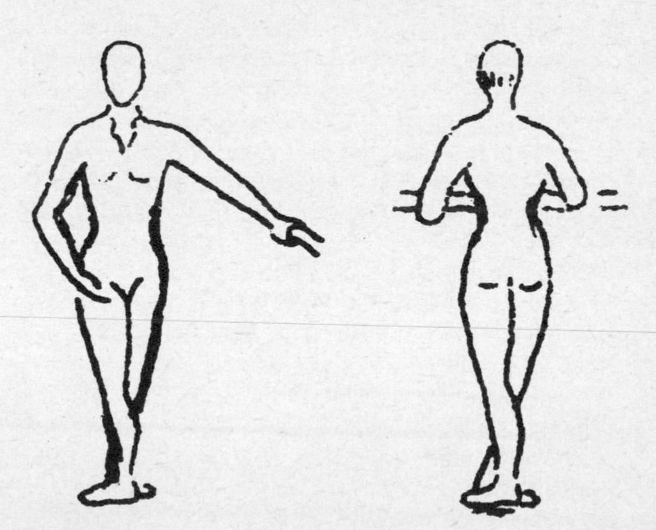

Fig. 68 Initial position with one hand on the barre

Fig. 69 With two hands resting on the barre

Closing movement for all exercise at the barre

As all exercises are executed with a certain amount of energy (some more, some less), at the end of each exercise there is a calm, smooth movement to close.

For technical reasons this ending is not adopted in exercises nos. 1 or 10.

Execution

Demi-plié as the foot closes into fifth front at the end of the exercise.

The head turns to the wall.

The arm lowers from second to position de repos.

Then with a slow movement:

- the knees straighten once more
- the head gradually turns to the opposite side
- the arm is raised from position de repos through first, opening to second with a smooth, fluid movement.

The arm lowers once more to position de repos; the head is erect.

To turn from the right side to the left

The initial position for exercises at the barre is right when the left hand rests on the barre and the right arm and leg are free. In this case, the right foot, which is the working foot and executes the exercise, must always commence in fifth position front while the left leg, which is behind, always functions as a support standing on the whole foot which must be firmly and solidly well placed on the ground, irremovably turned out.

When the right leg has to work, the body balances by taking the full weight onto the left leg and in this case the left foot, well turned out, will be and will continue to remain, in first position.

All exercises executed on the right side with the right leg are repeated on the left side with the left leg. Therefore, at the end of an exercise from the initial position right, the right foot crosses behind the toe of the left foot which is in first position. Then, balancing the weight on both legs, the feet rise onto half pointe and, making a half turn inwards towards the left, the body turns round as the left hand is released from the barre and the right, gripping it, takes its place; then the heels lower and automatically the feet will be well crossed in fifth position with the left foot front. The left arm lowers, well rounded, into position de repos.

After this movement, the pupil is in the initial position left ready to execute the same exercise on the left side with the left leg.

To avoid repetition, each exercise will be described on the right side with the right leg working.

The execution of the exercise on the left side with the left leg can be easily determined by substituting the indication left for right.

It is important to emphasize that the following rule must be strictly observed: as soon as the exercise has been completed on one side, it must immediately be repeated on the other side before continuing on to the next exercise.

The reason for this rule is both technical and physical, ensuring that there are equal amounts of work and relaxation on both legs so that training is always well balanced.

EXERCISE 1

PLIÉS

In this movement, the body descends as the knees slowly bend until they have reached their maximum; it then rises up until the knees straighten completely; the weight is evenly balanced on both legs.

The movement is executed more than once in each position, commencing in first.

Whatever the position, both descending and rising, plié is performed slowly and gradually, not jerkily.

The feet remain securely in the original position throughout (firmly together in the crossed positions; heels well turned out in the open positions). The weight is on the whole foot, the little toe does not leave the floor.

As the knees bend and straighten they must remain turned out in line with the shoulders and the feet.

When descending in first, third, fourth and fifth, the heels rise gradually and easily, only as much as is necessary to continue the plié and not more than this. In any case, never before this movement. At the depth of the plié the feet will be on half pointe with the weight evenly distributed over both legs (fig. 70).

When rising, the heels perform the same movement in reverse; they lower gradually and easily before the knees straighten, never after.

The heels are never raised during plié in second position. This rule must be strictly observed (fig. 70a).

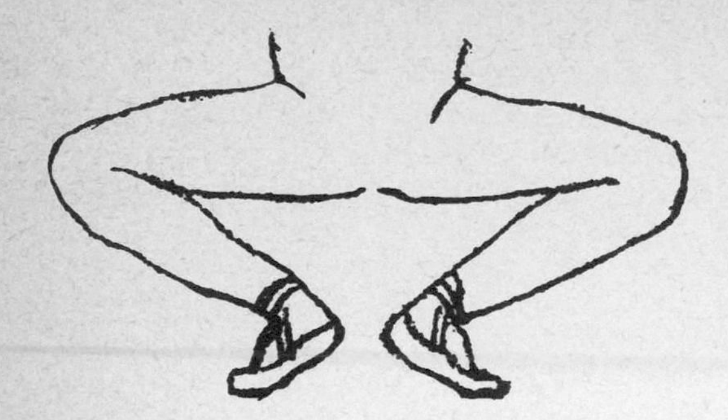

Fig. 70 Heels raised

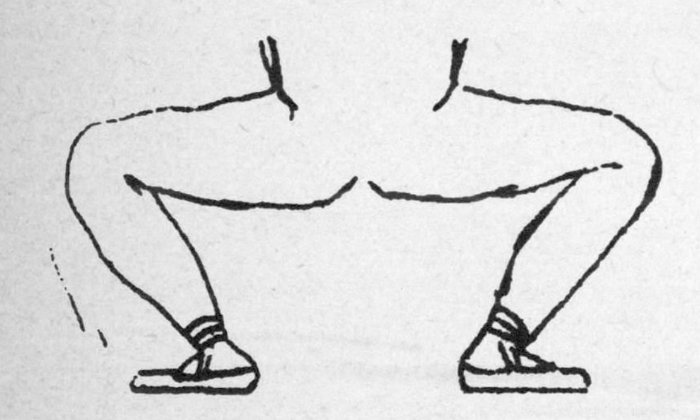

Fig. 70a Heels on the floor

The purpose of pliés is to exercise the muscles of the thighs, calves and insteps, open and turn out the legs and at the same time open the hips, forcing the internal muscles of the thighs and prepare good levers for jumping. It also develops elasticity and prepares the legs and feet to be light and smooth. Pliés also strengthen the lumbar region giving the dancer necessary stability.

Because of its particular qualities, plié is first in the order of exercises. It activates all the principal muscles of the legs and back, developing a strong sense of balance; it forces the turn-out of the legs, providing them with the necessary framework with which to perform all the other exercises.

Plié is the classic movement which gives suppleness; the whole body begins to feel an immediate and beneficial sense of lightness and agility, essential for the profitable continuation of the lesson.

Correct execution of pliés

Plié is executed slowly with the torso remaining upright; the lumbar region is held firmly in order to remain on balance.

The whole foot is firmly placed on the floor; the heels are gradually raised only when the plié has reached its deepest point – when the knees cannot bend any more.

Rising up, the heels lower until they are once more firmly on the floor; continue rising until the legs are completely straight with the thighs and calves firmly together.

The knees are well turned out in line with the shoulders and the feet, both descending and rising; the feet are turned out with the heels firmly together in first position; well crossed and held together in third and fifth positions; fully turned out in the open positions of second and fourth (in the last two positions, particularly in fourth, the weight must be equally distributed and both knees must bend evenly during the plié).

In this way perfection of execution will be achieved, easily, without force or fatigue, perfectly on balance, drawing by degrees all manner of benefits for the muscles.

The arms during pliés

The hand which is placed on the barre does not move; take particular care not to raise the elbow after rising up.

During the plié, the free arm complements the movement of the legs with a port de bras.

Before commencing the exercise, the free arm is raised from position de repos, passing through *first*, to *second* position; then, the palm of the hand faces down, the wrist is slightly raised with the fingers extended a little to give lightness to the movement; the arm gradually lowers at the same time and speed as the plié, passing through *demi-seconde*, arriving in *position de repos* as the plié reaches its deepest point.

As the body rises up, still smoothly but slightly faster, the arm coordinates with the legs, rising from *position de repos* to arrive exactly in *first* position as the legs are fully straightened. The arm opens to *second*, which is the original position, on the last beat of music, ready to recommence.

The head during pliés

As the knees bend, the head follows the port de bras with a slow and elegant movement; it turns to the shoulder of the supporting side to return looking straight ahead at the depth of the plié; it remains in this position on rising up, then turns to the opposite side following the arm as it opens from first to second position.

Both the movements of the arm and that of the head must be executed with lightness and grace without pulling the shoulder forward, which must remain quite still and in perfect line with the other.

N.B. In the first exercise we have shown immediately how, right from the start, some movements of the legs are combined with movements of all or some parts of the body.

As plié is a slow exercise, it forms part of the Adagio movements.

No more than two pliés should be executed in one position. More than this number would weaken the knees.

Pliés are executed in duple rhythm in 4/4 time, taking one whole bar to bend and one whole bar to rise and return to the original position.

COMMON FAULTS

In the execution of pliés, the following faults are to be avoided:

1. Raising the heels onto demi-pointe before bending the knees
2. Remaining on demi-pointe while the knees bend
3. Raising the heels to three quarter pointe
4. Over-turning out the feet
5. Descending or rising up jerkily

Subdivision of pliés

Pliés, as well as an exercise, are one of the classic movements in dance in both the adagio and in the vigorous trampoline-movement which gives impetus to jumps, and on alighting where it acts as a shock absorber.

For this reason, it is not always necessary to execute a full plié; depending on specific necessities, plié may be small or medium.

This movement is divided into 3 basic pliés, these are:

1. Plié à un quart (fig. 71)
2. Demi-plié (fig. 72)
3. Grand plié (fig. 73)

The difference between these pliés depends on how much the knees bend.

In grand plié the heels are raised only as much as is absolutely necessary to allow the knees to bend naturally to their maximum (fig. 73). It is a serious fault to raise them more than is necessary (fig. 74).

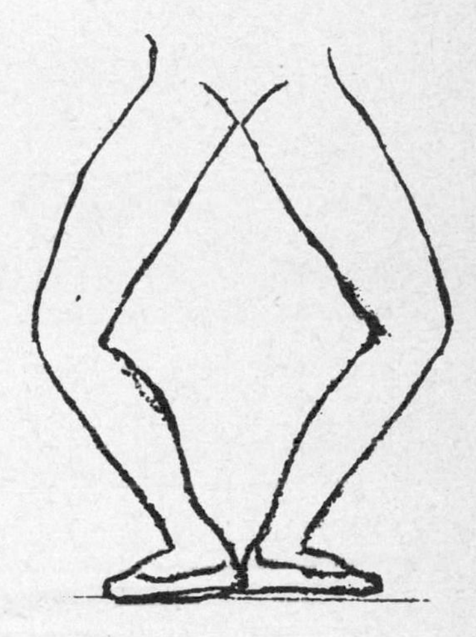

Fig. 71 Plié à un quart

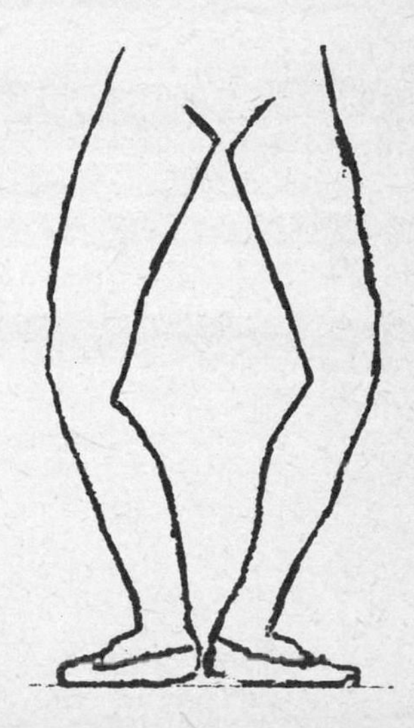

Fig. 72 Demi-plié

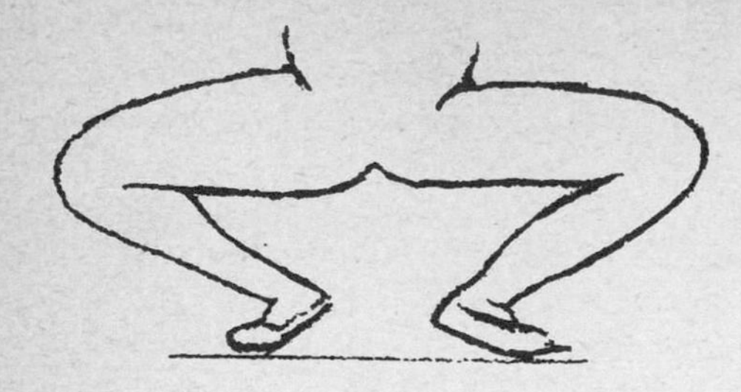

Fig. 73 Grand plié

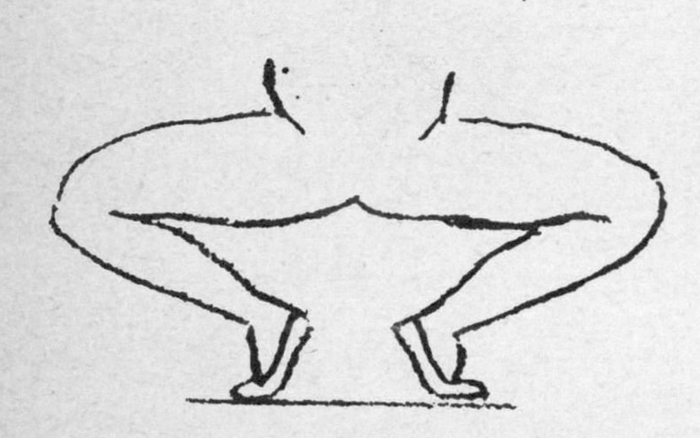

Fig. 74 Faulty grand plié

BREATHING

During plié, breathing must be rational. It must be deep and regular, never speeding up nor slowing down:

As the knees bend, in a calm and regular rhythm, exhale completely; rising up, still in a calm and regular rhythm, inhale deeply until the working arm is open in second position, completely expanding the chest and shoulders.

This rational breathing invigorates the heart and lungs giving the dancer greater stamina and an indisputable advantage to his health.

EXERCISE

Pliés in the five positions form one whole exercise; battement tendu to change from one position to the next, immediately transferring the weight onto both legs.

1. Pliés in first

Stand in the initial position for exercises at the barre; open the arm to second position.

Battement tendu to second and slide the right foot to first.

With the heels held well together and the feet turned out, bend the knees slowly making sure that they are turned out over the toes; as the heels are slowly raised, the weight is on half pointe. Rise up slowly, gradually lowering the heels until the knees are completely straight (fig. 75).

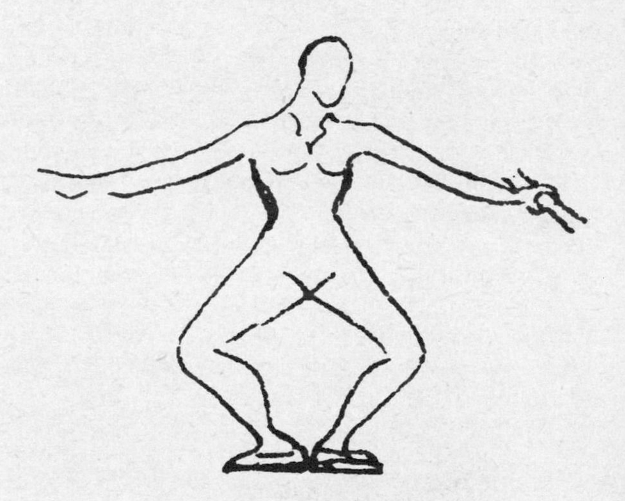

Fig. 75 Plié in first position

As the knees bend and then straighten, the port de bras and head movement are coordinated.

During the first part of the plié, the heels remain turned out in the same line of departure.

Rising up, the heels come together making any adjustment unnecessary.

As we have seen, breathing must be deep and even.

Care must be taken with the movements of the arm and the head.

2. Pliés in second position

The feet are in first position and the arm in second; battement tendu, sliding the foot to second position, quickly lowering the heel, taking the weight over both legs.

The feet are well turned out in line with each other; the distance between them is around 8 inches (20 cm).

The knees are over the toes during plié, maintaining the turn-out throughout the whole exercise.

The heels are never raised in this position.

The body is held upright with particular strength in the lumbar region at the depth of the plié, as there is the inevitable tendency to allow, even slightly, the torso to drop forward and the behind to stick out, forcing the knees to close and stability to be lost.

Care must be taken with port de bras, the movement of the head, and breathing.

3. Pliés in third position

The feet are in second position, the arm remains in second. Transfer the weight onto the supporting leg with the working foot still pointed in second position; slide the foot into third position gradually lowering the heel. Commence plié slowly, still maintaining the turn-out, raising and lowering the heels when descending and rising up, as explained previously.

Make sure that the feet crossed in third remain held together throughout the whole movement and that the heels never turn in, even for a moment.

Care must be taken with port de bras, the movement of the head and breathing.

4. Pliés in fourth position

The feet are in third position, the arm in second. Adjust the weight onto the supporting leg; battement tendu sliding the foot to fourth front, lower the heel quickly taking the weight evenly over both legs.

Crossing the feet in the open position relates to third position; however, the distance between the feet, which are parallel, is about 4 inches (10 cm).

Slow plié keeping the knees turned out, gradually raising and lowering the heels as explained above.

Great care must be taken so that plié is always executed evenly with the weight equally balanced over both legs.

During plié, as the heels rise, care must be taken to ensure that one heel does not come off the floor before the other; they always rise and lower in complete coordination.

Care must be taken with port de bras, the movement of the head and breathing.

5. Pliés in fifth position

Remain in fourth position, arm in second. Transfer the weight onto the supporting leg leaving the working foot pointed to fourth front on the floor; draw the foot into fifth position, sliding the pointe along the floor and gradually lowering the heel. Slow plié keeping the knees over the toes, gradually raising and lowering the heels as explained above.

Great care must be taken to ensure that the feet are held together throughout the whole movement as the heels must never turn in.

As usual, the movements of the arms and head are taken carefully and breathing is regular.

After the fifth and last plié, turn to the other side as explained on page 39 and repeat the exercise in the same way and at the same speed on the opposite side.

N.B. In first and second positions, both on the right side and the left, the position of the feet does not change and is the same for the right as for the left.

In the third, fourth and fifth positions: on the right side, the right foot will be in front; on the left side, the left foot will be in front.

So for these positions we have:

- one position with the right foot
- one position with the left foot

EXERCISE 2

GRANDS BATTEMENTS

In grand battement the fully stretched leg is raised to the front, to the side or to the back.

This movement is executed more than once in each of the three positions of the legs.

Grand battement is always strong and well accented; it is executed vigorously and whatever the direction, the feet always commence in fifth position:

a) If the leg is raised to fourth front, the working foot commences in fifth front.

b) If the leg is raised to fourth back, the working foot commences in fifth back.

c) If the leg is raised to second, the working foot can commence either in fifth front or fifth back.

The fully stretched working leg is raised until it is completely horizontal; the supporting leg is well stretched and the body remains firm throughout the movement.

The purpose of this exercise is to make it possible for the leg to work independently of the torso. The muscles are trained to execute this movement as easily and naturally as the other daily exercises, without rigidity in the thigh, abdomen or any other part of the body.

Grand battement releases the leg from the torso, training it to move quickly in all directions from the height of the femur; in particular it enables it to move with complete tension in the knee and in the hamstring and posterior tibial muscles.

The quality of this movement is strong, vigorous and energetic (fig. 76).

Fig. 76 Grand battement in second

Manner of executing grands battements correctly

When executing grand battement in any direction, the body remains in a position of "aplomb," firm and perfectly balanced without any swaying.

The supporting leg is fully stretched with the foot firmly on the floor, turned out in first position.

To fourth front: the fully stretched leg rises, with energy, from fifth position to fourth front at hip height; knee and foot are correctly turned out, instep arched, toes pointed, heel contracted and turned up.

Without a pause and with the same energy, the leg lowers, well sustained, returning to the original position of departure, closed front in a well-crossed fifth position.

To second position: the heel of the raised foot is contracted and down. The foot that commences in fifth position front, can close either in fifth back or in fifth front. In both cases the feet are tightly crossed.

To fourth back: raise the leg from the fifth, fully stretched, to hip height, well turned out with the foot arched and the heel down; as the leg lowers, well sustained, the lumbar spine must be held firmly in place as the foot closes into a well-crossed fifth.

While the leg is moving, the body must remain gymnastically strong and completely vertical.

The working leg is fully stretched and thrown into the air with vigor; it is lowered, well sustained, with the same amount of energy.

As the foot leaves the floor, it gradually begins to point, so that by the time it is in the air, it is already well arched. Lowering, the same movement will be reversed until the foot gradually closes into fifth with the whole foot on the ground.

We can see that a grand battement is composed of one complete movement in which the leg is raised and lowered.

This exercise must be executed with great energy: the leg rises to the height of the hip, exactly horizontal to the vertical line of the body (see: Book One, Part One, page 27, fig. 37).

This position can only be achieved gradually, with perserverance and a lot of practice. In this movement, the muscles of the working leg alone operate, the supporting leg is limited to remaining completely stretched with tense muscles being a solid base with the weight evenly balanced.

The other parts of the body remain in their correct position, naturally and easily, without any unnecessary strain.

Arms and head in grands battements

The hand holds the barre without straining and does not move throughout this exercise.

Before the exercise, the free arm is raised from position de repos, passes through first into second position where it remains until it lowers into position de repos only after completion of the whole exercise.

Throughout the exercise the head is held erect, naturally and easily, facing forwards without any tension in the neck; the face tranquil and the mouth smiling.

There are 32 grands battements in all; 8 in each position finishing the last 8 in second position.

More than this number should be avoided as it would result in damaging, rather than strengthening the leg muscles.

Grands battements are executed in a duple rhythm in 2/4 time, slightly andante and well accented. In the first temps of the bar the leg rises and lowers; in the second temps, the feet are held firmly together in fifth position.

So, in one half of each musical bar there is action, and in the other half there is a pause.

COMMON FAULTS

When executing grands battements the following errors are to be avoided:

1. Allowing the leg to drop like a dead weight when lowering. It must be sustained and "carried" back into the original position.
2. Raising the leg above hip height.
3. Bending the knee of the supporting leg in order to push the other leg higher.
4. Leaning back, sideways, or forwards, in order to lift the other leg more comfortably; the body always remains upright and perfectly "aplomb."

BREATHING

As grand battement is a vigorous movement, the pupil must avoid becoming breathless as this is extremely damaging. Breathing calmly, slowly, independently of the movement of the legs, must become a habit.

At the beginning of the exercise, inhale deeply for two whole bars or for two grands battements; exhale completely during the next two bars.

In this way, for every 8 bars, or grands battements, the dancer will inhale deeply twice, and will exhale completely twice.

If breathing is correct, the exercise is never tiring.

EXERCISE

Take the right arm to second where it remains throughout the exercise.

1. Grand battement to fourth front

Raise the straight right leg, with energy, to fourth front, to the height of the hip, well turned out with the pointe of the foot forced down; lower it immediately, still straight and well turned out, into fifth position front.

2. Grand battement to second

Raise the straight right leg, with energy, to second position to the height of the hip, well turned out, with the pointe forced down; lower it immediately, still fully stretched, into fifth front.

The next grand battement closes in fifth back, then again in fifth front, and so on following alternately. The last one closes in fifth back.

3. Grand battement to fourth back

Raise the straight right leg to fourth back to the height of the hip, well turned out with the pointe forced down; lower immediately, still fully stretched and well turned out, into fifth position back.

4. Grand battement to second and ending

After grands battements to fourth back, grands battements in second are repeated, after which the closing movement described on page 39 is executed, ending the exercise.

Turn to the other side and repeat the whole exercise with the left leg.

EXERCISE 3

BATTEMENTS TENDUS

In battement tendu the foot opens to second position, keeping the pointe of the well-arched foot on the floor; the foot returns to fifth position in the same way.

The movement is repeated many times with the same leg.

Battement tendu is most useful when executed to second position; however, it can be taken to fourth front and fourth back.

The movement is performed quickly, with energy in a strongly accented rhythm.

N.B. Battement tendu exercise ends with two very similar movements that follow in a fixed order, executed with the same leg:

a) battements tendus
b) battements dégagés
c) battements relevés (with movement of pointe)

The three movements form a complete exercise.

The purpose of this exercise is to allow the stretched leg freedom and independence of movement and to strengthen and arch the foot.

This movement trains the extensor muscles, strengthening the legs which then begin to acquire independence from the torso as well as freedom and agility.

The quality of this movement depends on the action of the leg as it springs, energetically and rhythmically, from an open position to a closed position; the leg becomes used to moving precisely and cleanly.

This movement is a gradual preparation for steps where the legs work completely independently of each other.

Manner of executing battements tendus correctly

During this movement, the body remains upright, without tension; the weight is over the supporting leg which is straight with the foot turned out, forming one line with the torso.

The working leg opens from fifth position to second, fully stretched and turned out. The foot slides along the floor gradually raising the heel, until it is fully pointed but never raised off the ground (fig. 77). Still fully stretched and turned out, sliding the pointe along the floor, gradually lowering the heel, the foot closes sharply from second position into a tightly crossed fifth.

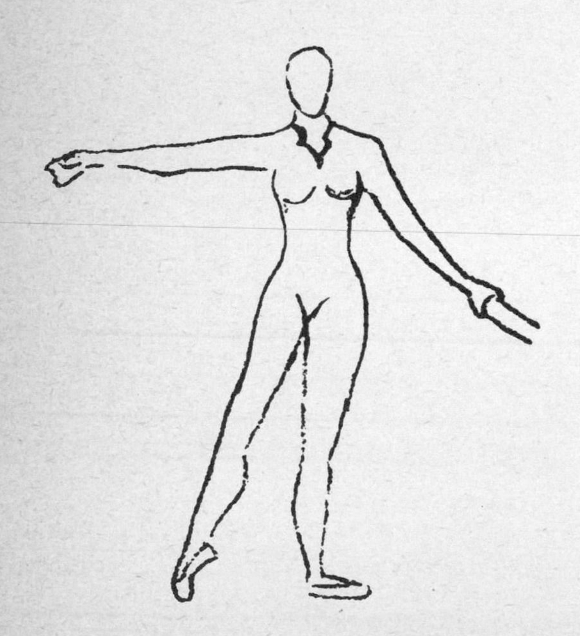

Fig. 77 Battement tendu in second

Without a pause and with the same energy, the leg opens once more to second position; the foot is well arched with the pointe forced down. Pausing for one beat, the movement is complete.

The exercise continues closing alternately into fifth; once to the front, once to the back.

N.B. This movement commences in second (open position); this gives the movement sharpness and agility.

Before the exercise, the free arm is raised from position de repos, passing through first into second position where it remains naturally during the exercise.

The head remains naturally erect with a serene expression, throughout the exercise.

Battement tendu is a strong, free movement; it is also used to change the feet smoothly from one position to another.

Sixteen battements tendus in second are the recommended quantity; more than this would cause tiredness without serving any useful purpose. It must be remembered that the exercise does not end here and is followed by another two similar movements.

Battements tendus are executed in a duple rhythm, in 2/4 time, moderato and well accented:

- in the first temps of the bar, the leg springs from second position to fifth, re-opening immediately to second;
- in the second temps, pause in second.

There is only one battement tendu for each bar, so closing and opening the leg occurs quickly, with a short pause in second between one complete movement and the next.

COMMON FAULTS

Common faults to be avoided:

a) Allowing the pointe of the foot to be raised off the floor, even for a moment; the foot must always remain in contact with the ground.
b) Bending the knee of the working leg when it is in second in order to arch the foot more easily. The knee remains fully stretched throughout.
c) Raising the hip as the leg goes to second. This type of movement, as well as being technically incorrect, is unattractive.
d) Allowing the foot, and the heel, to turn in when the

leg is in second. The foot and the whole leg must be well turned out and the heel pushed forward.

e) Closing, during the movement, in an incorrect fifth or even worse, into third, instead of fifth.

BREATHING

During battement tendu, breathing must be calm, regular and well coordinated with the movement.

Inhale deeply during the first two battements tendus, and exhale completely during the next two.

EXERCISE

Stand in the initial position for exercises at the barre on the right side; the right arm is in second, the head erect.

Slide the right foot along the floor from fifth position to second, pointe on the floor.

Begin the movement closing the foot, with energy, to fifth back, feet tightly crossed; open the leg immediately, still completely straight, to second position; after a slight pause, bring the foot into fifth front, crossing the feet tightly, opening immediately back to second, pointe on the floor. Continue the movement closing alternately into fifth, once to the front and once to fifth back.

At the end of the exercise, the right leg is in fifth front. The right arm remains in second position and the exercise continues with battements dégagés.

BATTEMENTS DÉGAGÉS

Battement dégagé is similar in appearance to battement tendu.

The leg opens from fifth position to second, well pointed but raised from the floor at least 1-1½ inches (3 or 4 cm), with an even movement, it closes again in fifth back opening once more to second, closing again in fifth front.

This movement must be executed evenly, quickly and easily, more than once with the same leg which is always well stretched.

The purpose of battement dégagé is to loosen and speed up the movement of the fully stretched leg, making the feet more supple by rapidly rising and lowering through the foot. During this movement the muscles are always sufficiently tense to maintain the leg extended and sustained; but the internal muscles of the thigh work mostly to release the leg and make possible very quick movements with the leg completely stretched.

The particular quality of this exercise is speed and dexterity when changing quickly from a closed position to an open position; this movement is performed in a relaxed and natural way. The exercise prepares the leg with rapid, easy movements to be able to execute steps where the leg opens, fully stretched, to second position with the foot well arched and raised a few inches off the ground; for example, it is the necessary preparation for assemblé, which originates from this movement.

Assemblé is a very important dance step since so many other steps originate from it.

Manner of executing battements dégagés correctly

The working leg opens, fully stretched and turned out, from fifth position front, to second; the heel is gradually raised as the foot slides along the floor until it rises, fully arched, about 1-1½ inches (3 or 4 cm) into the air. Without pausing, and with a continuous movement and the same energy, the leg closes once more in fifth.

Each battement dégagé closes alternately into fifth back and fifth front (fig. 78).

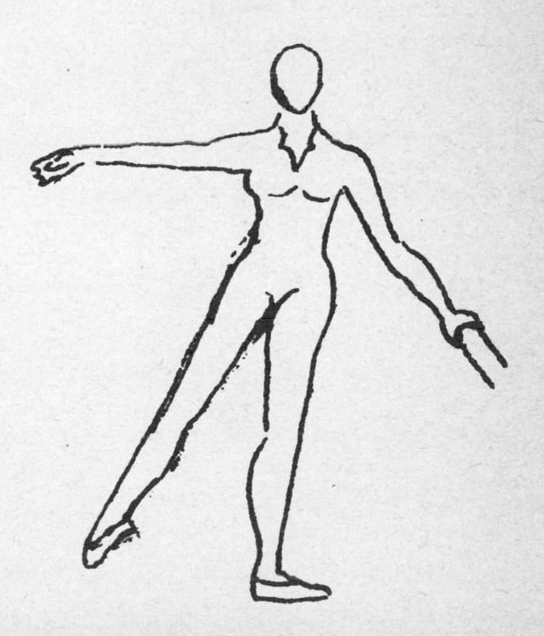

Fig. 78 Battement dégagé in second

Throughout battement dégagé, the body remains upright, firm and well balanced; the muscles are relaxed in a normal way and there is no tension, even unconsciously, in any part of the body. The leg works completely independently, with a quick, free movement and is well sustained throughout its whole length; the foot springs on command and never through reflex action.

N.B. This movement is not as easy as it first appears. The first part of the exercise, battement tendu, is the preparation; with constant practice, battements dégagés will be performed easily and freely. This is one of the faster exercises and must be executed diligently so that the movement is always completed; it is especially necessary to make sure that the feet are well closed in the fifth position. No part of the exercise should ever be "wasted" with the excuse of being too fast.

As before, the arm remains in second position throughout battements dégagés; the head stays erect.

The usual number of battements dégagés is 16. These are followed by 4 battements relevés to complete the exercise.

Remember that it is not the quantity but the quality that is important.

Battement dégagé is executed in a duple rhythm, in 2/4 time, molto mosso.

In the first temps of the bar, the leg opens to second and closes into fifth back. In the second temps, the movement is repeated, still smoothly and evenly. There are two battements dégagés to every bar.

COMMON FAULTS

It is a serious fault, during battements dégagés to open and close the foot only by moving the hip, neglecting the lower part of the leg which hangs like a rag.

BREATHING

In battement dégagés, executed in a fast rhythm, breathing is calm, serene and well coordinated with the movement.

During the first four battements dégagés, that is for two whole bars, inhale deeply. For the next four battements dégagés, that is for another two bars, exhale smoothly.

EXERCISE

The arm and the head remain in the same position as before; the exercise continues opening the right foot from fifth front, gradually raising the heel and arching the foot until it is pointed to second, about 1-1½ inches (3 or 4 cm) off the floor; without a pause, close the foot into fifth back.

Every battement dégagé closes alternately into fifth back and fifth front.

The arm remains in second as the exercise continues with battements relevés.

BATTEMENTS RELEVÉS

Essentially, battement relevé is a battement tendu with the added movement of lowering the heel, raising it immediately and precisely, strongly arching the pointe of the foot.

The leg is opened from fifth position to second; the pointe of the well-arched foot remains on the floor. The foot stays firmly in second position as the heel lowers and rises sharply forcing the foot to arch strongly; the foot then closes behind in fifth position with a decisive movement.

This movement is repeated in a series with the same leg; the action is sharp and swift.

Battement relevé follows battement dégagé without any interruption and in the same moderate, even rhythm as battement tendu. Battement tendu is the first movement of the exercise, battement relevé is the third and last.

The purpose of the exercise is to combine the movement of the leg with a complete and particular movement of the pointe; this gives the instep strength and elasticity when forming a strong, secure springboard for all steps of elevation.

By forcing the pointe on the floor, the spring-like movement of the heel, as it lowers and rises energetically, creates a well-arched foot. The movement is strong and decisive enabling the leg to acquire a consistent action.

In this way, the foot acquires a powerful spring-like movement, develops a strong arch and gradually takes the desired shape required both aesthetically and technically; this prepares the feet to support the whole weight of the body on the strong full pointe.

Manner of correctly executing battements relevés

Throughout the exercise, the torso is completely erect; the weight is firmly balanced over the supporting leg which is straight, with the foot well turned out forming one line with the torso.

The working leg, fully stretched and well turned

out, opens from fifth front to second position; the heel gradually rises as the foot slides along the floor until it is fully pointed (fig. 79).

In second position, pointe on the floor, the heel lowers (fig. 79a) with a decisive movement, then rises rapidly arching the foot as much as possible; to achieve a better result from this movement, the knee of the working leg is allowed to relax a little (fig. 80).

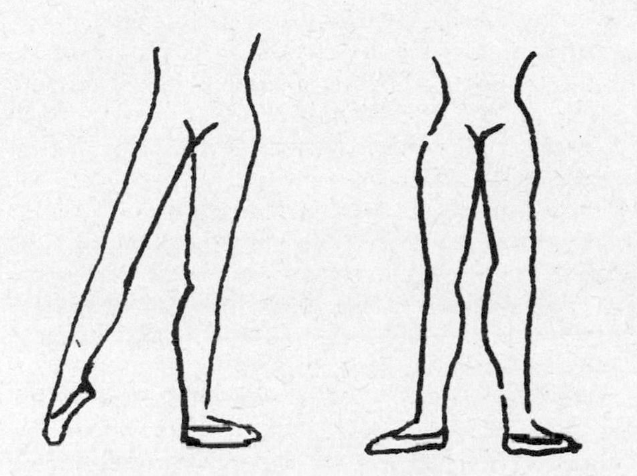

Fig. 79 Battement tendu

Fig. 79a The heel is on the floor

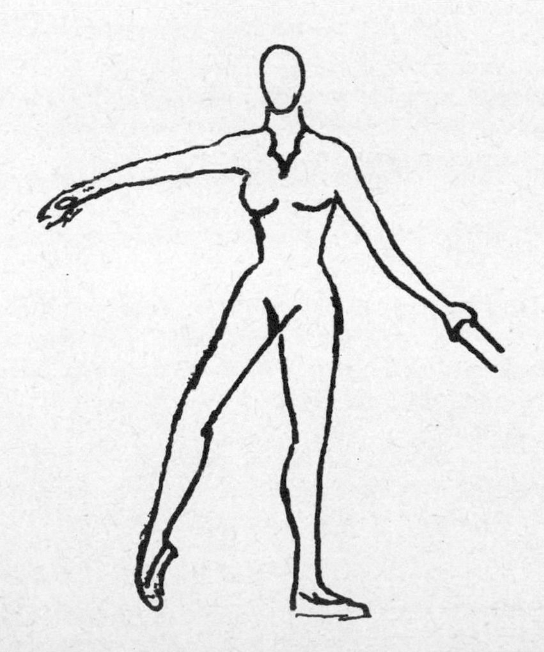

Fig. 80 Battement relevé

The foot closes with energy to fifth back, gradually lowering the heel until the whole foot is on the floor.

Each battement relevé closes alternately to fifth back and fifth front.

Battement relevé is executed in a precise, well-accented rhythm and it is important to ensure that the foot is well arched and the heel well turned out during the relevé. The fifths are firmly closed and well crossed.

Like battement tendu, this movement also commences in the open position of second.

During battements relevés the arm remains in second position. The head is erect and facing straight ahead.

Four battements relevés are sufficient; if well executed, these movements require the foot to make a considerable effort.

Too many would have the opposite effect of weakening the foot.

Battement relevé is executed in a duple rhythm in 2/4 time, moderato and well accented. During the first bar the heel lowers and rises; during the second bar the foot closes into fifth and opens immediately to second. So, for every two bars there is one battement relevé.

Although the two movements are different, they are both executed rapidly and decisively; because of this, there is a momentary pause between the first and second movement, and again between the second and third.

Common faults

During the relevé-pointe, it is a serious fault to withdraw the heel in order to arch the foot more. The heel is fully turned out throughout the movement.

Another serious fault is to raise the hip facilitating the movement of the leg to second.

Breathing

In battement relevé breathing is calm and regular. During the first bar, that is for the whole movement, inhale deeply. During the next bar, for the whole movement, exhale completely.

Exercise

Stand in fifth position, right foot front, arm in second, head erect. Open the right leg to second, pointe on the floor, to prepare for the exercise:

The heel lowers and rises with a decisive movement; slightly relax the right knee transferring the weight a little to the right; press on the pointe, strongly arching the foot.

After a moment, bring the body back, straighten the right leg, and close the foot into fifth back; open again immediately to second position, pointe on the floor.

N.B. After the last battement relevé, the exercise ends closing the foot in fifth front with the movement described on page 39.

The exercise is repeated in the same way and with the same timing starting with the left leg.

As we can see, this exercise is a combination of three different movements, each with the same purpose: to speed up and strengthen the legs and feet.

EXERCISE 4

RONDS DE JAMBE À TERRE

Ronds de jambe à terre are movements in which the pointe of the foot describes a semi-circle on the floor.

The straight working leg moves from fourth front to fourth back passing through second; then, passing through first position, returns to fourth front.

Ronds de jambe à terre are executed with outward and inward movements:

a) *En dehors* (outwards): moves from fourth front to fourth back.

b) *En dedans* (inwards): moves from fourth back to fourth front.

Ronds de jambe à terre is executed with a smooth, continuous movement, marked by a slight pause at the point of departure.

Ronds de jambe à terre en dehors and en dedans are followed by ronds de jambe soulevés which complete the exercise.

The purpose of ronds de jambe à terre is to enable the fully stretched leg to move smoothly and easily, loosen the movement in the hip socket and open the pelvis; the working leg is held well turned out with the pointe of the foot forced down and the heel pushed forward; the foot develops a smooth and graceful movement.

This exercise is executed calmly and easily which removes harshness and rigidity from the movement of the leg and gives it a certain elegance.

Manner of correctly executing rond de jambe à terre

During rond de jambe à terre, the weight is over the supporting leg ("aplomb") which remains fully stretched and well turned out with the foot in first position throughout.

The movement of the working leg, which is well turned out and fully stretched, is sure and decisive as it opens from fifth to fourth front or fourth back. As the leg goes from fifth to fourth front or back, the heel gradually rises, keeping the toes on the floor until the well-arched foot is in fourth position, on the floor; the leg remains straight and well turned out, foot fully pointed, for the whole rond de jambe.

The foot passes through first from fourth front (or back), and the exercise recommences. As the foot passes through first, the heel gradually lowers until the whole foot is flat on the floor, well turned out with the heels together. The movement continues, without pausing, gradually raising the heel until the foot is fully arched.

In this exercise, only the muscles of the legs are active. The supporting leg remains well stretched but not tense. The rest of the body is held firmly and naturally in position without unnecessary, harmful tension of the muscles. With care, the execution of rond de jambe à terre becomes simple, graceful and natural.

16 ronds de jambe à terre are sufficient for this exercise (8 en dehors and 8 en dedans).

Rond de jambe à terre is executed in a duple rhythm in 4/8 time, lento. In the first count of the bar, there is one whole rond de jambe; in the second count, there is a second complete rond de jambe. There are 2 whole ronds de jambe à terre to one bar which means 8 ronds de jambe à terre will take four bars of music.

Common faults

It is a serious fault, even for beginners, to allow the working leg, as it passes from one position to another, to turn in with the foot not completely arched and the pointe not well forced down and always in contact with the ground.

It is also an error for the feet not to be correctly turned out with the whole foot on the floor and the heels held together when the leg passes through first.

Breathing

During rond de jambe à terre, breathing must be calm and regular.

Inhale deeply during the first bar and for two whole ronds de jambe à terre; during the following bar and for two ronds de jambe à terre, exhale completely.

Inhale when rond de jambe à terre is preceded by a preparatory movement, as we will see later. In this case exhale during the first bar that is, at the beginning of the exercise, and so on.

EXERCISE

This exercise commences with a preparatory movement – this is none other than an incomplete grand rond de jambe à terre en dehors – and ends with a complete grand rond de jambe à terre en dehors.

These commencing and ending movements complete the exercise in a smooth and graceful manner.

Preparation

In the initial position for exercises at the barre with the right leg, demi-plié on both feet without raising the heels.

Slowly straighten the knee of the right leg, sliding the foot along the floor, gradually raising the heel until the foot is pointed to fourth position front.

At the end of this first movement, the right leg is in fourth front on the floor; the left leg is still in demi-plié.

The right arm is raised from position de repos to first following the movement of the leg; the head inclines over thc right shoulder (fig. 81).

The pointe of the right foot (with the leg fully stretched and turned out), describes a quarter circle on the floor, to second; gradually straighten the left leg during this movement so that it is completely straight by the time the right foot is in second position, still on the floor.

The right arm, following the movement of the leg, slowly opens to second; the head returns erect (fig. 82).

Rond de jambe à terre en dehors

After a short pause, at the end of the preparatory movement, the straight right leg describes another quarter circle to fourth back.

Gradually lower the heel, pass through first position, raise the heel once more and extend the leg to fourth front. Rond de jambe à terre en dehors always commences from fourth front. After a short pause, the right pointe describes a semi-circle, still on the floor, taking it to fourth back; pass through first once more and extend the leg again to fourth front on the floor.

Fig. 81 Right leg in fourth front

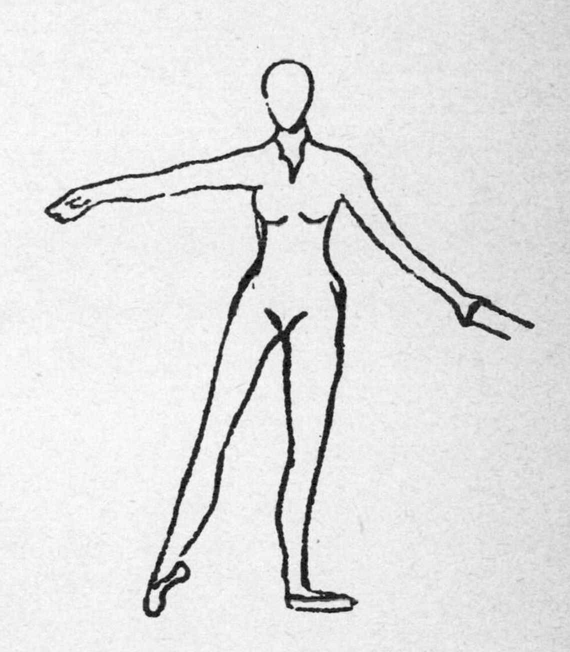

Fig. 82 Right leg in second after demi-rond de jambe

The left leg remains fully stretched throughout (fig. 83).

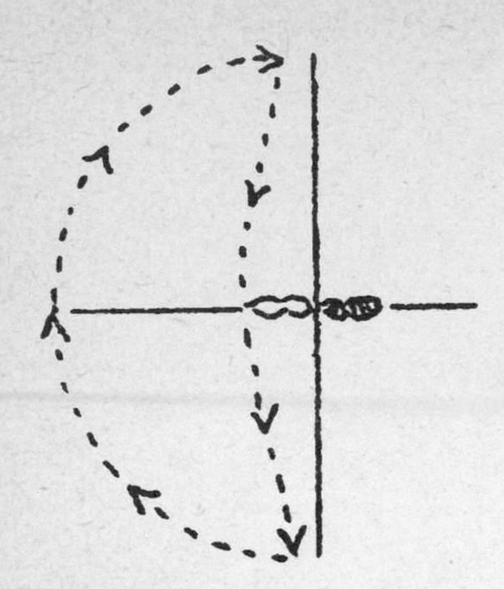

Fig. 83 Path of the right pointe in rond de jambe en dehors

Rond de jambe à terre en dedans

This is the same as the previous movement, but executed in reverse.

The right foot is in fourth front on the floor; gradually lower the heel, pass the foot through first, raise the heel once more extending the leg to fourth back; rond de jambe en dedans commences in this position.

After a slight pause, the pointe of the right foot, with the leg still straight, describes a semi-circle, passing through second position then first, extending once more to fourth back, on the floor.

The left leg remains fully stretched throughout (fig. 84).

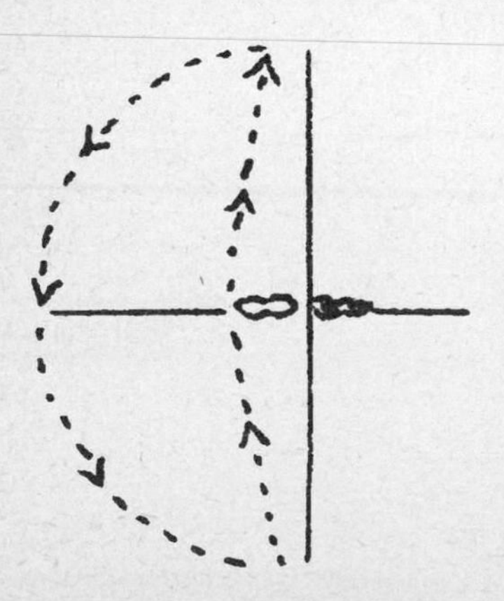

Fig. 84 Path of the right pointe in rond de jambe en dedans

After ronds de jambe à terre en dehors and en dedans, the last rond de jambe ends in first position; the right arm remains in second.

ROND DE JAMBE SOULEVÉ

Rond de jambe soulevé is a similar movement to rond de jambe à terre but raised at half height.

The circular movement is no longer executed with the leg completely straight, but with good use of the knee giving a smooth, graceful quality to the movement.

Rond de jambe soulevé is executed en dehors and en dedans:

a) *En dehors* (outwards): the movement commences to fourth front.
b) *En dedans* (inwards): the movement commences to fourth back.

The exercise is executed with strong, even movements.

Ronds de jambe soulevés follow ronds de jambe à terre and complete the exercise.

Through this exercise the leg acquires smoothness and agility, useful for charming, elegant movements. The movement of the foot also achieves a lightness and wonderful suppleness. The pelvis opens well.

This exercise is very important and we find it again as a dance step when practicing allegro steps. It also has a particular purpose which distinguishes it from the previous exercise.

Until now the exercises have been athletic in quality, with the primary purpose of developing the muscles, making them more supple. This is the first movement, that begins linking the physical development – the training of muscles and joints – with more polished and harmonious movements forming, in embryo, the first development of technique specifically for the classical dancer.

Manner of correctly executing the ronds de jambe soulevés

Throughout this exercise, the body is erect and firmly balanced over the supporting leg which is straight and firm, with the foot well turned out in first position.

Bearing in mind the purpose of the exercise, the movement of the working leg is very smooth, giving the appearance of natural unforced movement.

In the air, the leg, particularly the thigh, is held fully turned out, completely open in second.

As the foot passes through first, the movement of the leg must be correct; the whole foot is on the floor and the heels are together.

The movement of the foot, as it flexes on leaving and returning to first position, must be agile and free in order to give it a soft quality.

The gradual raising and lowering of the heel as the foot leaves or arrives in first, is controlled and completely natural.

In this exercise only the muscles of the leg are active and they work very smoothly; all the other parts of the body remain in their correct positions without tension and with the muscles relaxed.

The movement is even and uniform throughout the exercise.

During rond de jambe soulevé, the free arm remains in second position.

The head is erect.

Execute 16 ronds de jambe soulevés:
– 8 ronds de jambe soulevés en dehors
– 8 ronds de jambe soulevés en dedans

This number gives the leg the time to gradually improve the movement. A smaller number would be insufficient, a greater number is unnecessary.

Rond de jambe soulevé is executed in a rhythm in 4/8 time, lento, the same as the rond de jambe à terre. On the first count of the bar, there is one whole rond de jambe soulevé; the leg slows down slightly when in the air, and speeds up when passing through first.

On the second count of the bar, the whole rond de jambe soulevé is repeated.

As in the preceding exercise, there are 2 complete ronds de jambe soulevés for every bar; that is 8 for every 4 bars.

Common faults

When the leg is in the air it is a serious fault not to hold the thigh well turned out in second position.

It is also an error if the heels do not touch when passing through first.

Breathing

During rond de jambe soulevé, breathing must be kept calm and even without holding the breath or accelerating the rhythm. In the first bar, that is for two ronds de jambe soulevés, inhale deeply. In the next bar, that is for another two ronds de jambe soulevés, exhale completely.

Exercise

Rond de jambe soulevé en dehors

After rond de jambe à terre which ends in first, the right arm remains in second.

Throw the straight right leg to fourth front; open it to a high second; keeping the thigh well turned out in this position, bend the knee and continue the movement of the leg (from the knee to the foot) to fourth back. Lower the leg, gradually straightening the knee and, passing the straight leg through first, throw it once more to high fourth front to recommence the movement (fig. 85).

At the end of the exercise, the foot closes in first.

Fig. 85 Rond de jambe soulevé

Rond de jambe soulevé en dedans

After rond de jambe soulevé en dehors which ends in first, the right arm remains in second.

Throw the straight right leg to fourth back; open it to high second and, with the thigh well turned out in this position, bend the knee and continue the movement of the leg (from the knee to the foot) to fourth front; then gradually lower the leg, straightening the knee and, passing the straight leg through first, throw it once more to high fourth back to recommence the movement.

At the end of the exercise, close the foot into first position, lowering the right arm to position de repos.

Grand rond de jambe à terre en dehors and ending

Stand with the body well erect, the legs straight, the feet in first position; right arm in position de repos.

Demi-plié in this position without raising the heels.

The left leg is in demi-plié, the right leg opens to fourth front, sliding the fully pointed foot along the floor, gradually straightening the knee.

The right arm is raised to first, coordinating the movement with that of the leg.

The head inclines over the right shoulder (see fig. 81).

The pointed foot describes a semi-circle on the floor, taking the straight right leg from fourth front, passing through second to fourth back.

The right arm opens to second, coordinating with the leg. At the end of rond de jambe à terre, the head is inclined over the left shoulder.

Pause in this position with the leg extended to fourth back; bend the torso forward and down; the right arm is raised and extended, then lowers with the body until the hand touches the floor.

The body recovers to the upright position then bends strongly back. The arm follows the movement of the body and is taken back, well stretched.

The body returns upright gradually straightening the left knee; the right foot, pointed on the floor, draws in gradually lowering the heel until it closes in fifth back with both knees fully stretched.

Battement tendu taking the right foot to fifth front and execute the "closing movement" described on page 39.

The right arm lowers to position de repos; the head comes erect.

Turn to the other side and repeat the whole exercise on the left side.

N.B. In this grand rond de jambe à terre en dehors, the supporting leg, which acts as a pivot, is in demi-plié; therefore, the semi-circle described by the working leg is wider than usual.

As we have seen, the exercise begins with a preparation and has an ending which completes the whole exercise.

Therefore, the first musical bar is used as a preparation for the exercise.

After 16 bars the first part of the exercise finishes. After another 16 bars, the second part of the exercise finishes. Therefore, there are 4 bars for the ending.

EXERCISE 5

BATTEMENTS FRAPPÉS SUR LE COU DU PIED

Battement frappé sur le cou du pied does not commence in fifth position; the thigh is turned out in second position with the knee flexed and the heel placed on the cou de pied of the other leg.

In this movement the leg is extended very strongly into a low second position, then brought back to the initial position.

During battement frappé only the lower leg moves, the thigh remains completely still, without moving.

The purpose of this exercise is to train the thigh and lower leg muscles (rectus femoris, 3 vasti, tibialis and gastrocnemius) so that the legs become good levers, used for springing and for all energetic movements.

This movement is found very frequently in the most vigorous dance steps.

Battement frappé is one of the most energetic exercises and the initial movement can be compared with the crack of a whip. The returning movement is more moderate but just as lively.

This movement is followed by battement frappé avec petit battement sur le cou de pied, which completes the exercise.

Manner of correctly executing battement frappé

The body is erect; lumbar region held firmly, well balanced over the supporting leg which is well turned out with the foot in first.

In the initial position, the working leg is in second; the thigh remains firm and well turned out in this position throughout the exercise.

The knee is flexed with the heel placed on the cou de pied of the other leg.

The foot on the cou de pied of the supporting leg, is turned out and low, with the toes about 1 1/4 inches

(3 cm) off the floor. Only the lower part of the working leg moves during this exercise; the thigh remains well turned out in second.

The knee straightens sharply and the leg opens quickly to second with the ball of the foot sharply brushing the floor.

The leg in second position is straight with the foot fully arched, raised about 3 1/4 inches (8 cm) off the floor.

In this position, all the muscles of the thigh and leg are strongly contracted; there is no tension in the rest of the body.

The foot does not brush the floor when returning from second back onto the cou de pied of the other leg.

Throughout battement frappé, the free arm remains in second position; the head is erect.

16 battements frappés are sufficient in order to achieve the result required from this exercise.

More battements frappés are unnecessary and could damage the muscles by causing them to be overtired; the exercise is completed by another 16 battements frappés sur le cou de pied – preceded by petit battement – even more exhausting.

Battements frappés are executed in a duple rhythm in 2/4 time, slightly andante and strongly accented. There are two complete battements frappés for each bar: the leg opens to second (accent out) and returns onto the cou de pied, twice.

COMMON FAULTS

Battement frappé is a strong, lively exercise. If the movement to second is soft, with the muscles relaxed and flabby, it might just as well have not been executed.

It is also a serious fault if the ball of the foot does not strike the floor when opening to second.

BREATHING

Battement frappé is a very energetic exercise. Uneven and anxious breathing can be tiring and harmful. Great care must be taken to see that the pupil learns to breathe rationally.

Inhale deeply and evenly for two whole bars or four battement frappés; during the next two bars, for another four battements frappés, exhale completely, regularly and evenly, and so on.

There are 8 bars of music for 16 battements frappés, two to inhale, two to exhale.

A heavy exercise becomes easier to execute and less strenuous, when breathing is rational.

EXERCISE

Stand in the initial position for exercises at the barre; take the right arm to second position.

Preparation

Slide the right foot to second position, pointe on the floor.

Flex the knee without moving the thigh; place the heel of the working foot on the cou de pied of the left leg.

The pointe is slightly raised off the floor (fig. 86).

Fig. 86 Position of the foot at the moment of departure

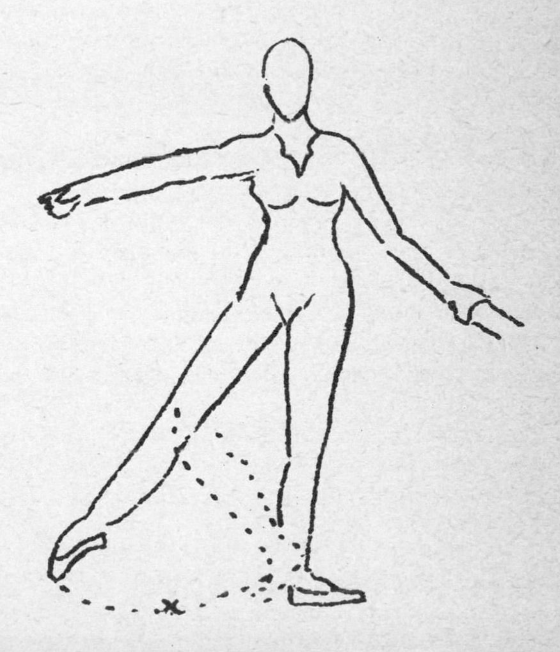

Fig. 87 Execution of battement frappé

Extend the knee and throw the leg strongly to second position; the foot is arched and raised about 3 inches (8 cm) off the floor.

Halfway through the movement, as the leg opens, slide the ball of the foot along the floor and continue until the foot is fully arched in second position, about 3 inches (8 cm) off the floor; the leg is completely extended, the muscles strongly contracted (fig. 87).

Without moving the thigh, bend the knee, bringing the foot briskly back onto the cou de pied of the left leg. The foot does not brush the floor during this movement.

For each battement frappé the heel is placed alternately, once in front and once behind, onto the cou de pied of the left leg.

Without pausing, the exercise continues with battement frappés avec petit battement sur le cou de pied.

BATTEMENT FRAPPÉ AVEC PETIT BATTEMENT SUR LE COU DE PIED

Battement frappé avec petit battement is similar to the previous exercise, but it is a compound step, preceded by petit battement sur le cou de pied.

The combination of these two movements, so different in quality, is the fortunate result of a great deal of experience.

This exercise can be surprisingly beneficial in a short space of time.

A very strong movement is preceded by an extremely swift, agile movement.

This exercise trains the leg to move easily particularly in the more difficult steps like fouettés and brisés.

This exercise enables the legs to perform more freely and become very nimble.

Because these two movements have been combined, the quality of this exercise is even more vigorous than the previous one, from which it follows on.

Manner of correctly executing battement frappé avec petit battement

The thigh of the working leg is in second position; the knee is bent with the heel placed on the cou de pied of the other leg.

The lower leg is free, moving easily and independently without any movement of the thigh.

The heel is on the cou de pied of the other leg; the toes are down, raised about 1 1/4 inches (3 cm) off the floor. Hold this position.

To execute battement frappé sur le cou de pied, slide the heel, still in contact with the other leg, from the front to the back of the cou de pied keeping the foot in exactly the same position. Continue, straightening the knee immediately so that the leg springs to second.

The foot returns placing the heel on the cou de pied behind the other leg. Next, slide the heel to the cou de pied front, spring the leg back to second position and so on, alternately front and back.

When the foot springs from behind, as the knee is flexed the foot will go behind the supporting leg; in this way, the petit battement will finish front before the foot springs to second once more, and so on.

The inside muscles of the leg contract strongly as the leg shoots into second with an arrow-like movement; none of the other muscles is tense in any way. Even those of the working leg are relaxed so that the movement of the foot can be free and not tense in any way.

Throughout the whole exercise, the free arm remains in second position, without tension. The head is erect as usual.

Execute 16 battements frappés avec petit battement. A greater number of battements would be wasted energy, remembering that there are already 32 battements in the complete exercise and that the compound battements and the simple battements are very vigorous; it can easily be seen that this exercise requires a great deal of energy.

If the correct technique is strictly followed, 32 battements can be taken without the body becoming overtired and the exercise will be very useful.

Battements frappés avec petit battements, like the previous movement, are executed in a duple rhythm in 2/4 time, slightly andante and strongly accented.

There are two complete battements frappé avec petit battements to each bar; fast petit battement in the first half of the bar with the leg springing quickly to second with the accent out, returning to its position a little more slowly.

The whole movement repeats immediately in the second half of the bar.

COMMON FAULTS

It is a serious fault to tense the muscles in petit battement; and it is obviously incorrect to take the leg to second with the muscles relaxed and flabby.

Breathing

Battement frappé avec petit battement is even more energetic than the previous exercise. When using so much energy it is important to build up stamina by breathing rationally and naturally right from the beginning.

For two whole bars, that is for four battements, inhale naturally and deeply. In the next two bars, that is for another four battements, exhale completely.

By breathing in this way, the exercise will finish without the body feeling uncomfortable in any way.

Exercise

At the end of the previous exercise, the right heel is in front of the left cou de pied (fig. 88). Petit battement taking the heel of the right foot to the cou de pied behind the left leg (fig. 89); without pausing, shoot the right leg to second, without allowing the thigh to move. During the movement, the right foot sharply brushes the floor and arrives in second with the pointe strongly arched.

Fig. 88 Petit battement front

Fig. 89 Petit battement back

Without moving the thigh, bend the knee taking the heel of the right foot behind the left cou de pied without sliding along the floor; continue in this way, alternately once to the front and once to the back (fig. 90).

At the end of the exercise, the right foot closes from second position into fifth front; demi-plié on both legs. Then continue with the closing movement described on page 39.

Fig. 90 Battement frappé

EXERCISE 6

RONDS DE JAMBE EN L'AIR

In this exercise the leg, held in second position at hip height, makes a circular movement from the knee, without moving the thigh.

This exercise allows the lower leg, from the knee to the foot, to work independently of the thigh. The knee acquires the smooth, free movement necessary for dancing.

Although there is a certain amount of liveliness in the movement, rond de jambe en l'air is essentially smooth and flexible; because of these characteristics it is one of the most frequent movements in the more graceful steps. It can often be found in the adagio due to its quality of smoothness and in the allegro because of its quality of lightness.

Correct manner of executing ronds de jambe en l'air

A watchful eye should be kept on the thigh in second position during rond de jambe en l'air, making sure that it is firmly held and well turned out at hip height as the lower leg moves.

When first learning this movement, it is permissible for the pupil to hold the thigh and help by pushing it back (fig. 91).

Fig. 91 Hand holding the thigh in rond de jambe en l'air.

The knee of the working leg moves easily and freely and the movement is executed without any tension. The foot is fully arched; the pointe describes a large ellipse in the air.

Every rond de jambe en l'air ends with a very stretched leg in high second position (fig. 94).

The lumbar region is firmly held so that the weight is well balanced and firm over the supporting leg.

In both rond de jambe en l'air en dehors and en dedans, the circular movement of the leg is always complete and well defined.

The exercise begins with a preparatory movement (figs. 92 and 93): développé to fourth front and demi-grand rond de jambe en dehors opening to high second position.

Execute 16 ronds de jambe en l'air with each leg:

– 8 ronds de jambe en l'air en dehors
– 8 ronds de jambe en l'air en dedans

At first, it is very tiring to hold the leg in second for such a long time but later on, with practice, it can be achieved quite easily.

This number of ronds de jambe has been proved to be correct. If they are executed accurately, ronds de jambe en l'air give the leg a smooth, graceful movement without unnecessary (or harmful) exertion.

Ronds de jambe en l'air are executed in a rhythm in 4/8 time, slightly andantino; in the first half there is one complete rond de jambe en l'air, in the second half the movement is repeated.

Common faults

It is a serious fault throughout the exercise not to hold the thigh completely still and well turned out at hip height.

Breathing

Breathing remains calm and even throughout. Inhale deeply during the first two bars, that is for four ronds de jambe en l'air; exhale completely during the next two bars, that is for four ronds de jambe en l'air.

Exercise

Preparation

Start in fifth position; slowly raise the right foot, well arched, sliding the pointe along the tibia until it is level with the knee; the thigh is fully turned out at hip height. Demi-plié on the left leg, développé and extend the right leg to fourth front; the right arm rises to first (fig. 92).

From fourth front, the right arm and the leg open to second position together as the left leg gradually straightens (fig. 93).

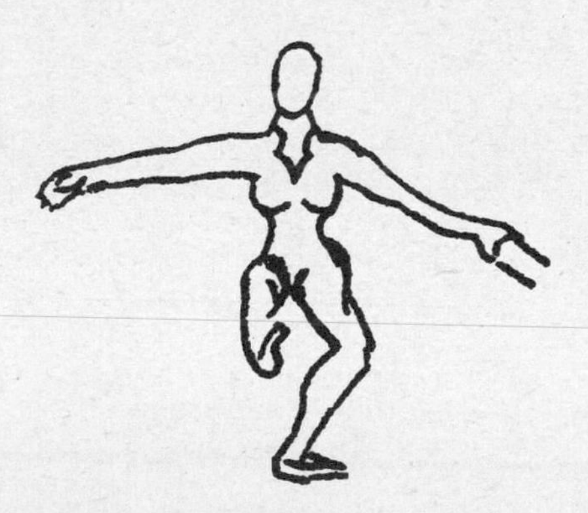

Fig. 92 Right leg extended to fourth front, left leg in demi-plié

Rond de jambe en l'air en dehors

Hold the thigh firmly in high second position; bend the right knee taking the pointe of the right foot *behind*. The pointe brushes the knee of the left leg, moves

Fig. 93 Right leg in second, left knee straight

Fig. 94 Movement of the right leg in rond de jambe en l'air

forward then the leg extends once more to second. During the movement, the right pointe describes a helicoidal shape in the air, from back to front.

After the circular movement, the leg extends once more to second. When eight ronds de jambe en l'air en dehors have been completed, the right leg closes from second into fifth position *back.*

Rond de jambe en l'air en dedans

Demi-grand battement extending the right leg to second at full height.

Execute the same movement with the foot, but in reverse: the thigh is held firmly in second, still at hip height; the right knee bends taking the right pointe *forward.* The pointe brushes the knee of the left leg, goes *backwards*, then the leg extends once more to second. During this movement the pointe of the right foot describes a helicoidal shape in the air, from front to back.

After 8 ronds de jambe en l'air en dedans, the right leg closes from second position to fifth front then continues with the ending described on page 39.

ROND DE JAMBE EN L'AIR FONDU AVEC GRAND BATTEMENT

This exercise is composed of grands battements and ronds de jambe en l'air.

The leg opens strongly from fifth position to second at hip height. Execute two ronds de jambe en l'air en dehors and close once more in fifth back.

The purpose of this exercise is to enable the leg to move easily in various types of movements in one count.

Both movements retain their specific characteristics, merging together in a combined harmony of vigor and grace.

Manner of correctly executing ronds de jambe fondus

Both movements of this exercise are executed as correctly and precisely, in the same manner as when executed separately. However, this exercise is based on rond de jambe en l'air and not grand battement, but *demi-grand battement.*

In demi-grand battement to second, the leg is raised from fifth front to second at hip height; the foot is fully arched. The thigh is held firmly in second during the movement of the knee which is lively and free.

After the two ronds de jambe en l'air, the leg lowers with demi-grand battement and closes behind in fifth.

When demi-grand battement opens from fifth front, the rond de jambe en l'air is *en dehors*; when it opens from fifth back, ronds de jambe en l'air is *en dedans*. Therefore, in this combined exercise, ronds de jambe en l'air en dehors and en dedans are always alternated.

This exercise is preceded by the same preparatory movement as ronds de jambe en l'air on page 58.

The head is erect and facing front, the free arm opens to second during the preparation and remains in this position throughout the exercise.

The exercise commences with the leg in second position at full height.

Ronds de jambe fondus avec grands battements are executed in a rhythm in 4/8 time, andante, taking one bar for each complete movement.

Common faults

It is important that each movement is executed exactly as when performed separately. The difficulty or speed of the movements of either rond de jambe en l'air or demi-grand battement does not excuse cutting short or in any way neglecting the individual technical execution.

Breathing

Throughout the exercise breathing is calm and even. Inhale during the first bar, or one whole rond de jambe fondu; exhale in the next bar.

Exercise

Preparation

The preparation is the same as for the previous exercise:

Développé the right leg to fourth front; raise the right arm to first; demi-plié on the left leg. Open the right arm and leg to second as the left leg gradually straightens once more.

Holding the thigh firmly in second position at full height, execute two ronds de jambe en l'air en dehors; demi-grand battement closing behind into fifth. Demi-grand battement raising the leg once more to second and, with the thigh held firmly, two ronds de jambe en l'air en dedans. Demi-grand battement closing in fifth front.

Continue the exercise always closing alternately fifth front and fifth back.

After the last demi-grand battement, close into fifth front and execute the ending movement described on page 39. The right arm lowers to position de repos.

N.B. This exercise does not follow the simple ronds de jambe en l'air, but is an alternative exercise.

EXERCISE 7

PETITS BATTEMENTS SUR LE COU DE PIED

Petits battements sur le cou de pied are movements performed by the foot, guided by the lower leg, while the thigh remains still.

The working leg is flexed in second position and with the heel in front of the cou de pied of the other leg.

The heel goes quickly behind the cou de pied and immediately returns front.

The purpose of this exercise is to train the leg and the foot to be supple and elastic in fast, continuous movements.

We have already seen petits battements combined with battement frappé and we will see them again in the adagi and more particularly in the allegro section.

This exercise is a necessary preparation for movements of a higher order as all the "beaten" steps derive from petits battements. Entrechats and brisés cannot be performed without first achieving a natural ease in faster footwork.

Petit battement is the usual exercise for speed and easy, clean movements of the feet.

Manner of correctly executing petits battements

During this exercise care must be taken to see that the thigh of the working leg is held firmly, well turned out in second position, with the muscles well relaxed and never tense.

The heel of the working foot is placed on the cou de pied of the supporting leg; the toes are slightly raised (fig. 95). The heel of the moving foot brushes the other leg, always remaining in contact with it when passing from the cou de pied front to the cou de pied back, and vice versa.

During the exercise there is no tension in any of the muscles; the foot moves freely and rapidly in a natural manner.

Initially, this movement is executed very slowly and only gradually increases speed. In this way it becomes natural and with constant practice gradually acquires all the necessary speed.

Later on, this movement is also executed on the half or full pointe of the supporting foot. Either way, the technique is the same; the supporting leg is always fully stretched.

After petits battements, followed by more petits battements with the supporting leg on half of full pointe, the more advanced pupils will continue the exercise with petits battements frappés en avant, in which the foot does not cross. The sole of the foot beats in front of the cou de pied of the supporting leg with a short, sharp movement. The knee of the working leg is brought slightly forward in order to beat more easily.

Throughout the exercise, the arm remains in position de repos. This is so that there is no tension in any of the muscles. The head remains still and erect.

Execute 64 petits battements on each leg divided in this way:

- 16 petits battements sur le cou de pied
- 16 petits battements sur le cou de pied with the supporting foot raised on the half pointe or full pointe.
- 32 petits battements frappés en avant with the supporting foot raised onto the half pointe or full pointe.

Bear in mind that beginners only need to execute the first 16 petits battements; the exercise will only be completed in the more advanced classes.

The exercise is taken in a duple rhythm, 2/4 march time, molto mosso.

Common faults

It is a serious fault to tense the muscles, even partially, during petits battements.

Breathing

Breathing is calm and even and the breath is never held.

Inhale during the first two bars; exhale for the next two bars.

Exercise

In the initial position, battement tendu opening the right leg to second position pointe on the floor. Without moving the thigh, flex the knee and place the heel in front of the left cou de pied; the toes are down and slightly raised (fig. 95). The right arm is in position de repos.

Without moving the thigh and with the heel still touching the left leg, take the foot to the back (fig. 96), and immediately return to the front again with the same quick movement; continue in the same way.

Fig. 95 Petit battement, right heel front

Fig. 96 Petit battement, right heel back

Petits battements sur la pointe

Without interrupting the petits battements movement, slightly flex the left knee, and stretch it quickly rising onto half or full pointe of the left foot; continue the rapid petits battements (fig. 97).

Fig. 97 Petits battements sur la pointe

Petit battement frappé en avant sur la pointe

After the previous movement, remain on the left pointe with the leg fully stretched.

The right leg is brought slightly forward and the sole of the foot beats rapidly in front of the left cou de pied.

During this movement, the right arm passes through first and fifth, lowering into position de repos, and repeats this movement once more making two ports de bras (fig. 98).

Ending

After the exercise, lower the left heel. Développé, extending the right leg to fourth front, en l'air.

The right arm rises to first from position de repos.

Grand rond de jambe en dehors taking the right leg to forth back en l'air and bending it into attitude.

The right arm is raised to fifth; the pose is attitude (fig. 99).

Fig. 98 Petits battements frappés sur la pointe

Fig. 99 Attitude position at the barre

Then, small demi-plié and relevé onto the left pointe. Remaining on balance, release the left hand from the barre and take the arm to fifth.

The pose is attitude with both arms in fifth en couronne.

In this position, lower the left heel. Replace the left hand on the barre and lower the right arm to position de repos. Extend the right leg to fourth back and close behind into fifth position.

Battement tendu taking the right leg to fifth front; small demi-plié and execute the ending described on page 39.

The head returns to the normal, upright position; the right arm lowers into position de repos.

EXERCISE 8

GRANDS BATTEMENTS ARRONDIS

In grands battements arrondis, the leg rises to fourth front at full height and with a broad, circular movement, goes to second at full height and closes behind in fifth.

This is a very strong movement. The leg rises to hip height and remains at this height until it closes behind in fifth.

Manner of correctly executing grands battements arrondis

The working leg must be fully stretched and turned out throughout the movement; it rises to at least hip height – even higher if possible – before it closes behind in fifth; the foot is fully arched.

The free arm remains in second and the head is erect, facing front.

After battement arrondi, battement tendu taking the foot to fifth front.

The movement is executed in a duple rhythm, 2/4 time, moderato and well accented. Battement arrondi in the first half of the bar, battement tendu in the second half.

BREATHING

Breathing is normal and calm. Inhale throughout the first whole bar and exhale in the next.

N.B. We have explained how to execute grands battements arrondis from fourth front to second.

This movement is generally found in the centre exercises, however, it can be taken at the barre as an exercise in stability.

In the centre, this movement is also executed with the leg going to second at hip height, taking it to fourth front, closing in fifth front.

EXERCISE

Take the right arm to second position.

Extend the right leg strongly to fourth front at full height (fig. 100); continue the movement with the same energy taking the leg to second at full height with demi-grand rond de jambe en dehors (fig. 101); without a pause, close behind in fifth.

The whole movement is executed in one bar only, very strongly.

Battement tendu taking the right leg to fifth front to repeat battement arrondi.

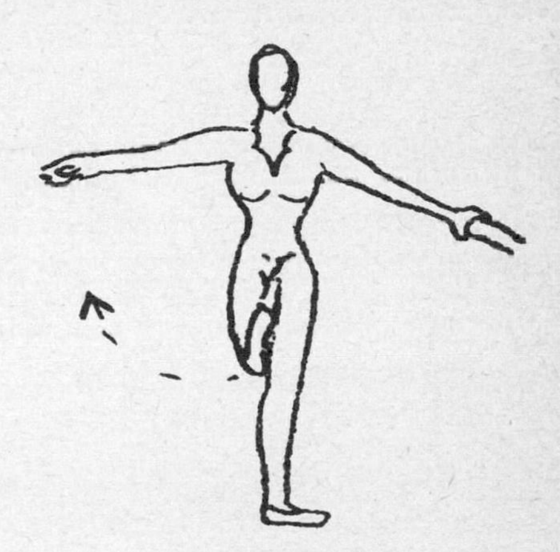

Fig. 100 The right leg in fourth front moving to second

Fig. 101 The right leg lowers from second to fifth back

EXERCISE 9

GRANDS BATTEMENTS À CLOCHE

In grands battements à cloche, the fully stretched leg goes from fourth front (or back), at full height, to fourth back (or front), at full height, passing through first position with a strong movement that resembles the swinging of a bell.

The forceful movement is executed with the fully stretched leg raised as high as possible to the front and back.

The purpose of this exercise is to loosen the leg in the hip socket. It must be executed with precision so that the movement does not become careless and thereby harmful.

The working leg is fully stretched and well turned out with the foot strongly pointed. The whole foot brushes the floor as it passes through first with the heels together. The body remains upright and well balanced over the supporting leg which is perfectly straight and firmly held. The arm stays in second with the head erect and still.

The exercise is executed in a duple rhythm, 2/4 time, slightly andante.

COMMON FAULTS

It is a serious fault to bend the knee of the supporting leg in order to push the other leg higher.

Another serious fault is to throw the leg up in a lazy and passive manner.

The leg is always controlled, sustained and active.

BREATHING

In strong movements it is much more important to control breathing, keeping it calm and even. Inhale during the first bar of music, exhale in the next bar.

Well-regulated breathing helps to avoid fatigue in strenuous exercises.

EXERCISE

Preparation

Take the right arm to second; battement tendu opening the right foot to second, pointe on the floor; slide the foot through first to fourth back, on the floor.

Movement

After the preparation, the right leg passes through first and is energetically thrown to high fourth front; without a pause, passing once more through first it is thrown to high fourth back, then again to fourth front and so on (fig. 102).

Fig. 102 Movement of grand battement à cloche front and back

N.B. Execute 7 battements à cloche ending with the right leg to high fourth front; then, continuing the movement, close the foot in fifth front; demi-plié and slowly straighten the legs while the right arm lowers, coordinating with the movement, through position de repos to first and opening gracefully to second. The head turns to the right shoulder.

Then, the right arm lowers to position de repos and the head returns to face front.

In battement à cloche, the movement is counted from when the leg arrives in fourth front and when it arrives in fourth back.

Battements arrondis and battements à cloche

For a rational distribution of movements, battements arrondis and battements à cloche have been combined into one exercise.

Exercise

Take four battements arrondis en dehors, then without a pause, battement tendu opening the right leg from fifth back to second, pointe on the floor, then continue the movement sliding the right foot through first to fourth back, pointe on the floor.

Without pausing, the right leg is thrown from fourth back to fourth front beginning battements à cloche.

After seven battements à cloche, the right leg ends in high fourth front; close in fifth front, demi-plié and execute the ending movement described on page 39.

The right arm lowers to position de repos and the head comes erect.

EXERCISE 10

GRANDS RONDS DE JAMBE DÉVELOPPÉS

Grand rond de jambe développé is a broad, fan-like movement of the fully stretched leg from fourth front (or back), at full height to fourth back (or front), at full height.

This is a movement of higher order and is a precise part of the study of the adages. It is of fundamental importance, requiring perfect execution and a rock-like stability.

This movement is practiced first at the barre, to allow the pupil to overcome all the technical and artistic difficulties, before taking it in the centre.

Every part of this movement is executed with great care.

During the développé, as the knee is flexed, the thigh remains well turned out in second with the pointe of the strongly arched foot brushing the supporting leg as it rises until it is in line with the knee. During développé to fourth front, the leg is still well turned out as it extends strongly at hip height, making a right angle with the vertical line of the body.

The leg remains at this height throughout grand rond de jambe; the lumbar region is firmly held with the body remaining perfectly vertical ("aplomb").

Holding the barre serves only to help to retain balance while overcoming the difficulties of the movement. Pupils are not to abuse the barre by leaning on it.

The arm remains in second and the head is erect throughout the movement.

Bear in mind that this is one of the most important and basic movements in the training of dance.

It is sufficient to execute 8 grands ronds de jambe développés on each leg, 4 en dehors and 4 en dedans. More than this would tire the body excessively to the detriment of the correct execution; this exercise is taken with great care in order to obtain the required advantages.

Exercise

Grand rond de jambe développé en dehors

Stand in the commencing position for exercises at the barre on the right side, the right arm is in second; open the right leg to fourth front, pointe on the floor, and execute ramassé des pieds.

Raccourci and développé to high fourth front; demi-plié on the left leg (fig. 103).

Slowly begin grand rond de jambe en dehors taking the fully stretched right leg to second as the left leg gradually straightens (fig. 104).

Without a pause, the right leg, still fully stretched, is taken to fourth back (fig. 105).

The right knee bends, the pointe brushes the left knee (fig. 106) and développé extending the leg to fourth front to repeat the movement.

Grand rond de jambe développé en dedans

After the last rond de jambe en dehors, the right leg is in fourth back (fig. 105).

Slowly begin grand rond de jambe en dedans, taking the right leg to second (fig. 104).

Without a pause, the right leg, still fully stretched, is taken to fourth front to end rond de jambe.

The right foot comes through raccourci, the pointe brushes the left knee (fig. 106); développé extending the leg to fourth back to repeat the movement.

Ending

The last rond de jambe ends with the right leg extended to fourth front.

The leg then closes, fully stretched, into fifth front. Demi-plié and execute the closing movement described on page 39.

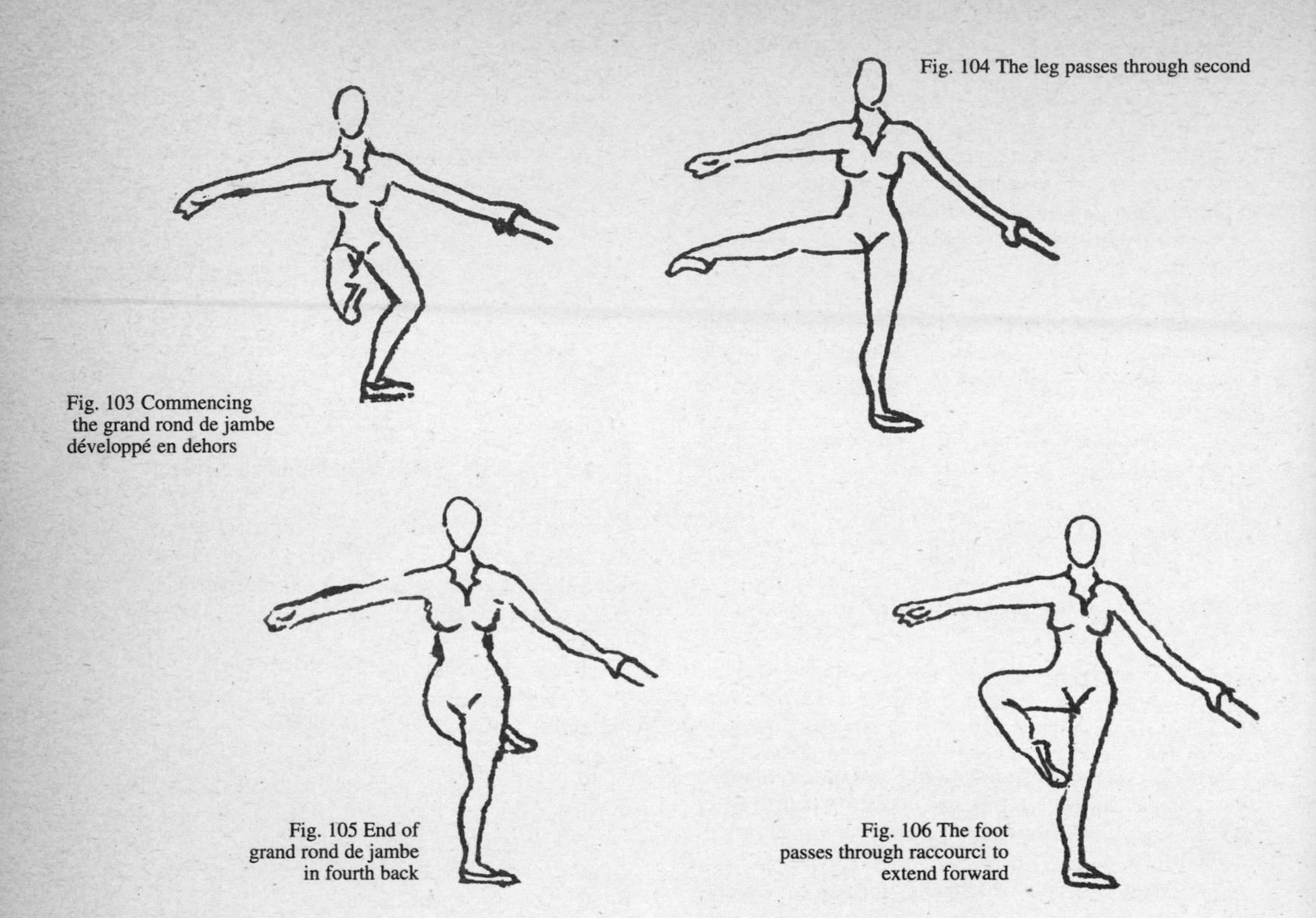
Fig. 103 Commencing the grand rond de jambe développé en dehors

Fig. 104 The leg passes through second

Fig. 105 End of grand rond de jambe in fourth back

Fig. 106 The foot passes through raccourci to extend forward

EXERCISE 11

GRANDS BATTEMENTS FONDUS AVEC PLIÉS

This exercise is composed of grands battements and demi-pliés.

In grand battement the leg is raised and lowered back into the original fifth position; demi-plié on both legs and straighten immediately.

This movement is executed very strongly and quickly in the three positions of the legs: fourth front, second and fourth back.

As well as a training exercise, this strong movement is also invaluable for limbering the legs after the various movements performed during the different exercises.

It is important that demi-plié occurs only after the leg has completed the grand battement and the legs are well crossed in fifth position; the next grand battement will occur only after the legs have straightened on completing demi-plié.

The free arm is in second and brought forward into arabesque during the grands battements to fourth back; it returns to second position for the last two grands battements in second which end the exercise.

2 grands battements fondus are executed in each position plus 2 more in second to end the exercise.

Breathing

Breathing is calm and regular, inhaling for two bars and exhaling for two bars.

Exercise

Stand in the commencing position for exercises at the barre, on the right side; the right arm is in second.

Execute two grands battements fondus avec pliés in each position:

1. 2 grands battements fondus to fourth front;
2. 2 grands battements fondus to second;
3. 2 grands battements fondus to fourth back; the right arm goes forward into arabesque.
4. 2 grands battements fondus to second; the right arm returns to second.

After the final grand battement in second, the right foot closes in fifth front; demi-plié and straighten, ready to execute the closing movement described on page 39.

EXERCISE 12

DÉTIRÉS

Détirés are manoeuvres in which the leg is stretched using the hand or the barre. The hand holds the foot and stretches the leg to fourth front then continues the movement opening it to second as high as possible.

This movement, which is effective to open the legs, is taken very carefully and gradually in order to avoid painful, torn ligaments.

As this movement is more a manoeuvre than a real exercise, it can be taken without music, slowly and not more than two times on each leg.

To make the movement clearer, it is divided into three temps (parts):

EXERCISE

1st Temps: raccourci with the right foot, thigh well turned out in second; take the foot in the right hand (back of the hand up).

2nd Temps: holding the heel firmly, slightly bend the supporting knee, extend the leg to high fourth front.

3rd Temps: still holding the heel firmly, take the leg, still extended, into a wide second straightening the left knee at the same time (fig. 107).

Détiré can be executed with the leg on the barre; the purpose is the same and it must be executed with equal care and attention.

To make it clearer, this détiré also is divided into 2 temps.

EXERCISE

Preparation

Stand facing the barre at about 4-6 inches (10-15 cm) distance; feet in fifth, right foot front.

1st Temps: raise the right leg, well stretched, to second and place the heel (Achilles tendon) on the barre; leg well turned out with the foot strongly arched.

2nd Temps: holding the barre firmly with the left hand, incline the torso to the right and extend the right arm, placing the hand on the leg letting it slide until it touches the pointe of the foot, lowering the head (turned right) onto the right leg (fig. 108); the supporting left leg leans to the right, still fully stretched. The body remains facing the barre, completely in line without distorting the pelvis. Recover to an upright position, lower the right leg and close in fifth.

EXERCISE 13

POINTE-WORK EXERCISE

"Pointe-work exercise" is the basis for the complex and difficult study of the pointes. This exercise is only executed by the more advanced pupils because it is an exercise of higher order.

Too much impatience at this initial stage can have disastrous results for the pupil, often causing irreparable damage. This is because the ankle, which is not yet strong, with insufficiently trained muscles, may not be able to support the stress and force of the exercise, with results that are easily imagined.

Through patience and resolution, combined with consistent and meticulous practice, the pupil gradually achieves a standard of preparation and security of movement which gives her complete self-confidence. Little by little, she can attempt more complicated and difficult exercises allowing her to obtain the results which are expected and which she has hoped for.

The movement itself is simple; it consists in rising sharply onto the pointes in various positions of the feet.

Pointe-work is a very intricate part of dance training. Due to its great importance its execution must be fully examined; here, we give an explanatory summary of the exercises at the barre.

Fig. 107 Détiré in second

Fig. 108 Détiré at the barre

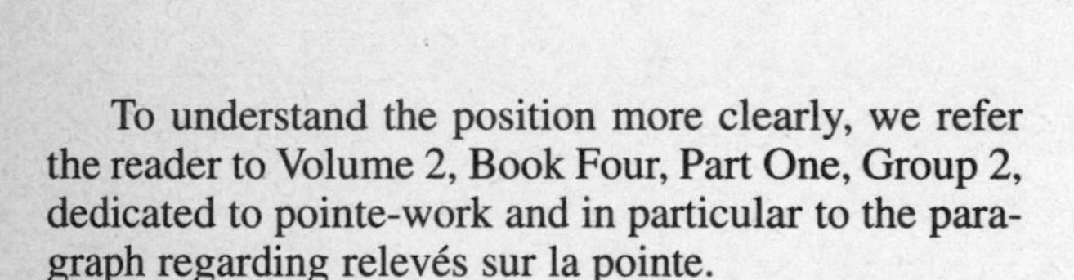

To understand the position more clearly, we refer the reader to Volume 2, Book Four, Part One, Group 2, dedicated to pointe-work and in particular to the paragraph regarding relevés sur la pointe.

Rising onto pointe is performed in two different ways depending on whether rising onto half pointe or full pointe.

Rising onto half pointe

To rise onto the half pointe, simply raise the heels lifting the body by means of the fully stretched leg muscles.

As the feet rise to half pointe in fifth, the feet move towards each other so that at the end of the movement the legs are held well together. Lowering the heels, the feet open just enough to allow them to return into their usual fifth position.

Rising onto full pointe

Rising onto full pointe, however, it is necessary to spring up in a particular way.

Small demi-plié and straightening with energy, spring up lightly, just enough to allow the feet to stretch through their full length and hold firm in order to place the tips of the toes on the floor and be able to support the whole weight of the body on them.

When springing into fifth, the feet draw in, tightly crossed with the legs fully stretched and firmly together. As the heels lower, the feet open just enough to return to the normal fifth position.

"The pointe exercise" is executed holding the barre with both hands with the back of the hands up and the thumbs down.

The head remains erect and still.

We also recommend that, in the initial stage, this exercise is taken without music to make it easier for the pupil to concentrate.

Exercises on the pointes are only given to female pupils; males must never rise sur les pointes.

COMMON FAULTS

It is extremely dangerous to spring onto pointe with the ankles weak and unsteady, the knees bent or the leg muscles relaxed.

EXERCISES ON POINTE

Stand facing the barre, holding with both hands, backs of the hands up; feet closed tightly in fifth, right foot front.

1. Relevé in first

Feet in first position, small demi-plié, spring quickly onto pointe, legs fully stretched (fig. 109).

Lower the heels in first with a slight demi-plié and straighten the knees calmly. Make sure that the heels return well held together.

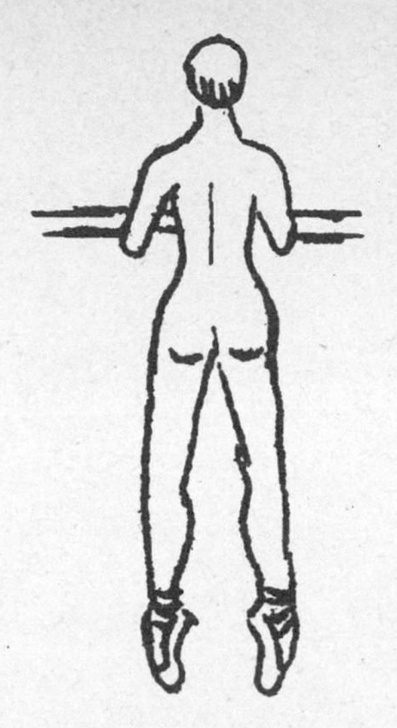

Fig. 109 Relevé in first

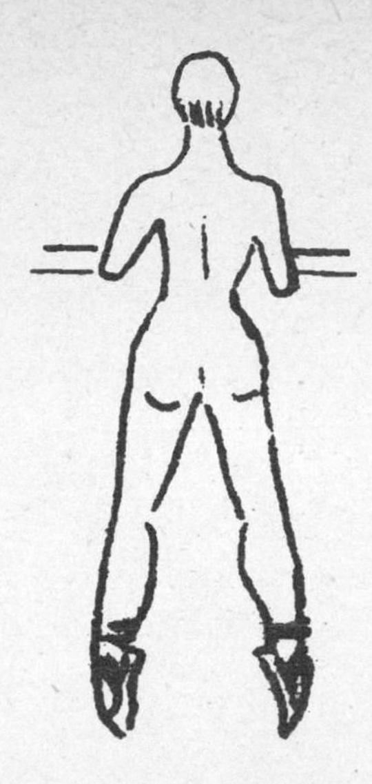

Fig. 110 Relevé in second

Fig. 111 Relevé in fourth

2. Relevé in second

Demi-plié with the feet in second position; spring quickly onto pointe, legs fully stretched (fig. 110).
Lower the heels in second with a small demi-plié and straighten the knees calmly.

3. Relevé in fourth

Demi-plié with the feet in fourth position, spring quickly onto pointe; legs fully stretched (fig. 111).
Lower the heels in fourth with a small demi-plié and straighten the legs calmly.

4. Relevé in fifth

Demi-plié with the feet in fifth; spring quickly onto pointe, legs fully stretched. During the movement, the feet must move towards each other so that the legs draw together (fig. 112).
Lower the heels with a small demi-plié in fifth and straighten the legs calmly.
During this movement the feet open to return to their normal fifth position.

N.B. The detail on page 70 of figure 112, shows a correct relevé in fifth (feet tightly together). The detail in figure 113, shows an incorrect fifth (feet not held together).

5. Échappé from fifth to second

Small demi-plié in fifth, spring into second on full pointe with the knees completely stretched.
Small spring, closing the feet once more tightly into fifth; demi-plié and stretch.

N.B. The detail on page 70 of figure 114, shows a correct échappé in second (the feet are the correct distance apart).
The detail in figure 115, shows a faulty échappé in second (the feet are not open enough, therefore they are not the correct distance apart).

6. Échappé from fifth to second, from second to fifth (demi-échappé)

1st Temps: small demi-plié in fifth, spring onto full pointe in second position extending the knees; lower the heels in second with a slight demi-plié.
2nd Temps: strong relevé onto pointe in second position; spring lightly back into a tight fifth, demi-plié and stretch.

7. Échappé to fourth from fifth

Small demi-plié in fifth, spring quickly onto pointe opening the feet to fourth, legs fully stretched.

Fig. 112 Correct relevé in fifth

Fig. 113 Faulty relevé in fifth

Fig. 114 Correct échappé in second

Fig. 115 Faulty échappé in second

Spring lightly back into a tight fifth; demi-plié and stretch.

COMPLETE EXERCISE

Several exercises on pointe have been grouped together to make one complete exercise for the more advanced student who needs to practice every day.

This exercise is executed at the barre in the order and rhythm indicated below.

The music for this exercise is no. 11 in the appropriate score (Part One, "Exercises at the Barre").

Preparation

Stand with both hands holding the barre; feet in fifth, right foot front:

EXERCISE

4 Échappés to second on full pointe
3 Échappés to fourth on full pointe (right foot front)
1 Échappé to second
3 Échappés to fourth (left foot front)
2 Demi-échappés to second and second to fifth
3 Relevés in fifth on full pointe (right foot front)
1 Échappé to second on full pointe
3 Relevés to fifth on full pointe (left foot front)
2 Demi-échappés to second and second to fifth
4 Échappés alternately in fourth and second

N.B. Rising onto pointe must be quick and decisive; hold for an instant on pointe before lowering the heels.

The feet change each time in échappé to second.

EXERCISE 14

LIMBERING

The "backbend" is a movement in which the torso, bending right back, forms the shape of an arch.

Care must be taken during this movement to see that the knees do not bend while the torso is arched and that the neck muscles are not harmfully tense.

Fig. 116 Backbend

EXERCISE

Stand in fifth position facing the barre, holding it firmly with both hands with the backs of the hands up.

Keeping the knees completely straight, gradually bend the torso backwards, arching as much as possible, pushing in the back (fig. 116).

Recover.

Change the feet in the fifth position and repeat the exercise.

The backbend must be executed carefully and gradually.

This exercise gives the body suppleness, strengthens the lumbar region and makes the torso more flexible and free.

Backbends are executed at the end of the exercises at the barre, no more than two or four times.

PART TWO
PORT DE BRAS

Port de bras is a series of movements of the arms executed in the centre of the room. Both arms move together and there is an active use of the upper body.

Exercises at the barre are mainly for the legs; the variety and quality of each exercise being designed to loosen and speed up the movements of the lower limbs. The other parts of the body have taken part only in harmonious complement.

In the first section we have already shown the great importance of the arms in dancing. Their soft, harmonious movement gives character and presence to the artist, enabling him to communicate his inner feelings and express and develop this most powerful interpretive art. It is therefore logical to have exercises suitable for the arms which are as important as those for the legs. These develop the muscles and, with a special technique, give them smoothness, softness, and precision of movement.

Port de bras is the first of the centre exercises, that is, executed without the support of the barre. Only the upper body, torso, head and particularly the arms, move. Therefore, port de bras is studied separately because the technique and execution are completely different from all the other exercises; they are in a group by themselves, clearly distinct from the other exercises. All the rules which teach how the arms move artistically in all ways and directions are contained in this group.

The *theory of port de bras* is the manner in which the arms pass from one position to another; this technique ensures that the arms are always in an artistically correct position.

Even the head and torso, with suitable training on their possibilities of movement, develop this action in coordination with the movements of the arms.

However, as we have said already, the rest of the body remains absolutely still in the correct position.

The greatest care must be taken to see that the arms are extended and rounded, without any angles at the elbows and wrists. Each time the arms move into a position, the elbows and wrists complete the movement in their particular way; this is discussed more fully in Book One, Part One, page 23. We also refer the reader to the same chapter, page 17, for the use of the hands in dance in general and in the development of movements in ports de bras in particular.

This coordinated movement of the arms, elbows and wrists, gives grace and harmonious smoothness to the expressive actions of the upper limbs.

During the port de bras exercises, the lower part of the body, from the waist to the feet, remains firm and solid with the feet well crossed in fifth and the legs fully stretched and held together.

The torso, from above the waist, makes twisting movements of about a quarter turn either to the right or the left.

Remember that it is a serious fault if, during the movements of the arms and the torso, the knees bend (even for an instant) or the legs are not held well together.

Finally, breathing must be corrected to ensure that the pupil is never out of breath. Respiration must be deep and normal and coordinated with the movement of the chest which contracts and expands continually: exhale as the chest contracts due to the movements of the arms; as the torso gradually expands, inhale deeply.

This exercise and its particular movements are extremely beneficial for the healthy development of the lungs.

First position of the arms is technically the most important because the arms must pass through this position when rising from one position to another.

There are eight exercises in this group of port de bras. Each exercise is executed four times consecutively on one side and the same number repeated immediately on the other side before continuing on to the next.

The name of each exercise is taken from the position in which the arms are at the end of a complete movement.

PORT DE BRAS EXERCISES

1. Port de bras in second (a).
   Port de bras in second (b).
2. Port de bras in third (a).
   Port de bras in third (b).
3. Port de bras in fifth.
4. Circular port de bras.
5. Circular port de bras with the feet in a large fourth.
6. Port de bras in arabesque; swinging the weight in a movement like a seesaw with the feet in fourth.
7. Port de bras in attitude; swinging the weight in a movement like a seesaw with the feet in fourth.
8. Port de bras in first and fifth; swinging the weight in a movement like a seesaw with the feet in fourth.

Initial position

Unless otherwise indicated, all the port de bras are performed in the centre of the room with the feet in fifth, right foot front.

The body faces slightly to the left diagonal; the head is erect and the shoulders down; arms in position de repos (fig. 117).

This is the position in which ports de bras are taken to the left. After the exercise, battement tendu taking the left foot front and the body to face the right diagonal; execute the same port de bras to the right.

Therefore, when executing port de bras to the left, the right foot is in fifth front; and vice-versa, to the right, the left foot is front.

Every port de bras is divided into four temps (parts) corresponding to the movements of the arms, and are executed 8 times for each exercise; 4 times to the right and 4 times to the left.

The music which accompanies the ports de bras can be found in the appropriate score (Part Two, no. 2).

1. Port de bras in second (a)

PREPARATION

Port de bras raising the arms through first to second (fig. 118).

EXERCISE

1st Temps: the torso turns left with the arms still in second; the head turns and inclines right.
2nd Temps: the right arm goes to first while the left lowers and, passing through position de repos, joins the right arm in first; the head comes erect.
3rd Temps: the torso turns front; the arms are in first and the head is erect.
4th Temps: the arms open to second; the head turns and inclines to the right shoulder (fig. 118).

The exercise is taken 4 times; then the arms lower into position de repos; incline and turn the head left (fig. 117).

Port de bras in second (b)

1st Temps: open the arms to demi-seconde, turning the torso left; the head is erect.
2nd Temps: raise the arms to first; head erect.
3rd Temps: with the arms in first and the head erect, the torso turns to the front.
4th Temps: open the arms to second; the head turns and inclines to the right shoulder (fig. 118). Lower the arms into position de repos, turning the torso left; the head is erect. Repeat nos. 2, 3 and 4 and continue.
The whole port de bras is executed 4 times.
At the end of the exercise, lower the arms into position de repos without changing the torso. The head inclines left (fig. 117).

2. Port de bras in third (a)

PREPARATION

Port de bras raising the arms through first to second.

Fig. 117 Initial position for port de bras left

Fig. 118 End of port de bras in second

EXERCISE

1st Temps: turn the upper body to the left as the right arm is taken forward, straight, without altering its height, palm of the hand facing down; the left arm, straight, goes back, lowering it a little with the palm of the hand facing down (the position of the arms is épaulée). The head turns and inclines right.

2nd Temps: the shoulders straighten bringing the right arm into first; the back left arm lowers, passes through position de repos to join the right arm in first; the head comes erect.

3rd Temps: the torso turns to face front with the arms in first and the head erect.

4th Temps: raise the left arm to fifth at the same time lowering the right to behind demi-seconde; the head turns left looking to the hand (attitude position, fig. 119).

Turn the torso left, the right arm is raised and extended forward with the palm of the hand facing down. The left arm extends and lowers backwards, palm of the hand facing down (the position of the arms arms is épaulée).

The head turns and inclines right; repeat nos. 2, 3 and 4 and continue.

The whole port de bras is executed 4 times. At the end of the exercise, lower the arms into position de repos without changing the torso. The head inclines left (fig. 117).

Port de bras in third (b)

1st Temps: open the arms to demi-seconde turning the torso left; the head is erect.

2nd Temps: raise the arms to first; head erect.

3rd Temps: the torso turns to face front with the arms in first and the head erect.

4th Temps: raise the left arm to fifth and at the same time lower the right arm behind demi-seconde; the head turns and looks to the left hand (the arms are in attitude position, fig. 119).

As the torso turns left, the right arm, passing through second, lowers into position de repos; the left, moving forward, joins the right in position de repos. Continuing, repeat nos. 2, 3 and 4 and so on.

The whole port de bras is taken 4 times. At the end of the exercise, lower the arms into position de repos, without turning the torso. Head inclines left (fig. 117).

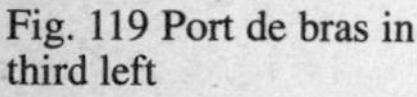

Fig. 119 Port de bras in third left

Fig. 120 Port de bras in fifth

3. Port de bras in fifth

PREPARATION

Open the arms to demi-seconde, turn the torso left; head erect.

EXERCISE

1st Temps: raise the arms to first.
2nd Temps: with the arms in first and the head erect, turn the torso front.
3rd Temps: take the arms to fifth; the head is slightly raised and turned right (fig. 120).
4th Temps: lower the arms to second, the head turns and inclines right (fig. 118); lower the arms to position de repos as the torso turns left. Head erect.
The whole port de bras is taken 4 times.
At the end of the exercise, take the arms to position de repos, without changing the torso. The head inclines left (fig. 117).

4. Circular port de bras

PREPARATION

Incline the torso slightly to the left side. Incline and turn the head left (fig. 117).

EXERCISE

1st Temps: the right arm passes through first to fifth. The left rises to demi-seconde (fig. 121).
2nd Temps: without a pause, lower the right arm to demi-seconde and at the same time, pass the left arm through second to fifth. Incline and turn the head right following the movement of the arms. Incline the torso slightly over to the right (fig. 122).
3rd Temps: pass through first and lower the left arm to position de repos.
4th Temps: continuing the movement, lower the right arm to position de repos; the torso and the head come erect.
The torso turns and inclines slightly left. The head inclines and turns left.
The port de bras is taken 4 times.
At the end of the exercise, lower the arms into position de repos, without changing the torso. The head inclines left (fig. 117).

5. Circular port de bras (feet in large fourth)

PREPARATION

Demi-plié and glissé sliding the right foot to fourth front towards the left diagonal. Transfer the weight onto the right leg in demi-plié; the left remains completely extended behind with the whole foot on the floor (fig. 123). The torso inclines slightly over the left side; the head inclines left. Arms in position de repos.

EXERCISE

1st Temps: the right arm passes through first to fifth. The left arm rises to demi-seconde. The lower back is strongly arched.
2nd Temps: without a pause, lower the right arm to demi-seconde and at the same time,

Fig. 121 First phase of circular port de bras

Fig. 122 Second phase of circular port de bras

Fig. 123 Circular port de bras in large fourth position

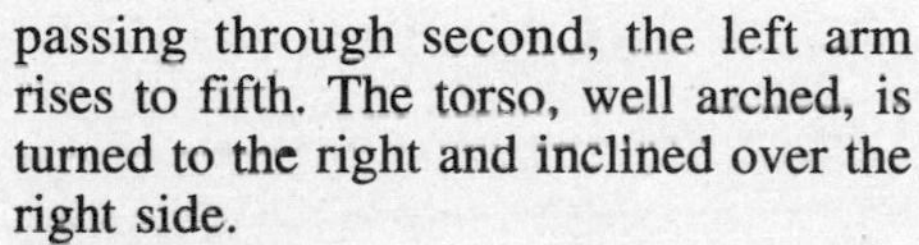

passing through second, the left arm rises to fifth. The torso, well arched, is turned to the right and inclined over the right side.

3rd Temps: the left arm passes through first into position de repos.

4th Temps: continuing the movement, the right arm lowers to position de repos. The torso and the head come upright.

The body turns left and inclines over the left side. Incline and turn the head left and repeat the movement. The complete port de bras is taken 4 times.

At the end of the exercise, the arms lower to position de repos. The head comes erect. The right leg, sliding along the floor, closes in front in fifth. The knees straighten.

6. Port de bras en arabesque

Exercise

1st Temps: demi-plié on both feet and slide the right leg to fourth front towards the left diagonal, transferring the weight onto the front leg.

Straighten both knees raising the left heel, the left foot remains pointed to fourth back.

Raise the arms to half first before opening.

The left extends forward slightly above shoulder height, palm of the hand facing down; the right moves back and down in alignment with the left, palm of the hand facing down. Head erect (fig. 124).

2nd Temps: demi-plié lowering the left heel; transfer the weight back onto the left leg; straighten the knees raising the right heel; the right foot remains pointed to fourth front.

The arms lower, then meet in half first before separating once more. The right arm extends forward slightly above shoulder height, palm of the hand facing down; the left moves back and down in alignment with the right, palm of the hand facing down.

The head turns to the right shoulder; the pose is épaulée (fig. 125).

Port de bras transferring the weight forwards and back with the feet in fourth, is taken 4 times.

Then the feet close in fifth and the arms are lowered (fig. 117).

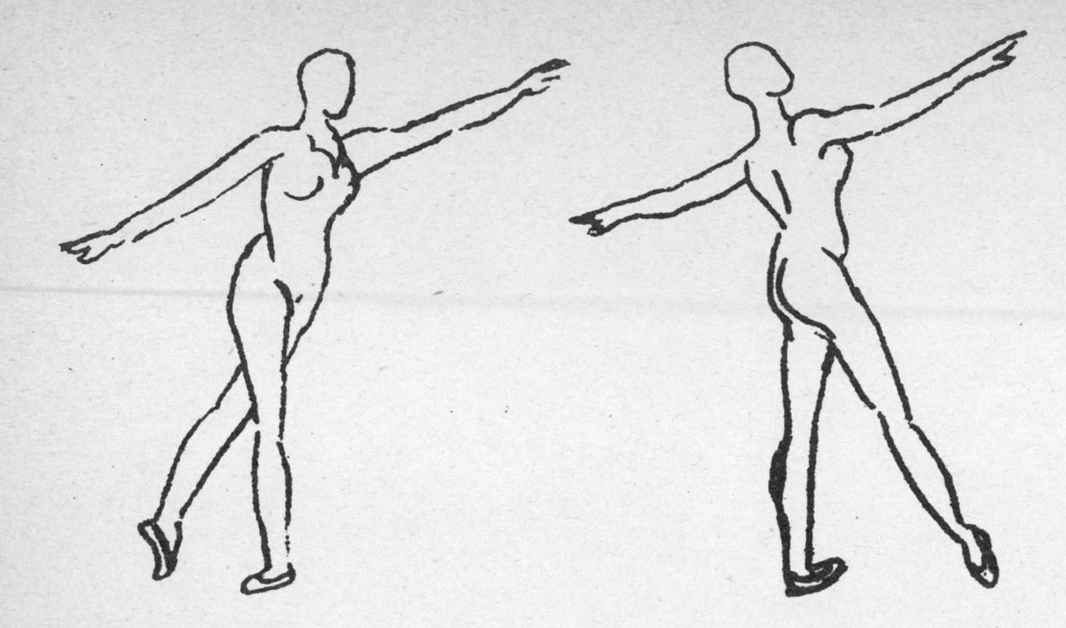

Fig. 124 Port de bras in open second arabesque

Fig. 125 Port de bras in arabesque croisée, second temps

7. Port de bras en attitude

EXERCISE

1st Temps: demi-plié on both feet and slide the right foot to fourth position front towards the left diagonal, transferring the weight onto the front leg.
Straighten the knees, raising the left heel; the left foot remains pointed to fourth back.
The arms rise to half first and open; the left continues into fifth, while the right moves to demi-seconde.
The head turns left looking to the left hand. The pose is attitude forward (fig. 126).

2nd Temps: demi-plié lowering the left heel, transfer the weight onto the left leg.
Straighten the knees raising the right heel; the right foot remains pointed to fourth front.
The arms lower and meet in half first to separate once more; the right arm rises to fifth, the left goes to demi-seconde.
The head turns right and looks to the right hand. The pose is attitude back (fig. 127).

The port de bras is taken continually changing weight forwards and backwards with demi-plié through fourth position, 4 times. Then slide the right foot into fifth front and straighten the knees.
Lower the arms to position de repos. The head turns left (fig. 117).

8. Port de bras in first and fifth

EXERCISE

1st Temps: demi-plié on both feet and slide the right foot to fourth front towards the left diagonal, transferring the weight onto the right leg.
Straighten the knees raising the left heel; the left foot remains pointed to fourth back.
The arms are raised to first; the head inclines, turned left (fig. 128).

2nd Temps: demi-plié lowering the left heel; transfer the weight onto the back leg.
Straighten the knees, raising the right heel.

Fig. 126 Port de bras in attitude forward

Fig. 127 Port de bras in attitude back

The right foot remains pointed to fourth front.
The arms are raised to fifth, the head turns gradually from the left to the right (fig. 129).

Lower the arms through second into position de repos.
The head is inclined right (fig. 130).
The port de bras is taken with a continual change of weight forwards and back-

Fig. 128 Port de bras in first forward

Fig. 129 Port de bras in fifth back

wards with balancé through demi-plié in fourth position, 4 times.
Slide the right foot to fifth front; straighten the knees. Lower the arms to position de repos. The head is erect. The pose is in the classic initial and final position for exercises in the centre of the room (fig. 131).

Fig. 130 End of the port de bras in fifth with the arms opening to second

Fig. 131 Closing into the initial and final position

PART THREE
EXERCISES IN THE CENTRE

Through practicing daily the pupil will, by degrees, be easily able to execute even the most difficult exercises with the greatest of ease according to the strictest technical requirements of dance.

Little by little, as the limbs become more supple and the various movements quicker, the pupil will develop a sense of balance and will gradually be able to do without the support of the barre.

Ports de bras enable the arms to move correctly in all positions and the upper body to incline and turn in every way, moving out of the upright central line of gravity, while still remaining on balance.

When the pupil has arrived at this level, he can most certainly begin to prepare for exercises of higher order.

This preparation consists of a series of movements called "exercises in the centre" because they are taken in the centre of the studio without holding the barre.

In these, the pupil learns to perfect all the movements of the legs and arms skillfully and with complete stability.

Another important purpose of these exercises in the centre is to strengthen the lumbar region which, more than anything else, has the most difficult task of strengthening the equilibrium.

The exercises in the centre are the same as those at the barre with the exception of a few small variations at the end of some movements.

Some of the barre exercises are not included in the centre practice for purely technical reasons. Their usefulness is limited to training the legs as they are of no particular use for balance and stability which is the purpose of this part of the program.

As the centre exercises are the same as those at the barre, the pupil does not have the anxiety of learning new movements and can concentrate his attention on staying on balance.

These exercises will not be described again and we refer the reader to the appropriate part of the chapter dedicated to exercises at the barre: Book Two, Part One, page 37.

In order to practice balancing, for technical reasons and particularly musically, the execution of the coda at the end of some of these exercises is quite different from those at the barre.

In the description of the centre exercises, only the actual execution of the movement which is different from that at the barre, partially or completely, will be illustrated.

In the centre, the arms which are free, perform the same movements. Their precise function is to help stability and balance.

N.B. The exercises in the centre, like those at the barre, are executed first with one leg or in one direction, then repeated with the other leg, in the opposite direction, before continuing on to the next exercise.

Bear in mind that, unless otherwise indicated, the initial position for all exercises in the centre is feet in fifth, right foot front, arms in position de repos, head erect (fig. 132).

TABLE OF EXERCISES IN THE CENTRE

1. *Pliés* (in the five positions)
   2 in each position

2. *Ports de bras*
   4 ports de bras in second
   4 ports de bras in third
   4 ports de bras in fifth

Fig. 132 Initial position for the exercises in the centre

4 circular ports de bras
4 circular ports de bras (feet in large fourth)
4 ports de bras en arabesque
4 ports de bras en attitude
4 ports de bras in first and fifth

Grands battements
4 to fourth front
4 to second
4 to fourth back

2a. *Ports de bras avec grands battements*
4 ports de bras in second
8 grands battements to fourth front
4 ports de bras in third
8 grands battements to second
4 ports de bras in fifth
8 grands battements to fourth back

3. *Battements tendus, dégagés et relevés*
16 battements tendus
16 battements dégagés
2 battements tendus relevés

4. *Ronds de jambe à terre*
8 ronds de jambe à terre en dehors
8 ronds de jambe à terre en dedans

5. *Battements frappés et avec petits battements*
8 battements frappés
16 battements avec petits battements sur le cou de pied

6. *Ronds de jambe en l'air*
8 ronds de jambe en l'air en dehors
8 ronds de jambe en l'air en dedans

7. *Petits battements sur le cou de pied*
32 petits battements

EXERCISE 1

PLIÉS

Pliés in the five positions form one complete exercise. Battement tendu to change the feet from one position to another, immediately centering the weight over both feet.

Stand in the centre of the room, feet in fifth position, right foot front; arms in position de repos; head erect (fig. 132).

Battement tendu to first.

EXERCISE

Port de bras through first to second.

Slow, full plié with the weight evenly over both legs; recover slowly completely straightening the knees.

During the descent, the arms lower coordinating with the movement of the legs, passing through demi-seconde to position de repos.

On rising, still in coordination, the arms rise to first then open to second.

As the body lowers, the head turns slowly left (the opposite side from the front foot in fifth, fig. 133).

Rising up, the head turns slowly right.

The exercise ends with the feet in fifth and the arms in position de repos which is the original starting position (fig. 132).

N.B. The exercise is performed in exactly the same way as at the barre so we refer the reader to Book Two, Part One, page 42.

Fig. 133 Full plié in fifth

EXERCISE 2

EIGHT PORTS DE BRAS

PREPARATION

Stand in the centre of the room in the initial position; feet firmly in fifth, right foot front; arms in position de repos. The body faces the left diagonal.

EXERCISE

The eight ports de bras form one complete exercise; it is executed alternately to the left and to the right:

- facing the left diagonal, 4 ports de bras no. 1;
- battement tendu taking the left foot to fifth front and the body to face the right diagonal;
- facing the right diagonal, 4 ports de bras no. 1; battement tendu taking the right foot to fifth front and the body once more to face the left diagonal.

Continuing in the manner described, all *eight* ports de bras are taken until at the end of the exercise 16 ports de bras will have been executed alternately: 8 to the left and 8 to the right.

N.B. For the description of each port de bras, see Book Two, Part Two, page 74, continuing to page 80.

GRANDS BATTEMENTS EN CROIX

After the eight ports de bras ending in the initial position, the exercise continues with eight grands battements with the right leg. Port de bras taking the arms to second.

EXERCISE

4 grands battements to fourth front
4 grands battements to second
4 grands battements to fourth back
Change feet and repeat with the left leg.

N.B. This exercise is the same as at the barre, see Book Two, Part One, page 45.

EXERCISE 2 (b)

PORTS DE BRAS AVEC GRANDS BATTEMENTS

This exercise is composed of two completely different movements: ports de bras followed by grands battements. Ports de bras are combined with grands battements to fourth front, second and fourth back.

The exercise is executed alternately on one side with the right leg and on the other side with the left leg, before continuing on to the next movement.

Stand in the centre of the room with the feet in fifth, right foot front; arms in position de repos.

EXERCISE

4 ports de bras in second (ending in second)
8 grands battements to fourth front (fig. 134)
Change feet and repeat with the left

4 ports de bras in third (ending with the arms in fourth, turn the head right)
8 grands battements to second (fig. 136)
Change feet and repeat with the left

4 ports de bras in fifth (ending with the arms in second)
8 grands battements to fourth back (fig. 135)
Change feet and repeat with the left

N.B. Change feet with battement tendu.

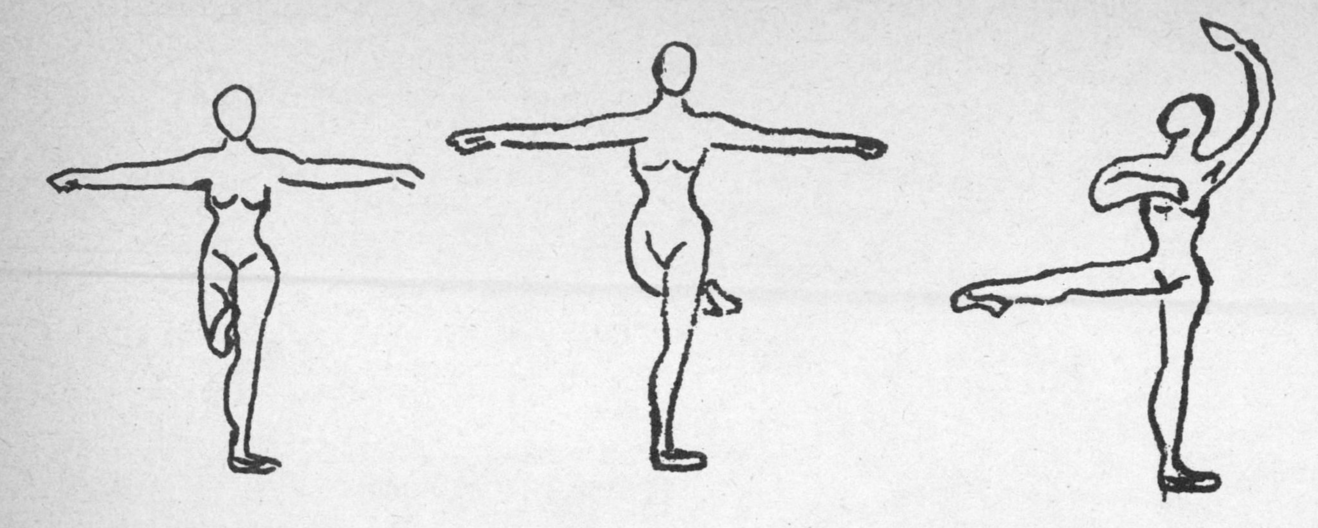

Fig. 134 Grand battement to fourth front

Fig. 135 Grand battement to fourth back

Fig. 136 Grand battement to second

EXERCISE 3

BATTEMENTS TENDUS ET DÉGAGÉS

Battement tendu is completed with two other movements which follow in an established and logical order.

The three movements together form one exercise and are always executed with the same leg.

The exercise is exactly the same as that at the barre, therefore, in order not to repeat ourselves, we refer the reader to Book Two, Part One, pages 47-50.

Stand in the centre of the room, feet in fifth position, right foot front. Arms in position de repos.

Take the arms to second with port de bras, then release the right leg to second, pointe on the floor (fig. 137). Then execute:

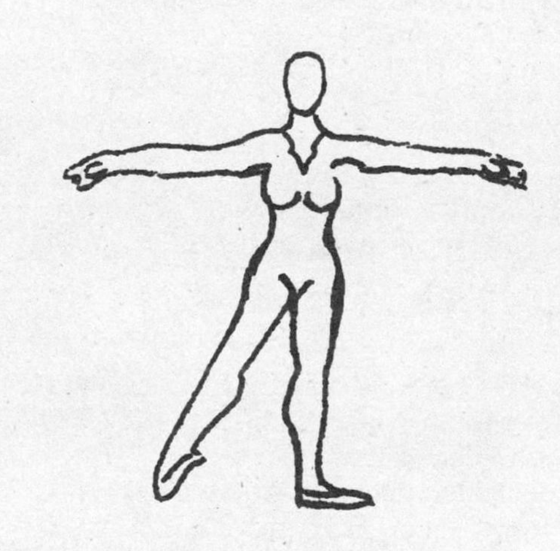

Fig. 137 Commencing position for battements tendus

Exercise

8 battements tendus
16 battements dégagés
2 battements tendus relevés

At the end of the exercise, lower the arms to position de repos. Then make a grande préparation to second and execute one turn en dehors to the right (see Volume 2, Book Four, Part One, Group Four).

EXERCISE 4

RONDS DE JAMBE À TERRE

Ronds de jambe à terre in the centre is exactly the same as at the barre; see Book Two, Part One, page 51.

Stand in the centre of the room in fifth position, right foot front; arms in position de repos.

Exercise

Prepare with demi-rond de jambe à terre en dehors plié.

8 ronds de jambe à terre en dehors (fig. 138)
8 ronds de jambe à terre en dedans (fig. 139)
1 grand rond de jambe à terre en dehors plié to close. Right foot behind in fifth.
2 changements (Volume 2, Book Four, Part One)

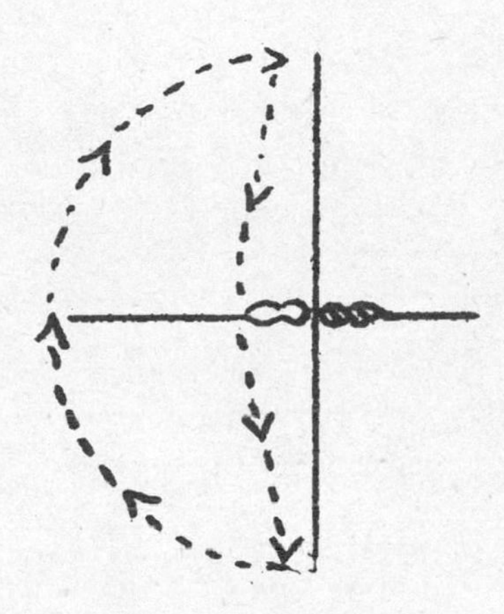

Fig. 138 Track of the right pointe in ronds de jambe en dehors

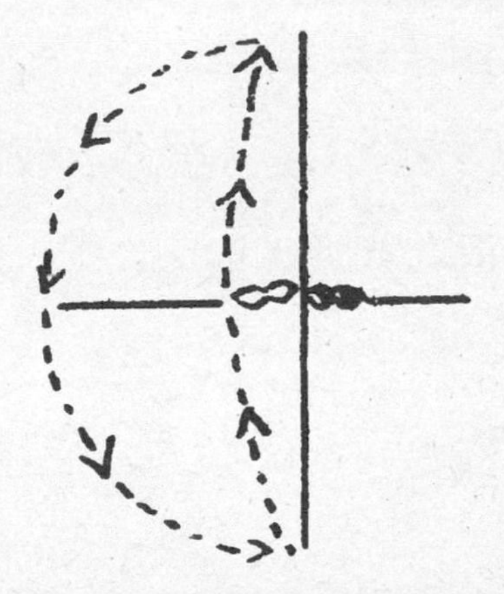

Fig. 139 Track of the right pointe in ronds de jambe en dedans

Variation for advanced classes

In the advanced classes, rond de jambe à terre can also be combined with a turn of the body. This is accomplished as follows:

Explanation

For every rond de jambe à terre, with a slight movement with the underneath of the supporting foot (without raising it from the floor), the body makes $^1/_8$ of a turn.

There are 8 consecutive ronds de jambe in the same direction so that, after the eighth rond de jambe, the body will have completed one whole turn.

The movement must be smooth, without any jerks or starts.

a) Executing ronds de jambe à terre en dehors with the right leg, the body will turn to the right.
b) Executing ronds de jambe à terre en dedans with the right leg, the body will turn to the left.

Exercise

8 ronds de jambe à terre en dehors turning right with the right leg
8 ronds de jambe à terre en dedans turning left with the right leg

Rond de jambe à terre is always executed with all its requirements; therefore, as the body makes the turn, the leg always passes from fourth front to fourth back or from fourth back to fourth front, describing the classic semi-circle with the pointe of the foot, and going to the front or to the back passing correctly through first position.

EXERCISE 5

BATTEMENTS FRAPPÉS ET BATTEMENTS FRAPPÉS AVEC PETITS BATTEMENTS

Battement frappé is a strong, vigorous movement, so its execution requires stability and perfect balance. This is followed by battement frappé preceded by petit battement sur le cou de pied, a more complicated and difficult movement which completes the exercise.

This exercise is exactly the same as at the barre. See Book Two, Part One, pages 55 and 57.

Stand in the centre of the room, feet in fifth, right foot front; arms in position de repos.

Port de bras taking the arms to second.

Open the right leg to second, flex the knee and place the heel on the left cou de pied.

Exercise

8 battements frappés (fig. 140)
16 battements frappé avec petits battements sur le cou de pied
After the exercise, the feet close in fifth, the arms lower to position de repos.

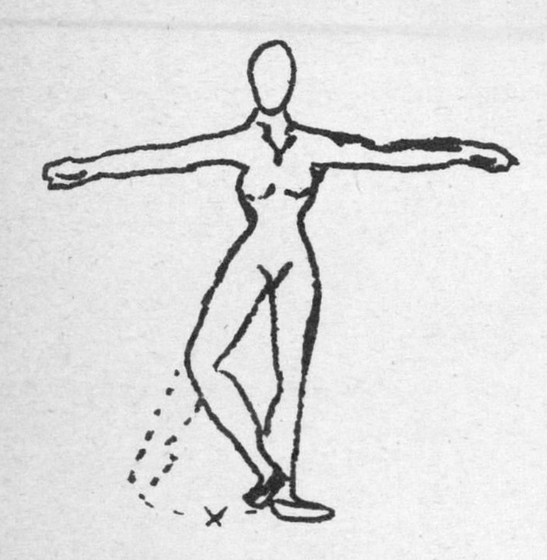

Fig. 140 Movement of battement frappé

Slide the right foot to fourth front transferring the weight onto the front leg raising the left heel; the left foot remains pointed to fourth back.

Enveloppé with the left leg, turn en dedans to the right; the arms are raised to fifth. End with the feet in fifth, left foot front. Arms in position de repos.

EXERCISE 6

RONDS DE JAMBE EN L'AIR

Rond de jambe en l'air in the centre is the same as at the barre with only one small difference. For the movement of rond de jambe en l'air, see Book Two, Part One, pages 58-59. A detailed explanation of the way it is executed follows:

Stand in the centre of the room in fifth position, right foot front; arms in position de repos.

Port de bras through first to second.

Développé extending the right leg to second.

Exercise

1. Execute 3 ronds de jambe en l'air en dehors (fig. 141).
   Lower the right leg, fully stretched, to second, pointe on the floor and slide the foot quickly to fifth back; at the same time, incline the torso left.
   The arms go to a low fourth (right arm in second); the right shoulder is taken slightly back; the head turns to the left shoulder (fig. 142).
   Bring the body upright; raise the right leg to second; the body faces front; the arms open again to second.

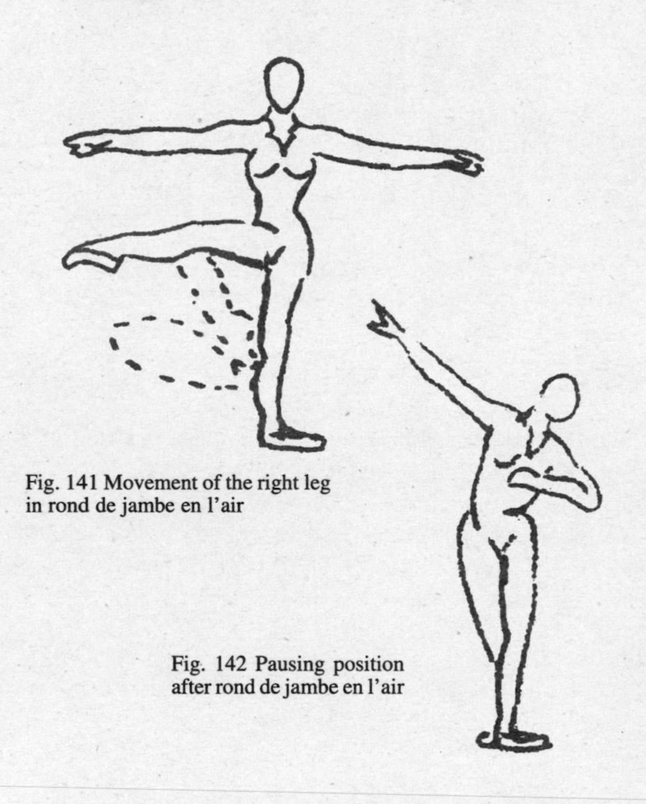

Fig. 141 Movement of the right leg in rond de jambe en l'air

Fig. 142 Pausing position after rond de jambe en l'air

2. Execute 2 ronds de jambe en l'air en dedans (fig. 141).
   Lower the leg, fully stretched, to second, pointe on the floor; slide the foot quickly into fifth front. At the same time incline the torso to the right.
   The arms go to a low fourth (left arm in second); the left shoulder is taken slightly back; the head turns right.

Exercise with the right leg

3 ronds de jambe en l'air en dehors
1 demi-grand battement, close fifth back

2 ronds de jambe en l'air en dedans
1 demi-grand battement, close in fifth front

2 ronds de jambe en l'air en dehors
1 demi-grand battement, close in fifth back

2 ronds de jambe en l'air en dedans
1 demi-grand battement, close fifth front

The exercise ends with the feet in fifth position, the arms lower to position de repos.

Battement tendu taking the left foot to fifth front and repeat the exercise with the left leg.

EXERCISE 7

PETITS BATTEMENTS SUR LE COU DE PIED

The movement of the petits battements sur le cou de pied in the centre is the same as at the barre except for one small variation. For the technique of the movement see Book Two, Part One, page 60. Below we give a detailed explanation of the exercise with the broad ending movement.

Stand in the centre of the room with the feet in fifth, right foot front; arms in position de repos.

Battement tendu taking the right leg to second; flex the knee and place the heel in front of the left cou de pied (fig. 143).

EXERCISE

15 petits battements with the right foot
1 jeté with the right leg

15 petits battements with the left foot
1 jeté with the left leg

ENDING

Développé extending the right leg to fourth front.

Grand rond de jambe en dehors taking the fully stretched leg to fourth back; bend into attitude.

The body turns slightly to the right.

The arms are raised to first, then open to second and the right is taken to fifth; the pose is attitude, facing diagonally right (fig. 144).

Relevé onto the left pointe, still in attitude.

Lower the left heel, demi-plié.

The right leg straightens and lowers to fourth back, transferring the full weight over it.

Straighten the knees and raise the left heel; the left foot is pointed to fourth front.

At the end of this movement, the right arm lowers to second and the left is raised to fifth. The body is en croisé en avant (fig. 145).

Close the feet in fifth and lower the arms to position de repos.

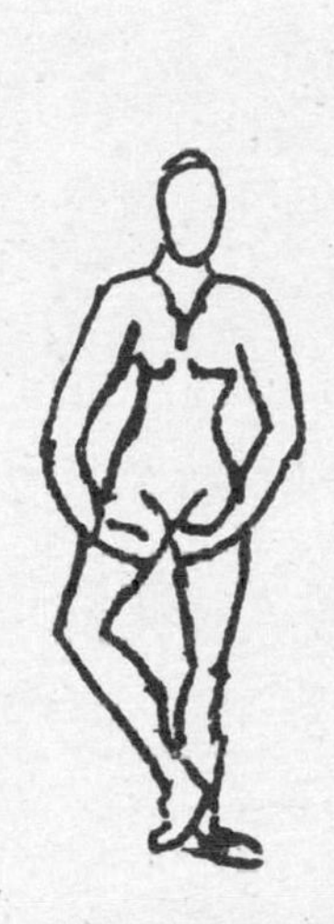

Fig. 143 Petits battements sur le cou de pied

Fig. 144 Ending movement: attitude

Fig. 145 Ending en croisé en avant

BOOK THREE

PART ONE
POSES

In Book Two of the practical section we discussed some of the dynamics of dance. Constant practice of suitable exercises gradually develops muscular sensitivity enabling the muscles to release the degree of strength and elasticity necessary for the various movements.

Through this muscular sensitivity the nuances of strength and speed are given. Training the muscular sense gives a spontaneity of musicality combined with stability in time and space.

In Book Three we deal with the static part of dance which, through a series of appropriate exercises based mainly on posture and adage movements, develops a fuller sense of rhythm.

Our body has innumerable ways of making positions and must be carefully trained into artistic poses. It is obvious that the unlimited positions that the human body can take, cannot be left to the whims of the dancer, which are often contrary to aesthetics and artistic plasticity. Therefore, even this, which is one of the most important aspects in teaching the art of dance, needs precise rules that govern and discipline the positions and movements in the technique of adage.

Consequently, it is essential that the pupil is well-prepared in the theory and practice of this important part of dance so that he will be able to move on to learn the *adagio* exercises which are some of the most important of higher order.

In this practical section the poses will be discussed. The dancer is taught to be technically correct in each position and to move with artistry.

Since slow or even static movements predominate in these exercises, the basic poses which are taught in this part of the method must be learned with precision.

The basic poses derive, for the most part, from movements of the arms and legs (see: Book One, Part One, pages 18 and 25) in a given direction of the body.

These movements and directions combine harmoniously together creating the principal poses. From these are derived all the others which, with the earlier movements and the adagio movements, support the whole practical section of the study of the adagi.

There are 8 basic poses and these will be treated individually.

1. En croisé en avant
2. À la quatrième en avant
3. Écarté
4. Effacé
5. À la seconde
6. Épaulé
7. À la quatrième en arrière
8. En croisé en arrière

POSES

1. Position en croisé en avant

Stand in the centre of the room facing the left diagonal; feet in fifth, right foot front. Arms in position de repos.

Port de bras taking the arms to third position left; head erect.

Adjust the weight onto the left leg. Raise the right leg to fourth front at half height, well stretched and turned out with the pointe of the foot forced down and the heel forward.

From the waist up, turn the torso to the front, and incline slightly over the right side.

The right foot points towards the left; the head inclines a little to the right shoulder (fig. 146).

Fig. 146 En croisé en avant

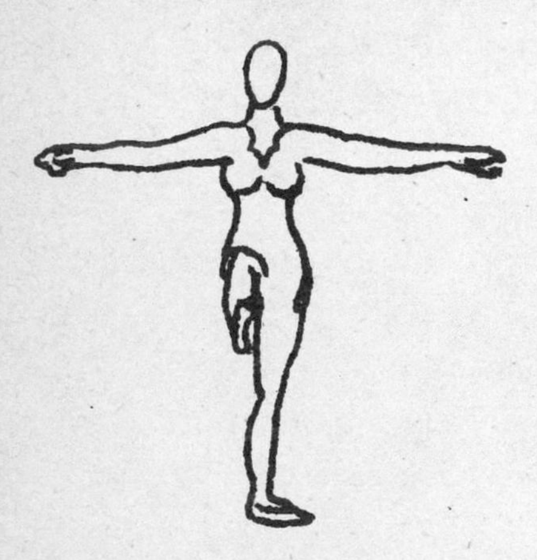

Fig. 147 À la quatrième en avant

2. Position à la quatrième en avant

Stand in the centre of the room in fifth position, right foot front; arms in position de repos.

Port de bras taking the arms to second position.

Adjust the weight onto the left leg. Raise the right leg to fourth front at hip height, well stretched and turned out, pointe of the foot forced down, heel turned out. Head erect and facing front (fig. 147).

3. Position écartée

Stand in the centre of the room in fifth position, right foot front, facing the left diagonal. Arms in position de repos.

Port de bras taking the arms to third position right.

Adjust the weight onto the left leg. Raise the right leg to second at half height; the foot, well arched, points to the right diagonal.

The right shoulder moving forward, and the left moving back cause the body to face the left diagonal.

The head turns right, slightly raised, looking to the hand of the right arm which is in fifth (fig. 148).

Fig. 148 Écarté

Fig. 149 Effacé

4. Position effacée

Stand in the centre of the room in fifth position, right foot front. Arms in position de repos. The body faces the right diagonal.

Port de bras taking the arms to third position left.

Adjust the weight onto the left leg. Raise the right leg to fourth front at half height, fully stretched and turned out, pointe forced down, heel turned out.

The head turns left (fig. 149).

5. Position à la seconde

Stand in the centre of the room with the feet in fifth position, right foot front. Arms in position de repos. Head erect and facing front.

Port de bras taking the arms to second.

Adjust the weight onto the left leg. Raise the right leg to second at hip height, fully stretched, with the pointe well forced down (fig. 150).

Fig. 150 À la seconde

Fig. 151 Épaulé

6. Position épaulée

Stand in the centre of the room turned to the left. Feet in fifth position, left foot front. Arms in position de repos.

Take the arms, well stretched, into arabesque; the right straight forward and above shoulder height, the left back and below shoulder level, in alignment with the right.

Raise the right leg to fourth back at hip height, fully stretched and well turned out with the pointe of the foot forced down.

The head is turned to the right shoulder (fig. 151).

7. Position à la quatrième en arrière

Stand in the centre of the room with the feet in fifth position, left foot front. Arms in position de repos. Head erect.

Port de bras taking the arms to second position.

Adjust the weight onto the left leg. Raise the right leg to fourth back at hip height, well stretched and turned out with the pointe of the foot forced down, heel turned out (fig. 152).

Fig. 152 À la quatrième en arrière

Fig. 153 En croisé en arrière

8. Position en croisé en arrière

Stand in the centre of the room facing the right diagonal. Feet in fifth, left foot front. Arms in position de repos. Head erect.

Port de bras taking the arms to third position left.

Adjust the weight onto the left leg. Raise the right leg to fourth back at half height, turned out and bent, with the pointe of the foot forced down.

From the waist up, turn the torso front, inclining slightly over the right side.

The head, turned front, is slightly inclined to the right (fig. 153).

ARABESQUE AND ATTITUDE

As well as the eight basic "poses" described in the previous chapter, two other poses, very important in the study of dance, must be added. These are distinct from all other poses for their classic beauty, perfection of line and particularly for their unique individual characteristics. These are very different from the poses described previously.

These characteristics are due to the very nature of these poses. They form themselves, since they do not arise from any movement of legs or arms. They are different also because they are outside the rules that discipline the movements and positions in dance and, above all, the basic principles of balance. They move away from the perpendicular line of the centre of gravity, finding their balance only in the virtuosity of the dancer.

The poses, arabesque and attitude, are the most beautiful and artistically perfect, having been created for the harmony and grace of dance and inspired by sculptures and paintings of the most illustrious masters of the past, for example, the marvelous classical pose, the attitude of Giambologna (Jean de Boulogne).

In arabesque, the body is held upright on one leg which is straight or in demi-plié while the other is extended and raised to fourth back. The arms are almost always completely stretched with the palms of the hands facing down.

In the first, second and fourth arabesque, one arm is extended forward and the other straight back in alignment with the first.

The arms can be lowered, raised, brought forward or back and still remain in the arabesque position as long as they strictly observe what has already been written on the theory of port de bras (Book One, Part One, page 23 which is, as the arms move, they must remain in alignment with each other.

In the third and fifth arabesques, both arms are raised in front, one below the other, parallel; even in this case, as they move, the arms are still in arabesque as long as they remain parallel.

N.B. In arabesque or attitude, the supporting foot is not completely turned out.

ARABESQUE

There are five basic arabesque positions:

1. First arabesque (ouverte and croisée)
2. Second arabesque (ouverte and croisée)
3. Third arabesque (ouverte and croisée)
4. Fourth arabesque (ouverte and croisée)
5. Fifth arabesque (ouverte and croisée)

1. First arabesque ouverte

Stand in the centre of the room, turned to the right side. Feet in fifth position, right foot front. Arms in position de repos. Head erect.

Raise the right arm in front, extended above shoulder height; palm of the hand facing down.

Raise the left arm behind, well stretched, below shoulder level, in alignment with the right; palm of the hand facing down.

Raise the left leg, stretched, to fourth back at hip height, turned out with the pointe of the foot forced down.

Torso well erect. Look at the right hand (fig. 154).

First arabesque croisée

Remain in the same position as the preceding exercise; feet in fifth but with the left foot front.

Raise the left arm, extended forward above shoulder height, palm of the hand facing down.

Raise the right arm behind, extended to fourth back below shoulder level, in alignment with the left, palm of the hand facing down.

Raise the right leg, well stretched to fourth back at hip height, turned out with the pointe of the foot forced down.

Torso well erect. Look at the left hand (fig. 155).

Fig. 154 First arabesque ouverte

Fig. 155 First arabesque croisée

Fig. 156 Second arabesque ouverte

Fig. 157 Second arabesque croisée

2. Second arabesque ouverte

Stand in the centre of the room turned to the right side. Feet in fifth, right foot front. Arms in position de repos. Head erect.

Raise the left arm, extended forward, above shoulder height, palm of the hand facing down.

Raise the right arm behind, extended below shoulder level, in alignment with the left, palm of the hand facing down.

Raise the left leg, well stretched, to fourth back at hip height, turned out with the pointe of the foot forced down.

Torso well erect. Look at the left hand (fig. 156).

Second arabesque croisée

Remain in the same position as the previous exercise, feet in fifth but with the left foot front.

Raise the right arm, extended forward, above shoulder height, palm of the hand facing down.

Raise the left arm, extended behind, below shoulder level, in alignment with the right, palm of the hand facing down.

Raise the right leg, well stretched, to fourth back at hip height, turned out with the pointe of the foot forced down.

Torso well erect. Look at the right hand (fig. 157).

Fig. 158 Third arabesque ouverte

Fig. 159 Third arabesque croisée

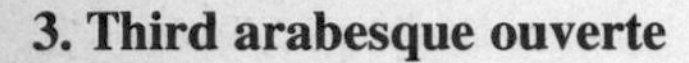

3. Third arabesque ouverte

Stand in the centre of the room turned to the right side. Feet in fifth, right foot front. Arms in position de repos.

Raise the right arm, extended forward above shoulder height, palm of the hand facing down.

Raise the left arm in front, slightly bent, below and parallel to the right, palm of the hand facing down.

Raise the left leg, well stretched, to fourth back at hip height, turned out, with the pointe of the foot forced down.

Torso erect. Look at the right hand (fig. 158).

Third arabesque croisée

Remain in the same position as the previous exercise, feet in fifth but with the left foot front.

Raise the left arm, extended forward above shoulder level, palm of the hand facing down.

Raise the right arm in front, slightly bent, a little lower and parallel to the left, palm of the hand facing down.

Torso erect. Look at the left hand (fig. 159).

4. Fourth arabesque ouverte and croisée

The fourth arabesque, ouverte or croisée, is exactly the same as the second arabesque, ouverte or croisée; the only difference being that the supporting leg is in demi-plié, and the torso reaches slightly forward (figs. 160 and 161).

5. Fifth arabesque ouverte and croisée

The fifth arabesque is exactly the same as the third arabesque, ouverte or croisée, the difference being that the supporting leg is in demi-plié, and the torso reaches slightly forward (figs. 162 and 163).

Arabesque sur la pointe

The first, second and third arabesques are taken with the foot of the supporting leg on half pointe or full pointe (fig. 164).

There are three ways of executing arabesque on half pointe or full pointe:

1. Take the arabesque position then, holding the arms and the well-stretched raised leg firmly in position, make a small demi-plié and strongly stretch the supporting leg, rising onto the half or full pointe (arabesque en relevé).
2. Jeté, springing onto the fully stretched leg on half pointe or full pointe, taking the weight over the supporting leg; at the same time, the other leg and both arms take the arabesque position (arabesque en piqué sur la pointe).
3. Small demi-plié in fifth and strongly straighten the legs, rising onto half or full pointe of one foot, as the other leg and both arms take the arabesque position (arabesque à temps de pointe).

N.B. The fourth and fifth arabesques are executed only on the whole foot. Turns taken in arabesque are en dehors when they turn towards the supporting leg, and en dedans when they turn towards the raised one.

Fig. 160 Fourth arabesque ouverte

Fig. 161 Fourth arabesque croisée

Fig. 162 Fifth arabesque ouverte

Fig. 163 Fifth arabesque croisée

Fig. 164 Arabesque sur la pointe

ATTITUDE

In attitude, the body is erect with the lumbar region held firmly; the supporting leg is fully stretched; the other is well turned out, raised to fourth back with the knee bent, pointe of the foot forced down.

The arms are in third position; the high arm corresponds to the raised leg.

The head is turned to the high arm, looking at the hand.

The position of attitude depends on which arm and which leg are raised, for example:

1. The attitude is *right* when the right arm and leg are raised (fig. 165).
2. The attitude is *left* when the left arm and leg are raised (fig. 166).

N.B. In attitude the arms are generally in third, but it is also possible to have one arm in fifth and the other in demi-seconde.

Turns which can be executed in attitude positions are *en dehors* when the turn is towards the raised leg; and *en dedans* when turning towards the supporting leg.

The poses in attitude never vary, but the positions are classified according to the direction of the body in respect of the audience. Therefore there is:

Fig. 165 Attitude right

Fig. 166 Attitude left

Attitude sur la pointe

To rise onto pointe, stand in attitude then, firmly holding the position, small demi-plié and sharply straighten the supporting leg, rising onto half or full pointe (fig. 170).

In attitude, the position can also be taken in two ways:

– Piqué sur la pointe
– Temps de pointe

Fig. 170 Attitude sur la pointe

a) *Attitude to the front*, which faces the audience (fig. 167);
b) *Attitude ouverte*, when the raised leg is towards the audience (fig. 168);
c) *Attitude croisée*, when the supporting leg is towards the audience (fig. 169).

Fig. 167 Attitude facing front

Fig. 168 Attitude ouverte

Fig. 169 Attitude croisée

LINKED POSES

From the basic poses, from arabesques and attitudes, the dancer can create all those positions that his taste and artistry could require. These are almost unlimited and continually adapted for the artistic demands of choreographers.

As we have already said, the dancer must always be in perfectly coordinated positions when dancing.

Therefore, great care is taken to show this, especially at the beginning, during pauses, and at the end of every dance.

To make it easier for the pupil to study the many and various artistic ways in which these positions can be taken, we have decided to link certain poses into one exercise; these poses have been chosen from amongst the most beautiful and useful and they are combined into one flowing, and highly artistic, movement.

In this exercise there is a slight pause between one movement and another which allows the dancer to take the pose carefully, and the maestro to observe and correct possible errors. In this way, the pupil gradually acquires a natural sense of harmony and moves with easy spontaneity.

At this point, any hard, mechanical look begins to disappear, allowing the sensitivity of the dancer to show itself in most harmonious poses.

This exercise is executed with a musical accompaniment in 3/4 waltz time. It can be seen that the music not only conducts and draws out but encourages the completion of dance movements with an artistically attuned pliability.

The dancer must accustom himself to thinking that his dancing must never be just a sterile series of rational movements.

We could almost say that the movements must arise from the very soul and be imprinted therefore at the highest spiritual sensibility.

The body, by now supple from daily continuous repetition of the training exercises, must be directed, through gradual schooling, to become at one with the music, in order to melt into poses and movements of fascinating refinement.

Exercise with poses

Stand in the centre of the room with the feet in fifth position, right foot front, facing diagonally right.

Arms in position de repos. Head erect.

The exercise must be executed slowly and evenly, pausing in every position before moving onto the next pose.

For one part of the poses, the pupil faces the audience and for the other part, the back is turned; there are a series of poses in effacée and croisée.

The position of the "pose" always refers to the position of the arms.

1. Pose in attitude right to the right (back)

Demi-plié and slide the left leg to fourth back, transferring the weight onto the back leg. The knees straighten, the right foot remains pointed to fourth front.

During the movement, the arms are taken to the position of attitude right. The right arm passes through first to fifth, the left goes to demi-seconde.

The head turns and inclines right (fig. 171).

Fig. 171 Attitude right back

2. Pose in attitude left to the right (forward)

Demi-plié and balancé transferring the weight forward onto the right leg. The knees straighten, the left foot remains pointed on the floor, to fourth back.

Fig. 172 Attitude left forward

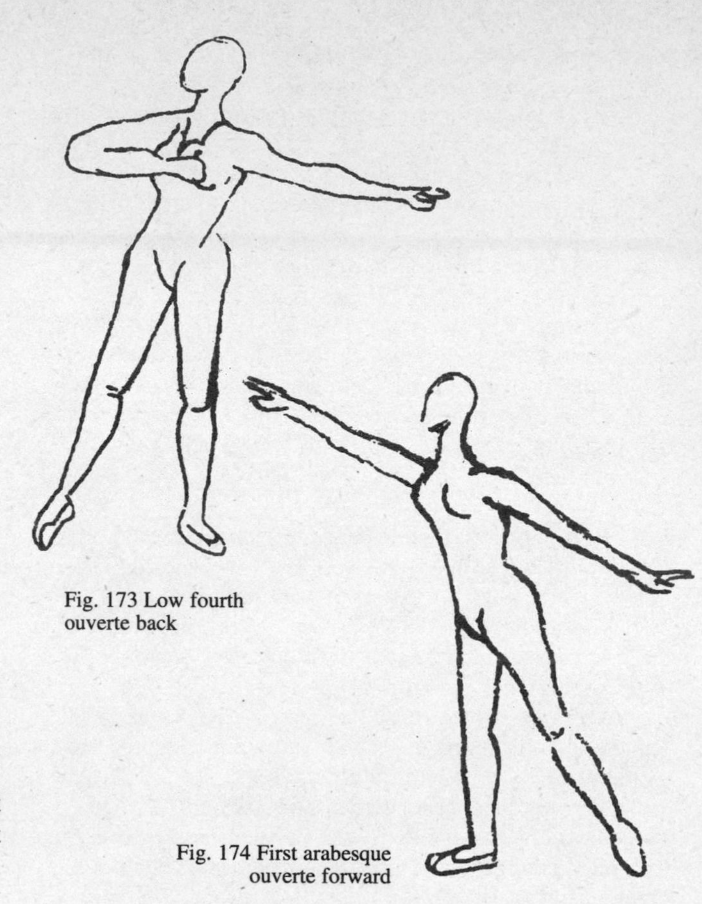

Fig. 173 Low fourth ouverte back

Fig. 174 First arabesque ouverte forward

During the movement, the arms pass through first to attitude left: the left arm is raised to fifth, the right opens to demi-seconde.

The head turns to the left shoulder (fig. 172).

3. Pose in low fourth left ouverte (back)

Demi-plié and balancé transferring the weight back onto the left leg. The knees straighten; the right foot stays pointed on the floor, to second.

During the movement, the arms are taken to low fourth left: the right arm rises to first, the left lowers in second.

The torso inclines slightly over the left side, in line with the right leg extended in second.

The head turns right (fig. 173).

4. Pose in first arabesque ouverte (forward, to the right)

Demi-plié and balancé transferring the weight forward onto the right leg. The knees straighten, the left foot remains pointed on the floor, to fourth back.

During the movement, the arms lower to position de repos before rising to arabesque: the right extends forward and the left stretches back.

The head is turned right, looking at the right hand (fig. 174).

5. Pose in first arabesque croisée (forward, to the right)

Demi-plié, slide the left leg to fourth front transferring the weight onto the left leg. During the movement, the back will turn to the audience. Straighten the knees, the right leg remains pointed on the floor, to fourth back.

At the same time, the arms lower to position de repos before rising, in reverse, to first arabesque: the left arm extended forward and the right back.

Look at the left hand (fig. 175)

Fig. 175 First arabesque croisée, forward

Fig. 176 Low fourth croisée, back

6. Pose in low fourth right croisée (back, to the right)

Still with the back turned to the audience, demi-plié and balancé, transferring the weight back onto the right leg. The knees straighten, the left foot remains pointed on the floor to second.

During the movement, the arms are taken to low fourth right: the left arm goes to first and the right stays in second.

The head turns and inclines left (fig. 176).

Attention – With no. 6 the series of poses to the right end; the exercise continues, without a pause, repeating the same poses to the left, reversing, however, the order of succession commencing, therefore, with pose no. 6 (the first turned to the left) and ending with pose no. 1 thus:

7. Pose in low fourth left croisée (to the left, back)

Demi-plié lowering the left heel; transfer the weight onto the left leg and at the same time turn the torso to the left. The knees straighten, the right foot remains pointed on the floor, to second.

The back is still turned towards the audience.

During the movement, the arms reverse positions from low fourth: the left arm extends to second, the right bends into first.

The torso, slightly inclined over the left side, is in line with the right leg pointed to second.

The head turns right (fig. 177).

8. Pose in first arabesque croisée (forward, to the left)

Still with the back to the audience, demi-plié and balancé transferring the weight forward onto the right leg. As the knees straighten, the left foot remains pointed on the floor, to fourth back.

During the movement, the arms lower to position de repos before rising, quickly, to arabesque position: the right arm extends forwards and the left back.

The head turns right, looking at the hand (fig. 178).

9. Pose in first arabesque ouverte (forward, to the left)

Demi-plié and slide the left leg to fourth front, transferring the weight onto the left leg. During this movement, the body turns to face the audience. The knees straighten, the right foot remains pointed on the floor, to fourth back.

Fig. 177 Low fourth croisée, back

Fig. 178 Arabesque croisée, forward

At the same time, the arms lower through position de repos and reverse into first arabesque: the left arm extends forward and the right back.

The head looks at the left hand (fig. 179).

10. Pose in low fourth right ouverte (to the left, back)

Demi-plié and balancé transferring the weight back onto the right leg. The knees straighten, the left foot remains pointed on the floor, to second.

During the movement, the arms go to low fourth right: the right arm stretched to second and the left raised to first.

The torso is slightly inclined over the right side and comes into line with the left leg extended in second. The head is turned left (fig. 180).

11. Pose in attitude right (forward, to the left)

Demi-plié and balancé transferring the weight forward onto the left leg. The knees straighten, the right leg remains pointed on the floor, to fourth back.

During the movement the arms pass through first to attitude right: the right arm is raised to fifth and the left opens to demi-seconde.

The head turns to the right shoulder (fig. 181).

12. Pose in attitude left (to the left, back)

Demi-plié and balancé transferring the weight back onto the right leg. The knees straighten, the left foot remains pointed on the floor, to fourth front.

During the movement, the arms pass through first and reverse the attitude position: the left arm is raised to fifth and the right opens to second.

The head turns left (fig. 182).

Attention – With no. 12, the 12 poses end (6 to the right and 6 to the left). After another 3 complementary poses, the exercise ends thus:

13. Pose in low fourth left (to the right), torso inclined

Turning the torso to the right, transfer the weight onto the left leg and slightly bend the knee; the right leg extends to second, pointed on the floor.

The torso inclines from the waist, over the right side as the arms go to low fourth: the right to first, the left opening to second continuing the line from the left shoulder.

The head is turned right, looking at the right foot (fig. 183).

Fig. 179 First arabesque ouverte, forward

Fig. 180 Low fourth ouverte, back

Fig. 181 Attitude right, in front

Fig. 182 Attitude left, back

14. Pose in low fourth right (to the left) torso inclined

Turn the torso left, transfer the weight onto the right leg and slightly bend the knee. The left leg extends to second, pointed on the floor.

The torso inclines from the waist, over the left side, the arms, reversing the position, are taken to low fourth right: the left to first, the right extended to second continuing the line from the right shoulder.

The head is turned left, looking at the left foot (fig. 184).

15. Pose in first and ending

Recover bringing the body upright; the weight is still over the bent right leg. Slide the left leg in demi-plié to fourth back.

Fig. 183 Low fourth left with the torso inclined right

Fig. 184 Low fourth right with the torso inclined left

Slowly straighten the knees; the weight is gradually transferred back onto the left leg; the right foot remains pointed on the floor, extended to fourth front.

During the movement, the arms lower to demi-seconde, pass through position de repos to half first position, palms of the hands facing up.

The head turns to the right shoulder (fig. 185).

Ending

Glissé sliding the right foot to fifth front. The arms lower to position de repos. The body turns front.

Pirouettes en dehors sur le cou de pied

The exercise with linked poses is completed by the execution of pirouettes:

– grande préparation for pirouette in second and one turn en dehors to the right sur le cou de pied;

– then, grande préparation as before and one turn en dehors to the left sur le cou de pied;

– repeat as above, this time with two turns to the right, then two turns to the left (see: Volume 2, Book Four, Part One, Group Four).

Fig. 185 Pose in first

PART TWO
ADAGIO MOVEMENTS

When the pupil is able to execute, with accuracy and mastery, the various poses which have been described, the first part of the Teaching Program, concerning static and plastic positions preparatory to the "exercises of a higher order," is complete.

The dancer has now achieved a greater sense of expression which allows him to demonstrate his artistry.

In the following chapter, we will be studying the second part of the Program dealing with "movements." This is closely connected with the first part.

In this section we will examine all the movements which the body must execute to model itself in the various poses. It is a complex and difficult study because all these movements are very slow and must be executed with mathematical precision. This is developed with grace and harmony, so it links elegantly, with finesse and art, to the stillness of the poses.

When the pupil also knows this second section perfectly, he can certainly be moved on to the studies of "higher order," that is, to the study of "Adagio."

The study of the adagi is, without a doubt, the most difficult part of the method, because the exercises are composed of very slow movements. Every minute imperfection can be seen immediately; therefore, great care must be taken in the execution.

The adagi are composed of a limited number of specific "movements" plus a few other general movements.

There are 15 basic and specific adagio movements; these are listed below in alphabetical order:

ADAGIO MOVEMENTS

1. Ballotté
2. Demi-ballotté
3. Demi-contretemps d'Adage
4. Détourné d'Adage
5. Développé
6. Grand rond de jambe
7. Pas de bourrée sur la place
8. Raccourci
9. Ramassé des bras
10. Ramassé des pieds
11. Relevé
12. Relevé-coupé
13. Temps de cuisse
14. Temps de cuisse du haut
15. Tour de promenade

We will give a detailed explanation of the technique of all these movements and try to clarify, as much as possible, the correct manner of execution.

It is important to understand that they must always be executed correctly and precisely; we repeat, there is no room for even the slightest error in Adagio.

1st MOVEMENT

BALLOTTÉ

Technically and more especially choreographically, sometimes the leg which is in the air has to be changed by raising the other leg (but in the opposite direction) in a single movement, in one count of music, gracefully and in coordination with other movements. Ballotté fortunately answers to these needs. It is very smooth, and the change from leg to leg is light and supple.

In order to achieve the coordination required in

this movement, the demi-plié must be very smooth and elastic.

Exercise

This movement commences with the leg raised to fourth front, fourth back, or to second.

Stand in the centre of the room with the feet in fifth position, right foot front. Arms in position de repos.

1. Ballotté to high fourth front

The arms are taken to first as the right leg is raised to fourth front. Demi-plié on the left leg; take the body forwards off balance; quickly lower the right leg transferring onto it the weight, then raise the left leg, fully stretched, to high fourth back.

During the movement, the arms open to second.

2. Ballotté to high fourth back

The left leg is in high fourth back. Demi-plié on the right leg; take the body backwards off balance and quickly lower the left leg transferring the weight onto it, then raise the right leg, fully stretched, to high fourth front.

The arms are held in second.

3. Ballotté to high second

Take the arms to second. Raise the right leg, straight, in second. Demi-plié on the left leg; take the body to the right off balance, quickly lowering the right leg; transfer the weight onto the right leg and raise the left leg, fully stretched, to high second (fig. 186 and 187).

After the movement, the left leg lowers into fifth position front; the arms end in position de repos.

2nd MOVEMENT

DEMI-BALLOTTÉ

Only the basic principal of the demi-ballotté movement is related to ballotté. The technique and the execution are notably different.

The name itself indicates that this is only half of the movement.

In demi-ballotté, when one leg lowers, the other, rising, does not take the same position on the opposite side. Instead of completing the movement, the foot is drawn in and the heel is placed on the cou de pied of the supporting leg where it remains waiting to execute another movement.

Exercise

Développé extending the right leg to fourth front. Arms in second.

Demi-plié on the left leg at the same time as the straight right leg lowers, pointed on the floor, to fourth front (fig. 188).

Gradually straighten the left leg as the right, still stretched, slides the pointe along the floor, to close

Fig. 186 Part of ballotté in second with the right leg

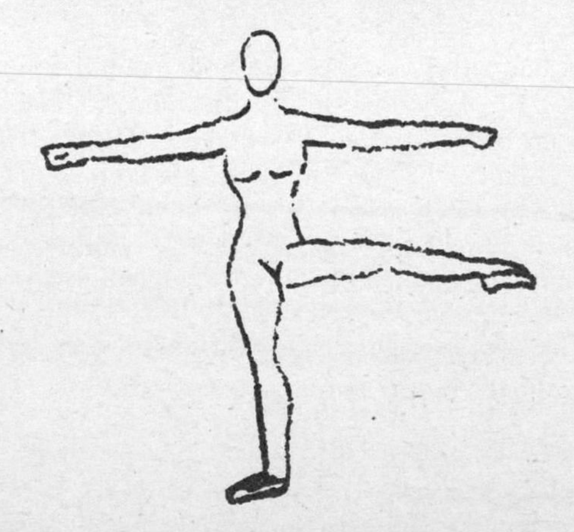

Fig. 187 After ballotté with the right leg, the left leg remains extended in second

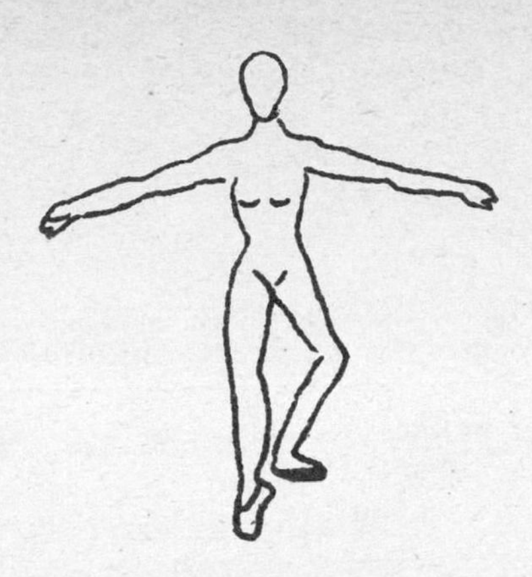

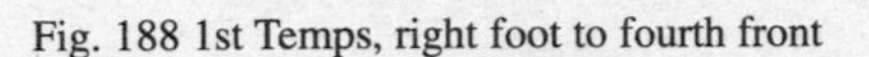

Fig. 188 1st Temps, right foot to fourth front

Fig. 189 2nd Temps, relevé

Fig. 190 3rd Temps, coupé; left foot raised behind

tightly into fifth front. The arms gradually lower to position de repos.

Relevé onto half pointe; coupé, sharply lowering the right heel, drawning in the left foot and placing the heel behind the right cou de pied (figs. 189 and 190).

N.B. Demi-ballotté to fourth back and to second are executed in the same way.

3rd MOVEMENT

DEMI-CONTRETEMPS D'ADAGE

This is an auxiliary movement which is used as a preparation for a following step, to make it more graceful.

As well as making a simple movement more graceful, it is often very useful in some "contra tempo" (against the beat) movements. In this case, demi-contretemps d'Adage is executed in the first temps of the musical bar, so that the dancer will commence on the upbeat.

EXERCISE (in 4 temps)

Stand in the centre of the room with the feet in fifth position, right foot front. Arms in position de repos.

1st Temps: rise onto the half pointe, knees straight. Raise the left leg, straight, to fourth back at half height; lower it until it beats against and bounces off the calf of the right leg, returning immediately to fourth back.
The arms open to demi-seconde.

2nd Temps: from fourth back, the left leg falls, passing through first to fourth front on the floor.
At the same time, the right heel lowers and both knees bend.
The arms close into position de repos.

3rd Temps: transfer the weight onto the left leg and straighten the knees; the right foot remains pointed on the floor, to fourth back.
The arms are raised to first.

4th Temps: slide the right foot in, close behind in fifth. The arms lower once more to position de repos.

CONTRETEMPS D'ADAGE

This movement is exactly like the demi-contretemps d'Adage. The only difference is that the first movement is eliminated, so it is executed with one movement and in one count only.

Exercise

One temps: rise onto half pointe as the left leg rises, straight, to second at half height.
Then:
lower and, passing in front of the right leg, place it, on the floor, in crossed fourth front. Demi-plié on both knees.

N.B. This "movement" acts like a trampoline for another step or when taking a position, for example, arabesque or attitude sur les pointes, etc.

4th MOVEMENT

DÉTOURNÉ D'ADAGE

Détourné d'Adage has an original, peculiar characteristic. The leg no longer has to move in order to change from one position to another; on the contrary, unlike any of the other movements, the whole body moves to change the position of the leg. In this way, the leg which is placed in a given position, without moving, will then arrive into another different position.

The procedure is simple and practical and represents real skill in composing the adagi.

Détourné d'Adage combines all the usefulness of a slow and original movement which allows the leg to change position without moving, with nobility of grace and style.

Exercise

Stand in the centre of the room with the feet in fifth position, right foot front. Arms in position de repos.

Slide the left leg to fourth back, pointed on the floor.

Raise the arms and open them to second position.

The right foot, which is flat on the floor, executes small movements (raising imperceptibly first the heel, then the toes) causing the body to turn to the left, well upright, with the weight over the right leg.

Little by little, the body turns slowly to the left; the left leg, on the other hand, remains on the same spot and, rotating, allows the body to continue turning left.

When the body has made a half a turn to the left, and the back is to the audience, the left leg will automatically be in fourth front, in respect of the body.

At this point, the body continues turning slowly, taking with it the left leg which remains pointed to fourth front, on the floor.

After the turn, the body will be facing front with the left leg pointed, on the floor, to fourth front.

Throughout the movement, the arms remain in second.

N.B. The détourné d'Adage movement is executed with the foot on the floor and with the leg raised in the following positions:
a) with the leg in fourth back
b) with the leg in fourth front
c) with the leg in second

The technique for executing the movement in all three positions is exactly the same as that described above.

Bear in mind, however, that each of these positions has its own rule depending on the position of the leg, therefore:

1. Fourth back

If the left leg is pointed or raised to fourth back, the body can turn one way only and that is to the left; therefore, the left leg, rotating, after the body has turned half way, will be in fourth front.

2. Fourth front

If the left leg is pointed or raised to fourth front, the body can turn one way only and that is to the right; therefore, the left leg, rotating, after the body has turned half-way, will be in fourth back.

3. Second

If the left leg is pointed or raised in second, the body can turn either to the right or to the left, therefore;
a) if the body turns left, the left leg extended in second, rotating, after the body has made a quarter of a turn, will be in fourth front;
b) if the body turns right, the left leg extended in second, rotating, after the body has made a quarter of a turn, will be in fourth back.

5th MOVEMENT

DÉVELOPPÉ

Développé is a classic Adagio movement and for this reason is of great importance. Therefore, its execution must be perfect.

Almost always in adagio, the leg is raised by means of a développé; because of its intrinsic qualities and slowness, it harmonizes better with all the other adagio movements.

Although the leg which executes the développé always moves in the same way, the supporting leg can: remain straight with the whole foot on the floor, make a demi-plié during the movement, or rise onto pointe during the movement.

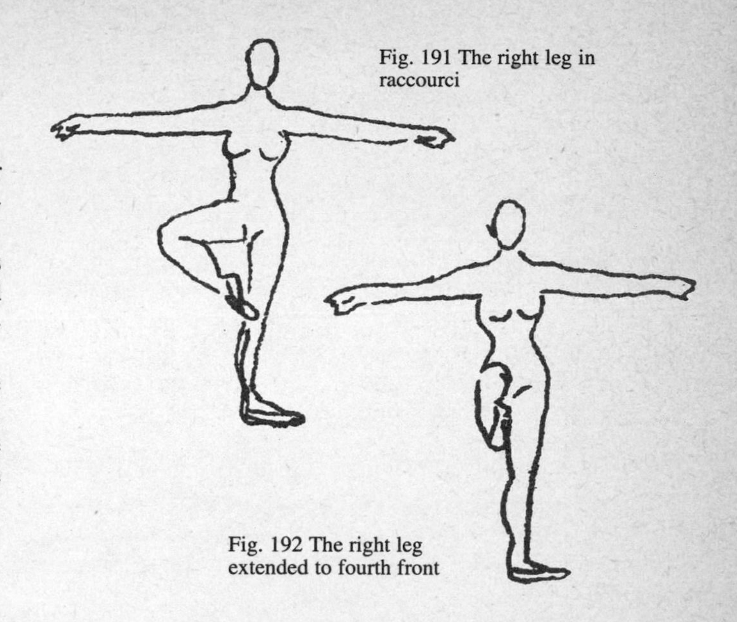

Fig. 191 The right leg in raccourci

Fig. 192 The right leg extended to fourth front

EXERCISE (in 2 temps)

Stand in the centre of the room with the feet in fifth position, right foot front. Arms in position de repos.

1st Temps: adjust all the weight onto the left, supporting leg which remains firm and fully stretched throughout the movement.
The right foot is slowly drawn up to raccourci, well turned out, (with the knee in second position); the pointe of the foot, fully arched, slides along the tibia of the left leg until it is at knee height (fig. 191).

2nd Temps: extend the right leg slowly (still well turned out with the pointe of the foot fully stretched) to high fourth front (fig. 192), fourth back or high second position.

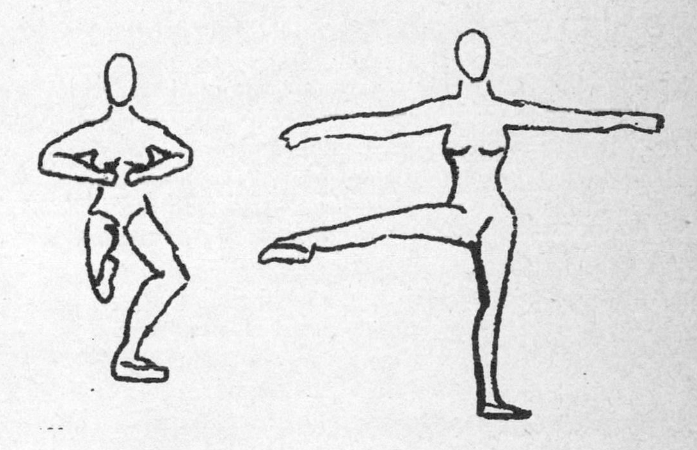

Fig. 193 The right leg extended and the left leg in demi-plié

Fig. 194 The right leg is carried to second and the left leg extends

Développé with demi-plié on the supporting leg

1st Temps: exactly the same as the preceding movement.

2nd Temps: as the supporting left leg gradually bends into demi-plié (knee well turned out); the right leg (at the same time), extends slowly to fourth front (fig. 193).

3rd Temps: the right leg, fully stretched, is carried to second with a quarter of grand rond de jambe en dehors, straightening the left leg (fig. 194).

Développé sur la pointe

This movement is exactly the same as développé with the straight leg, executed a little faster; the only difference is that the supporting leg is on pointe.

The pupil rises onto the pointe of one foot while the other leg, with développé, extends to high fourth front, fourth back or to high second.

Lower the heel only after the end of the développé.

6th MOVEMENT

GRAND ROND DE JAMBE

Grand rond de jambe is a movement of higher order forming part of the "group" of Adagio movements.

As it is of great importance, it has already been included in the exercises at the barre (Book Two, Part One, pages 65) as a daily exercise.

In Adagio, the grand rond de jambe is, of course, taken without the use of the barre. Therefore, it is even more important to execute it taking extra care to make it precise and perfect.

The leg which extends to fourth front (for grand rond de jambe en dehors) or to fourth back (for grand rond de jambe en dedans) must always be well turned out, at hip height, straight, with pointe of the foot strongly lowered.

During the rond de jambe movement, the leg remains exactly at its initial height, while the body, with the lumbar region well supported, remains in perfect "aplomb" firmly balanced.

Grand rond de jambe en dehors

Stand in the centre of the room with the feet in fifth position, right foot front. Arms in position de repos.

1st Temps: développé, extending the right leg to high fourth front. The arms go to first.

2nd Temps: slowly and evenly, remaining at the same height, the right leg moves from fourth front, through second to fourth back. The arms open to second as the leg passes through second.

N.B. The movement ends here. In order to continue, a third part is executed:

3rd Temps: from fourth back, raccourci with the right leg, taking the thigh to second; the pointe of the foot brushes the knee of the left leg; développé, extending the leg to fourth front.

Grand rond de jambe en dedans

1st Temps: développé, extending the left leg to fourth back.
The arms are raised to first.

2nd Temps: with a slow and even movement, keeping the leg at the same height, the left leg passes through second from fourth back to fourth front.
The arms open to second.

N.B. The movement ends here. To continue, a third temps is executed:

3rd Temps: from fourth front, raccourci with the left leg taking the thigh to second; the pointe of the foot brushes the knee of the right leg; développé, extending the leg to fourth back.

7th MOVEMENT

PAS DE BOURRÉE SUR LA PLACE

The execution of an adagio requires the body to be perfectly on balance, particularly if the adagio commences sur les pointes. Therefore, a dancer who is about to perform an adagio feels worried about the stability of her placing.

Pas de bourrée sur la place, cleverly and gracefully, enables the dancer to easily manoevre that slight displacement of the body; a movement of the feet, raised on half pointes or full pointes, gives the reassuring sensation of being completely on balance.

EXERCISE

Small demi-plié and sharp relevé springing onto half or full pointes, straightening the legs. After a short pause, the knees softly relax and, with the legs tightly together, the feet commence moving very slightly, lifting (an eighth of an inch or, a few millimeters) off the floor and lowering alternately; the weight, following the movement of the feet, is able to change from one leg to another.

This movement gives a feeling of being on balance.

If the adagio does not remain on pointe after the pas de bourrée sur les pointes, the heel of one foot lowers quickly, while the other foot is drawn in to place the heel on the cou de pied of the supporting leg.

If the front leg begins the movement, the heel of the back foot lowers and the front foot draws in and is placed in front of the cou de pied.

If the back leg begins the movement, the heel of the front leg lowers and the back leg draws in and is placed behind the other cou de pied.

8th MOVEMENT

RACCOURCI

In dance the working leg is not always straight or fully stretched when it is moving. Often it is flexed or bent as it moves; this happens particularly during the execution of adagi.

A leg which draws in before extending into a given position, gives the movement smoothness and a graceful softness.

This movement is usually linked with développé and therefore to the extension of the leg.

EXERCISE

The movement can be executed commencing:

a) from fifth position
b) from fourth front or back, and from second; pointed on the floor, at half height or at full height.

Whichever is the initial position, the knee of the leg which bends must be well turned out. The pointe of the foot is on the cou de pied front or back, or level with the knee of the supporting leg.

9th MOVEMENT

RAMASSÉ DES BRAS

Theory has shown us the various basic positions of the arms; practice has taught us how to execute the various movements with technique and precision; but even though the arms are correct, their movements still present certain imperfections so that they can appear a little mechanical and wooden. To avoid this, we prepare with the ramassé des bras which gives them grace and charm.

This simple movement gives excellent results.

The arms acquire the voluptuous and majestic movement which can be compared to a swan's legs as it glides along the water.

EXERCISE

Stand in the centre of the room with the feet in fifth, right foot front. Arms in position de repos.

Open the arms to demi-seconde; with the palms facing down, the hands follow, slightly late, the movement of the arms and continue the movement even when the arms, without pausing, lower to position de repos; the hands, which have opened more than usual, are the last to return to their place (Book One, Part One, page 18).

From position de repos the arms rise, passing through first, to continue into the other positions.

10th MOVEMENT

RAMASSÉ DES PIEDS

Ramassé des pieds has the same purpose for the lower limbs as the ramassé des bras has for the upper limbs.

The leg which must execute a slow movement in order to go into a given position, does so with much more grace by substituting the softness of ramassé des pieds for the hardness of the usual movement.

The very simplicity of this movement gives the action of the foot great elegance, rendering it indispensable in the adagio movements.

Executed once, before the leg is taken with développé into a given position, ramassé des pieds becomes a complement to the développé itself.

If the movement is repeated many times in succession before the leg completes another movement, it becomes a movement itself.

EXERCISE

Stand in the centre of the room with the feet in fifth, right foot front. Arms in position de repos.

N.B. This movement is executed to fourth front, fourth back, or to second.

1. Ramassé des pieds to fourth front

Point the right foot to fourth front, on the floor; raise the pointe slightly off the floor, lower immediately, sliding the pointe along the floor, with the knee well turned out; draw in the right foot and place the heel in front of the left cou de pied. Continue with the movement for développé.

2. Ramassé des pieds to fourth back

Pointe the left foot to fourth back, on the floor; raise the pointe slightly off the floor, lower immediately, sliding the pointe along the floor, with the knee well turned out; draw in the left foot and place the heel behind the right cou de pied. Continue with the movement for développé.

3. Ramassé des pieds in second

Pointe the right foot to second, on the floor, raise the pointe slightly off the floor, lower immediately, sliding the pointe along the floor, with the knee well turned out; draw in the right foot and place the heel front or back of the left cou de pied. Continue with the movement for développé.

11th MOVEMENT

RELEVÉ

Relevé is a simple movement in which the dancer rises onto half or full pointes with the whole body perfectly balanced on both feet.

Relevé is particularly important, especially for the adagi where this movement is used a great deal; it forms part of that series of movements that train the muscles to maintain equilibrium.

During relevé both feet rise onto half or full pointes or, with greater difficultly, the rise is onto one foot only.

The technique of this movement is different for the relevé onto half pointes and the relevé onto full pointes even if the final result is the same.

Relevé is part of the pointe-work movements, therefore, it also follows the rules of these steps in its manner of execution.

A detailed description of relevé can be found in the chapter dealing with pointe-work exercises; see Volume 2, Book Four, Part One, Group Two.

Relevé on two feet

Stand with the feet in fifth position; small demi-plié and straightening the knees strongly, rise onto the half pointes or full pointes of both feet.

Legs strongly stretched and tightly together; arms in position de repos.

Relevés are executed in all positions. In the closed positions the legs are tightly together; in the open positions they do not touch.

Relevé on one foot

The raised leg takes any position (fourth front or back, second, arabesque, attitude, etc.), the arms take a position complementary to the legs; small demi-plié on the supporting leg and straightening the knees with energy, rise onto the half pointe or full pointe. The muscles of the leg contract strongly; the lumbar region is held firmly.

12th MOVEMENT

RELEVÉ-COUPÉ

Relevé-coupé is composed of two quite distinct movements. We have included them in this chapter under one name as if dealing with one single movement because of the frequent use of this double movement in the Adagio exercises.

In any case coupé, when it is executed in this way, cannot be separated from relevé (Book Four, Part One).

Like the relevé, the coupé can only be prepared by rising onto half or full pointe. This necessary association of the two movements justifies a name of its own.

This is only used when other steps do not occur between these two movements, in which case the name of each movement is clearly distinct.

EXERCISE

Feet tightly closed in fifth, right foot front; arms in position de repos.

Small demi-plié; relevé strongly onto half or full pointe. Coupé, quickly lowering the left heel, placing the right heel in front of the left cou de pied.

If, after relevé, the right heel lowers on the coupé, the left heel is placed behind the right cou de pied.

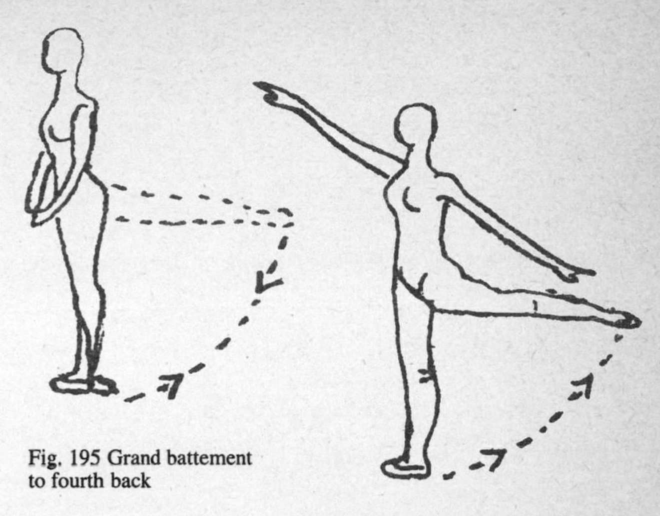

Fig. 195 Grand battement to fourth back

Fig. 196 The leg is raised to arabesque

13th MOVEMENT

TEMPS DE CUISSE

Temps de cuisse is a vigorous and rapid movement, followed immediately by a second slower, more graceful movement which takes the leg into a pose which usually is arabesque but which can also be fourth front or back, or second; however, it is always a pose with a straight leg.

This movement has the same purpose as développé. But where développé is a slow, smooth and soft movement, the temps de cuisse is executed with animation, agility and with a straight working leg.

EXERCISE

Temps de cuisse in arabesque to the right

Stand in the centre of the room with the feet in fifth position, right foot front. Arms in position de repos.

Turn the body diagonally right.

Grand battement to fourth back with the left leg; immediately close behind in fifth, then raise the leg once more to high fourth back, in arabesque ouverte.

During grand battement the arms are in position de repos. As the leg rises to arabesque ouverte, the arms go straight into first arabesque: right arm extended forward above shoulder height, left arm straight back below shoulder level, in alignment with the right (figs. 195 and 196).

14th MOVEMENT

TEMPS DE CUISSE DU HAUT

Temps de cuisse du haut differs from the previous movement since it commences with the leg raised.

This movement, incomplete by itself, prepares a second, and usually more energetic movement.

It always commences with the leg raised to fourth back or to second.

EXERCISE

Développé to extend the leg to fourth back or to second; temps de cuisse du haut is executed in one of these positions. Lower the leg, well stretched, to fifth back raising it again to the original starting position.

In effect, this movement is none other than grand battement executed from a raised position.

15th MOVEMENT

TOUR DE PROMENADE

The purpose of these turns is not so that the dancer can demonstrate his virtuosity, but rather to allow the dancer to animate his plastic but static pose and show off the pose at all angles.

For this reason, the pupil must learn to execute them naturally and with imperceptible movements of the supporting foot, avoiding jerky, hopping movements. The turn must be completely smooth, even and gliding, giving the impression that the dancer is standing on a ball-bearing and turning without moving the feet.

Essentially, it can be compared with a statue placed on a revolving platform which is presented for the audience to admire from every angle.

EXERCISE

This movement is usually taken when the pupil is in one of the following positions:
a) high second
b) arabesque
c) attitude

Standing in position in the centre of the room, raise the left leg into the desired position (arabesque, attitude, second).

The position, which must be technically perfect, is held firmly throughout the whole movement.

Pivot on the right leg with the whole foot on the floor and (lifting imperceptibly first the heel and then the toes) very slowly the body makes one full turn, returning to the pointe of departure in exactly the same position taken at the beginning.

PART THREE
THE ADAGI

This is one of the most delicate and difficult parts of dance training. Its importance, as we will see, is immense and fundamental.

Unfortunately, all too often it is erroneously neglected in many schools. This deficiency derives from the fact that often the precise functions and purposes behind the study of these adagi have not been understood.

Dance too often is thought to be an energetic art whose only value is in its amazing feats of virtuosity. Subsequently, an incorrect attitude based on this idea develops, considering it worthwhile to study for this purpose alone. Dynamics in the training of dance are the basic means by which the muscles develop amazingly, achieving complete independence of movement, and the limbs become more supple enabling them also to acquire the virtue of absolute independence. However, only through the slow, static exercises is it possible to perfect the movements.

The study of adagi allows the maestro to discern each minute nuance in the development of the movements executed by the pupil. This allows him to correct even the smallest imperfection, thus passing on his artistic sensitivity. The pupil is gradually trained always to mold himself very naturally, in even the most transient pose, artistically and with impeccable technique.

The adagi are composed of various movements which link the different poses in perfect harmony.

These compositions have been created by carefully linking together complementary movements; long experience has proved this to have positive results. Every pose and movement has been studied in depth and in the sequence of the compositions all possibilities of their development are presented.

From the first adagi linking the simplest poses, the pupil gradually learns to overcome the difficulties step by step, until the highest degree of technical ability is achieved.

This perfection in the adagio exercises does not consist merely of technical virtuosity but rather, in a combination of this with tones of gracefulness, now languid, now lively. This gives to the movements and poses something divine and spiritual, with touches of subtle yielding and sensuality drawing one to the height of sublime beauty.

The adagi in the Cecchetti method are sensibly divided into number and composition in order to form a complete series.

Every adagio has its own technical and rhythmical characteristics. These, taken in rotation, train the pupil to execute movements and poses in different orders, completely eliminating damaging habits.

As in the other exercises, all the adagi have been composed to purposely chosen music which brings out the particular qualities of each one.

The third part of the "Music Score for the Exercises," from the "Method of Classical Dance by E. Cecchetti," is dedicated to the study of the adagi.*

Therefore, for each one of the exercises described here, corresponding reference will be made to the musical score.

* As explained in the preface, the musical score will be published separately.

EXERCISE 1

TROIS RELEVÉS

(Score no. 1, 3rd Part)

This adagio is based on three relevés performed with the leg in high fourth position front, in high second and in high fourth back.

The relevé is executed after the leg has been taken to one of these positions by means of a développé and is correctly placed, with the arms in second position.

As the supporting foot is raised to half or full pointe, the leg muscles contract strongly.

The lumbar region must be firmly held in order to achieve a perfect balance.

EXERCISE

Preparation

Stand in the centre of the room with the feet in fifth position, right foot front. Arms in position de repos.

1. Plié

Full plié in fifth position; then recover slowly, completely straightening the knees.

2. Relevé-coupé

Demi-plié on both feet, relevé strongly onto half or full pointes. The body turns slightly to the left diagonal.

The head inclines slightly to the right shoulder.

After a short pause, the feet move alternately in pas de bourrée sur la place. Coupé, sharply lowering the left heel; the right foot draws in placing the heel sur le cou de pied in front of the left leg; at the same time, the body turns to face front once more and the head comes erect.

During the preparatory movement, the arms stay in position de repos (fig. 197).

3. First relevé with the right leg to fourth front

Ramassé des pieds with the right leg and développé quickly to fourth front.

Ramassé des bras and, moving in coordination with the right leg, raise the arms through first to open in second.

With the leg in high fourth front and the arms in second, small demi-plié on the left leg and relevé, rising sharply with the leg fully stretched, perfectly on balance onto half or full pointe of the left foot (fig. 198).

Lower the left heel then lower the right leg, well stretched, pointed to fourth front, on the floor; slowly draw in the foot placing the heel onto the cou de pied of the left leg.

The arms lower to the position de repos.

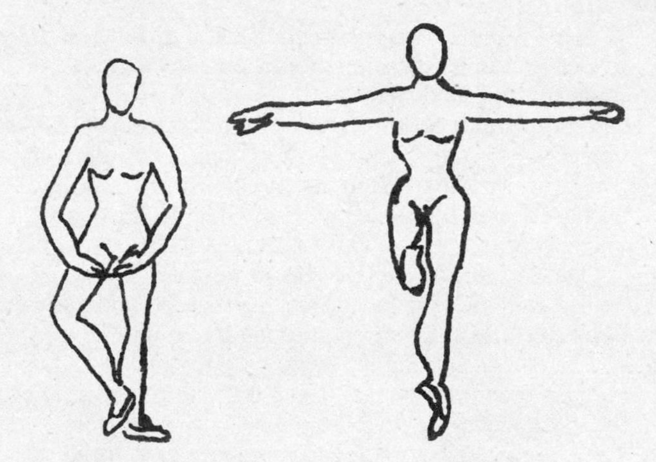

Fig. 197 After coupé with the left leg

Fig. 198 First relevé to fourth front

4. Second relevé with the right leg in second

Ramassé des pieds with the right leg and développé quickly to second (fig. 199).

Ramassé des bras and, moving in coordination with the right leg, raise the arms through first, opening to second.

In high second position with the arms in second, small demi-plié on the left leg and relevé, rising sharply, with the leg well stretched, perfectly balanced onto half or full pointe of the left foot (fig. 200).

Lower the left heel and lower the right leg, well stretched, pointed to second, on the floor; slowly draw in the foot placing the heel behind the left cou de pied.

The arms lower to position de repos.

Fig. 199 Beginning of développé to second

Fig. 201 Third relevé in fourth back

Fig. 200 Second relevé in second

5. Third relevé with the leg to fourth back

Ramassé des pieds and développé quickly to fourth back.

Ramassé des bras and, moving in coordination with the right leg, raise the arms through first opening to second.

With the leg in high fourth back, and the arms in second, small demi-plié on the left leg and relevé, rising sharply, with the leg well stretched, perfectly balanced, onto half or full pointe of the left foot (fig. 201).

Lower the left heel and lower the right leg, well stretched, pointed to fourth back, on the floor; slide the foot behind into fifth.

The arms lower to position de repos.

Repeat the whole exercise immediately with the left leg.

EXERCISE 2

GRAND ROND DE JAMBE EN DEHORS ET EN DEDANS

(Score no. 2, 3rd Part)

This adagio consists of two grands rond de jambe executed alternately on both legs. The exercise commences with rond de jambe en dehors with the right leg; rond de jambe en dedans is executed with the left leg.

The exercise is repeated commencing on the left leg.

This simple exercise requires great precision. The leg which performs the movement must adhere closely to the rules of technique which characterize grand rond de jambe. As the leg passes from fourth front, through second to fourth back, the movement must be completed with the leg always at the same height, in other words, 90° to the supporting leg. During rond de jambe, care must be taken to ensure that the knee of the working leg is well turned out in fourth and gradually rotates upwards as it passes from fourth front to second; in second it is perfectly turned upwards and it gradually rotates outwards once more while passing from second to fourth back. The leg must rotate naturally; the buttock is never raised, with the false idea of simplifying the movement.

The same rules, naturally, are valid for rond de jambe en dedans.

Throughout the movement, the pointe of the foot must be forced down and in alignment with the knee.

By executing rond de jambe with care, the error of "spreading" the legs can be avoided.

EXERCISE

Preparation

Stand in the centre of the room with the feet in fifth position, right foot front. Arms in position de repos.

1. Plié

Full plié in fifth; recover slowly, completely straightening the legs.

2. Relevé-coupé

Demi-plié on both feet and relevé, rising onto half or full pointe. The body turns very slightly to the left. The head inclines slightly over the right shoulder.

After a short pause, the feet move alternately with pas de bourrée sur la place. Coupé, sharply lowering the left heel placing the right heel on the cou de pied in front of the left leg.

The arms remain in position de repos throughout the preparatory movement.

3. Développé with the right leg to fourth front and grand rond de jambe en dehors

Ramassé des pieds with the right leg into développé to fourth front.

Ramassé des bras, and coordinating with the movement of the right leg, the arms are raised to first.

The right leg is in fourth front (arms in first); demi-plié on the left leg (fig. 202).

The right leg commences grand rond de jambe en dehors; as the leg moves to second, the left knee gradually straightens and the arms open to second (fig. 203), while the right leg continues the movement finishing in fourth back.

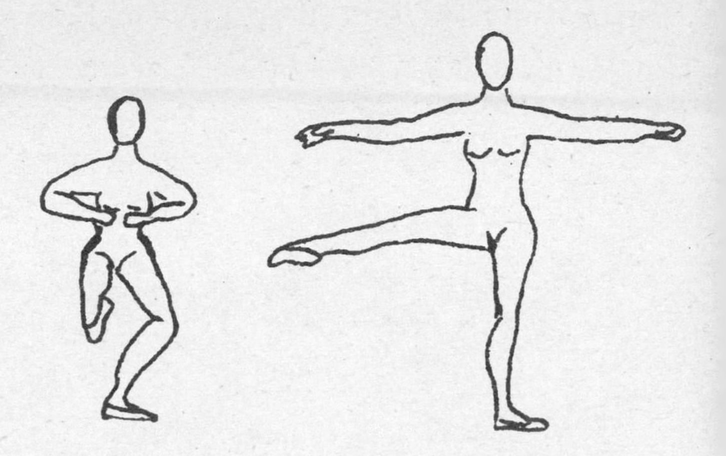

Fig. 202 Commence rond de jambe en dehors

Fig. 203 Rond de jambe moving: passing through second

4. Ballotté to fourth back with the right leg

Small demi-plié on the left leg (fig. 204), take the body backwards off balance, ballotté to fourth back immediately transferring the weight backwards, onto the straight right leg.

The left leg is raised, fully stretched, to fourth front; the left foot draws in, placing the heel in front of the right cou de pied.

Petit battement sur le cou de pied, taking the left foot behind the right cou de pied (fig. 205).

The arms are still in second position.

5. Développé with the left leg to fourth back and grand rond de jambe en dedans

Développé with the left leg to high fourth back; rond de jambe en dedans with the left leg, passing through second, taking the leg to fourth front (fig. 206).

The arms, which have been in second until now, rise slowly to fifth at the end of rond de jambe with the left leg which ends in fourth front.

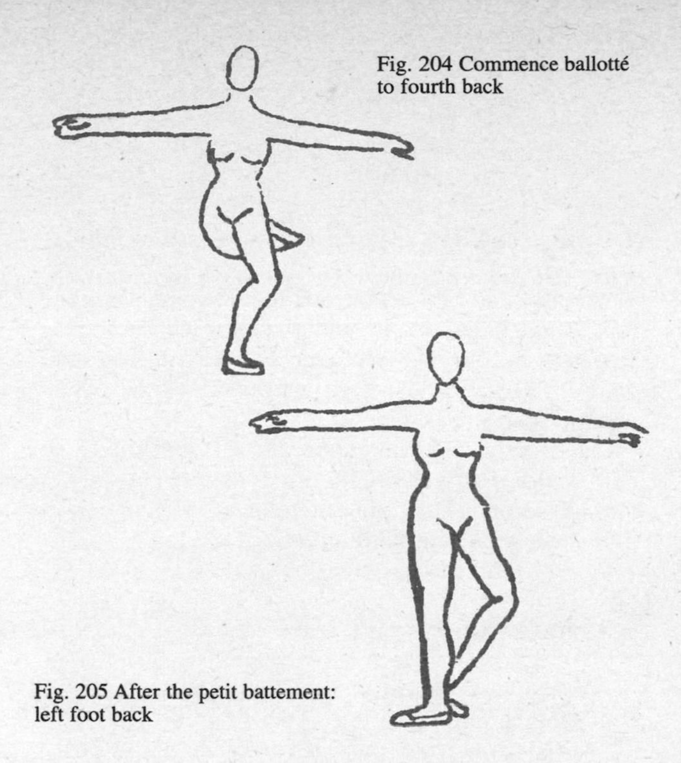

Fig. 204 Commence ballotté to fourth back

Fig. 205 After the petit battement: left foot back

6. Relevé with the left leg in fourth front

Small demi-plié on the right leg and relevé strongly onto the half or full pointe of the right foot (fig. 207).

Lower the right heel; lower the left leg and close in fifth front.

The arms lower to position de repos.

Repeat the whole exercise with the left leg.

EXERCISE 3

GRAND FOUETTÉ

(Score no. 3, 3rd Part)

Grand fouetté d'Adage is a collection of poses which are created from slow, calm movements, so are formed very naturally and smoothly.

The quality of the exercise is of soft, delicate grace.

The poses follow on through the various movements: poses in attitude, second, fourth and first arabesque.

Particular care must be applied to the many arm movements which are very important in this adagio.

The exercise, executed on both legs, ends with a single coda, so it is a good idea to commence the adagio once with the right and once with the left in fifth front so that the coda also will be performed alternately with one leg and then the other. This avoids the danger of habitually performing movements on one side only, which is very damaging.

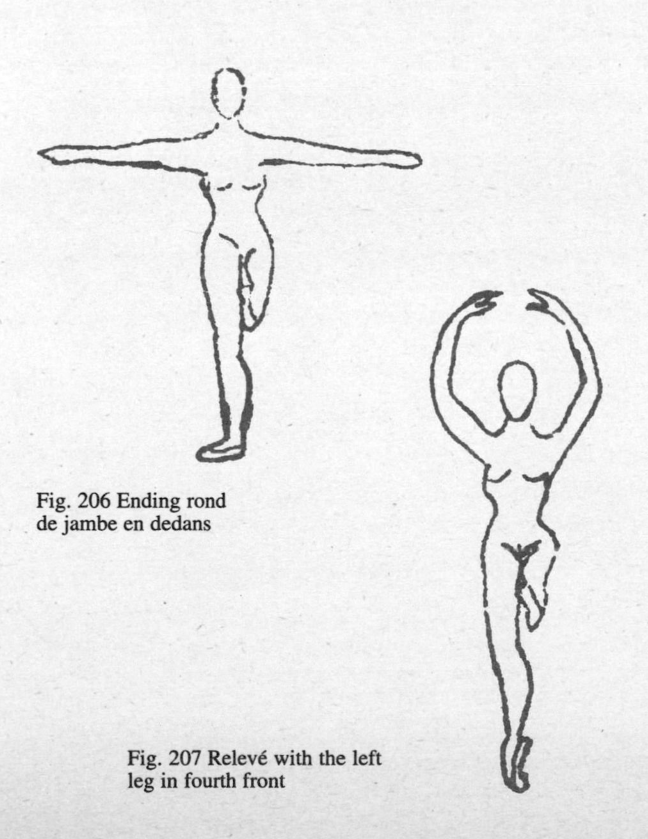

Fig. 206 Ending rond de jambe en dedans

Fig. 207 Relevé with the left leg in fourth front

EXERCISE

Preparation

Stand in the centre of the room with the feet in fifth position, right foot front; arms in position de repos.

FIRST PART

1. Relevé onto both feet

Demi-plié and relevé onto half or full pointes.

At the same time, take the arms to attitude, passing

through first: the left arm rises to fifth and the right opens to demi-seconde.

2. Circular port de bras and coupé

After a short pause, move the feet alternately with pas de bourrée sur la place, as the arms perform a circular port de bras, that is: the left arm lowers and, passing through second, goes into position de repos. The right arm is raised from second to fifth then, continuing the movement lowers, passing through first and meeting the left in position de repos (fig. 208).

The torso follows the movement of the arms and inclines slightly left; when the arms have reached position de repos, it inclines slightly right gradually coming upright as the arms, little by little, continuing their windmill-like movement, rise once more, first the left followed by the right.

Coupé, sharply lowering the left heel, as the right foot draws in placing the heel sur le cou de pied.

In coordination with this movement, the arms have arrived in low fourth with the right arm in second, and the left in first (fig. 209).

3. Développé with the right leg to fourth front

Développé extending the right leg to high fourth front.

The arms remain in low fourth right.

4. Grand rond de jambe en dehors with the right leg

Small demi-plié on the left leg. Commence grand rond de jambe en dehors with the right leg. As the leg passes from fourth front to second, the left knee gradually straightens; the right leg continues the movement to fourth back.

During the rond de jambe, the left arm gradually rises so that it arrives in fifth just as the right leg passes through second. The right arm remains in second position, the arms are in third left (fig. 210).

5. Attitude with the right leg

As the right leg arrives in fourth back, the knee bends into attitude position.

At the same time, during the second phase of the rond de jambe, passing from second to fourth back, the arms reverse positions: the right arm goes to fifth and the left, lowers to second (third right). The arms end in attitude right (fig. 211).

Fig. 208 Relevé and circular port de bras

Fig. 209 Coupé and arms to low fourth

Fig. 210 At the beginning of rond de jambe, the arms are taken to third left

Fig. 211 At the end of rond de jambe the arms are taken to third right

6. Second arabesque croisée with the right leg

The torso turns slightly left as the arms lower to execute ramassé des bras.

The torso turns right once more while the arms are raised to second arabesque (right arm extending forward above shoulder height and the left stretching back below shoulder level, in alignment with the right).

The right leg extends to fourth back.

Fig. 212 From second arabesque pass to fourth arabesque

7. Fourth arabesque croisée with the right leg

Slow demi-plié on the left leg, still in second arabesque croisée (fig. 212).

8. Facing front with the right leg in fourth back

Slowly straighten the left knee. Gradually turn the body to face front. As the body turns, the arms rotate until they are in second position.

The right leg remains in high fourth back.

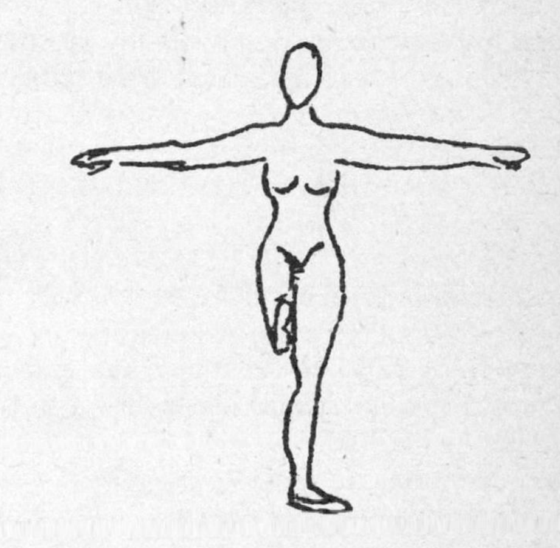

Fig. 213 From fourth back raccourci of the right and extend to fourth front

9. Raccourci of the right leg and développé to fourth front

The right leg bends and, with a développé extends to high fourth front.

At the same time the arms lower to rise once more through first and open to second (fig. 213).

10. Ballotté to fourth front with the right leg

Small demi-plié on the left leg and transfer the weight forward onto the right leg which quickly lowers, well stretched, as the left leg is raised to fourth back.

The arms remain in second position (fig. 214).

11. First arabesque ouverte with the left leg

Slightly turn the torso to the left, lower the arms; ramassé des bras and raise them to first arabesque: the right arm extends forward, slightly above shoulder height, the left back slightly below shoulder level, in alignment with the right.

As the arms move, the torso and then the whole body turn to the right (fig. 215).

Fig. 214 After ballotté with the right to fourth front

Fig. 215 First arabesque ouverte

12. Facing front with the left leg in fourth back

Slowly turn the body to the front; the left leg is still in high fourth back.
The arms rotate, moving into second position.

13. Temps de cuisse du haut with the right and chassé

Lower the left leg strongly, well stretched, into fifth back and immediately raise it.
Then, lower it once more into fifth back, still straight, and with chassé push the right leg away to fourth front, pointed on the floor, with the leg straight; the left (which has taken the place of the right) is in demi-plié.
The arms go to low fourth left.
The head is inclined right (fig. 216).

14. Grand rond de jambe à terre en dehors

Keeping the left leg in demi-plié, grand rond de jambe à terre en dehors taking the right leg to fourth back, pointed on the floor.
At the same time, the arms reverse the low fourth position, opening the right to second and bringing the left into first. The head inclines left (fig. 217).

Fig. 216 Beginning of grand rond de jambe à terre en dehors

Fig. 217 End of grand rond de jambe à terre

15. Close the right leg into fifth back

The left leg straightens slowly, as the right leg, straight, gradually closes behind into fifth.
The arms lower to position de repos.
The head comes upright.

SECOND PART

Grand fouetté is ended on the right side and continues on the left side in the same manner and order ending in fifth position, left foot behind.
Arms in position de repos.

CODA, at the end of the whole exercise.

1. Relevé on both feet

Demi-plié and relevé onto half pointes or full pointes.
The arms rise to fifth. The head turns right (fig. 218).

2. Petit pas de bourré marché sur les pointes in a circle

In this position make one turn to the right, moving the feet with very close, small steps (pas de bourrée marché) describing a circle with a diameter of about one yard and returning to the point of departure.
Sharply lower the left heel, bringing the right heel in front of the left cou de pied.
The arms lower to position de repos (fig. 219).

3. Développé to fourth front with the right leg

Développé with the right leg to high fourth front.
The arms pass through first to open in second.

4. Ballotté into fourth front with the right leg

Small demi-plié on the left leg; transfer the weight forward onto the straight right leg which lowers quickly as the left leg is raised, stretched, to fourth back.
The arms remain in second position.

5. Temps de cuisse du haut with the left leg in fourth back

Close the straight left leg, strongly behind in fifth: with a rebound, raise it immediately, still straight, to fourth back at half height.

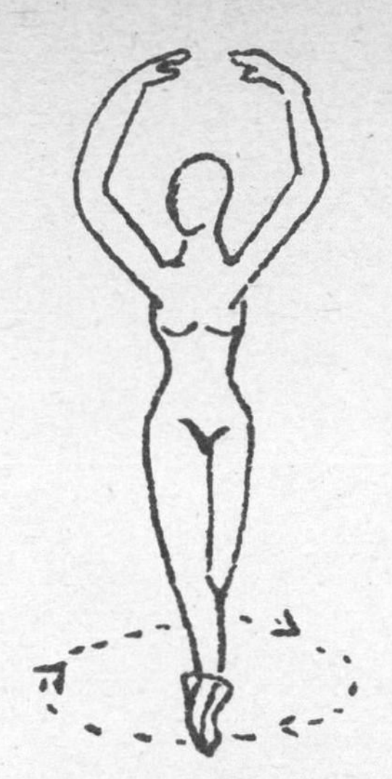

Fig. 218 Relevé and pas de bourrée marché in a circle

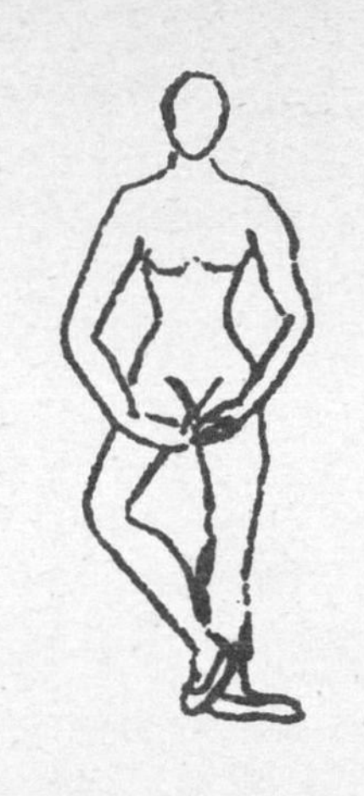

Fig. 219 Coupé with the left, right sur le cou de pied

6. Enveloppé fouetté turn to the right with the left leg

With the left leg, stretched, execute a strong fouetté à terre enveloppé, giving the body the impetus to turn en dedans to the right on the right leg.

During the turn the left leg stays held in raccourci in front.

Arms in position de repos (fig. 220).

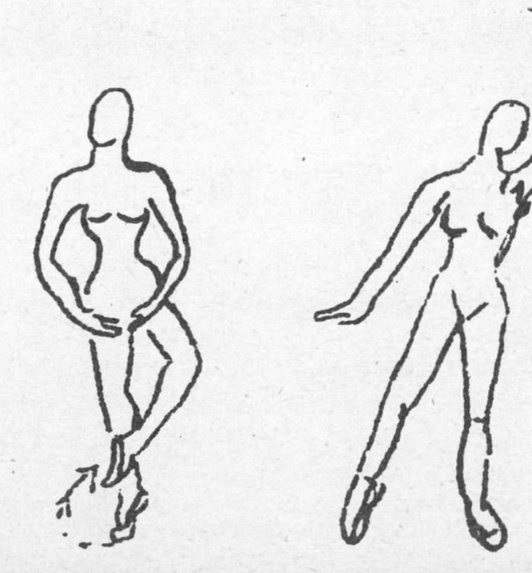

Fig. 220 Enveloppé turn to the right　Fig. 221 Final pose effacée

7. Final pose effacée to the right

Having ended the turn slightly facing right, place the left foot on the floor, as the right extends to fourth front, pointe on the floor.

The body turns in position effacée to the right.

The torso inclines back in alignment with the right leg.

The left arm is raised to fifth, the right is taken to demi-seconde (fig. 221).

The head turns to the left shoulder.

EXERCISE 4

COUPÉ FOUETTÉ

(Score no. 3, 3rd Part)

The quality and purpose of this exercise is different from the previous exercises. It is composed of slow passages and rapid energetic movements combined together for the precise purpose of developing muscular sensitivity. This trains the legs in particular, to perform sudden and powerful movements and the muscles of the body to contract to maintain equilibrium.

EXERCISE

Preparation

Stand in the centre of the room with the feet in fifth, right foot front. Arms in position de repos.

FIRST PART

1. Relevé et coupé

Demi-plié and relevé onto half or full pointes. The body turns slightly towards the left diagonal. The head inclines slightly to the right shoulder.

The arms remain in position de repos.

After a short pause, the feet move alternately with pas de bourrée sur la place. Coupé, quickly lowering the left heel; the right foot draws in, placing the heel on the left cou de pied.

2. Développé to fourth front with the right leg

Développé raising and extending the right leg to high fourth front.

The arms are taken to first.

Fig. 222 Double rond de jambe en l'air en dedans

3. Ballotté to fourth front with the right leg

Small demi-plié on the left leg, transfer the weight forward onto the right leg which quickly lowers, fully stretched, as the left leg is raised to fourth back.

The left foot draws in placing the heel behind the right cou de pied.

Arms are still in first.

4. Développé to second with the left leg

Développé raising and extending the left leg to high second.

The arms open to second.

5. Double rond de jambe en l'air en dedans with the left leg

Quickly execute double rond de jambe en l'air en dedans and extend the left leg, fully stretched, to second (fig. 222).

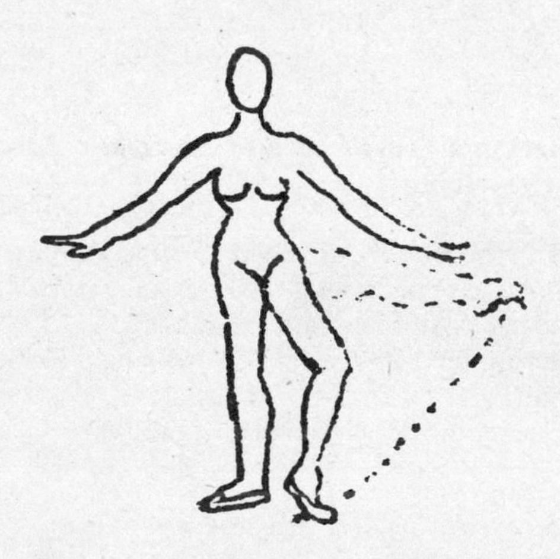

Fig. 223 Fouetté with the left leg behind the right

6. Fouetté à terre with the left leg behind the right

Fouetté lowering the left leg with energy, whipping the floor with the tips of the toes behind the right. Immediately, bend the knee and place the heel behind the right cou de pied (fig. 223).

The arms lower to demi-seconde.

The left foot executes two rapid petits battements sur le cou de pied of the right leg.

7. Développé to second with the left leg and close in fifth front

Développé, raising and extending the left leg to high second; lower immediately and close into fifth front.

The arms go through first, open to second and lower into position de repos.

SECOND PART

8. Relevé et coupé

Demi-plié and relevé strongly onto half or full pointes, straightening the knees with energy. The body turns slightly to the right. The head inclines slightly towards the left shoulder.

After a short pause, the feet move alternately with pas de bourrée sur la place. Coupé, quickly lowering the left heel as the right foot draws in, placing the heel onto the left cou de pied.

The arms remain in position de repos.

9. Développé to fourth back with the right leg

Développé extending the right leg to high fourth back.

The arms are taken to first.

10. Ballotté to fourth back with the right leg

Small demi-plié on left leg; take the body backwards off balance and lower the right leg, transferring the weight onto it, at the same time raising the left to fourth front.

The left foot draws in placing the heel in front of the right cou de pied.

The arms remain in first.

11. Développé to second with the left leg

Développé extending the left leg to second.

The arms open to second.

12. Double rond de jambe en l'air en dehors with the left leg

Quick double rond de jambe en l'air en dehors with the left leg and extend to second.

13. Fouetté à terre with the left leg

Fouetté devant immediately lowering the left leg straight, brushing the floor with the tips of the toes (fig. 223).

Bend the left knee, placing the heel on the right cou de pied.

The arms lower to demi-seconde.

Execute two rapid petits battements sur le cou de pied.

14. Développé to second with the left leg and lower closing into fifth front

Quickly développé the left leg to high second and rapidly lower it once more, stretched, to close in fifth front.

The arms, passing through first, open to second and lower to position de repos.

N.B. Repeat the whole exercise immediately starting with the left leg.

The movements numbered 5 - 6 - 7, are executed consecutively with great energy and extremely quickly, since they all take place in one bar of music only.

The same goes for the movements numbered 12 - 13 - 14.

EXERCISE 5

ROND DE JAMBE DÉVELOPPÉ

(Score no. 3, 3rd Part)

This exercise combines grand rond de jambe en dehors et en dedans with développé, as well as other movements.

These are some of the most useful and important movements in the development of this part of dance training and are frequently used in the various exercises of the Adagio.

Special care must be taken when executing grand rond de jambe, not just for technique but also for its own particular asset, which is to train a very strong sense of balance.

For this reason, and based on the results of previous experience, steps have been taken to ensure that this movement is combined with others and preceded or followed by those completely different in quality.

Therefore, in the various exercises, we find grand rond de jambe together with very fast movements, for example: enveloppé, pirouettes, etc., or in static poses.

EXERCISE

Preparation

Stand in the centre of the room with the feet in fifth position, right foot front. Arms in position de repos.

1. Plié

Full plié, evenly on both feet.

During the plié the right arm remains in position de repos, the left opens to demi-seconde (fig. 224).

Fig. 224 Plié and preparation for the turn

Fig. 225 Tire-bouchon turn to the right

2. Turn in tire-bouchon en dehors to the right

Commence rising and, close the left arm with energy to position de repos, giving the body the impetus to turn en dehors to the right on the half pointe of the left leg; at the same time, the right foot is drawn up right away, placing the heel onto the left cou de pied (fig. 225).

3. Développé to second with the right leg

After the two pirouette turns, développé, immediately extending the right leg to second position.
The arms pass through first and open to second.

4. Raccourci and développé with the right leg to fourth front

Holding the thigh firm, bend the right leg.
The arms lower to position de repos.
Développé, extending the right leg to fourth front.
The arms rise to first.

5. Grand rond de jambe en dehors with the right leg

Slowly, grand rond de jambe en dehors with the right leg: from fourth front, passing through second, to fourth back.
The arms, accompanying the movement of the leg, open to second.

6. Grand rond de jambe en dedans with the right leg

Slowly, the right leg repeats the grand rond de jambe movement in reverse (en dedans): from fourth back, passing through second, to fourth front.
The arms remain in second.

7. Grand rond de jambe en dehors with the right leg

With a slightly quicker movement, the right leg executes a third grand rond de jambe (en dehors): from fourth front, passing through second, to fourth back.
The arms remain in second and at the end of the movement lower into position de repos.

8. Raccourci and développé with the right leg to second

From fourth back the right foot goes through raccourci and, with développé, extends to second.
The arms pass through first and open to second.

9. Enveloppé turn to the left ending with the right leg in second

Enveloppé with the right leg giving the body impetus to turn en dedans to the left, on the left leg.
The arms lower and remain in position de repos during the turn (fig. 226).

Fig. 226 Enveloppé turn to the left on the left leg

Fig. 227 First arabesque ouverte to the left

After the turn, développé, extending right leg to high second position.

The arms, passing through first, open to second.

10. First arabesque ouverte with the right leg

Turn the torso to the left, leaving the right leg pointed to the same direction: it rotates into fourth back as the body turns.

From second position, the arms rotate into arabesque: the left extends forward above shoulder height, the right below shoulder level, in alignment with the left (fig. 227).

11. Relevé in first arabesque

Still in first arabesque ouverte, small demi-plié and strong relevé onto half or full pointe.

12. Facing front with the right leg in second and closing

Lower the left heel. Turn the torso to the right facing front. The right leg rotates from fourth back and returns into second position.

The arms rotate returning to second position.

Lower the right leg, closing into fifth back; the arms lower to position de repos.

Repeat the whole exercise immediately with the left leg.

EXERCISE 6

DÉVELOPPÉ CECCHETTI

(Score no. 6, 3rd Part)

The développés, from which this exercise takes its name, are characteristic of this exercise. The execution of the développés present a certain difficulty in this adagio, because they are always preceded by fast turns and are taken in the directions: fourth front, second and fourth back.

However, this difficulty can be overcome quite quickly with practice; it is better not to allow inaccuracy in the execution right from the beginning as it is then difficult to correct.

This adagio is divided into three parts.

EXERCISE

Preparation

Stand in the centre of the room with the feet in fifth position, right foot front. Arms in position de repos.

FIRST PART

1. Plié

Full plié, evenly on both feet.

The right arm remains in position de repos, while the left opens to demi-seconde (fig. 224).

2. Tire-bouchon turn en dehors to the right

Commence rising, closing the left arm with energy into position de repos, giving the body impetus for two turns en dehors to the right on the left half pointe; immediately, the right foot draws up, bringing the heel in front of the left cou de pied; as the left leg gradually straightens during the two turns, the pointe of the right foot brushes the other leg, gradually rising until the end of the turns when the thigh is well turned out in high second, and the pointe of the foot touches the completely straight, left knee (fig. 228).

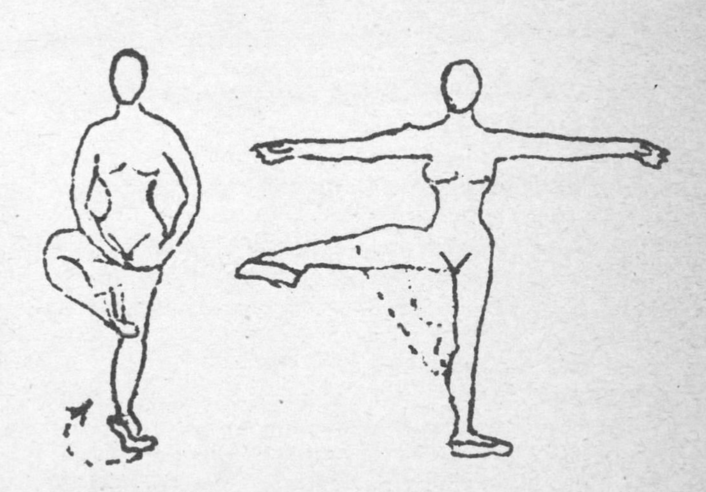

Fig. 228 Tire-bouchon turn to the right

Fig. 229 After the turn, développé to second

3. Développé with the right leg to second

After the turns, the right leg is ready to extend with développé to high second position.

The arms, passing through first, open to second (fig. 229).

4. Ballotté in second with the right leg

Demi-plié on the left leg and take the body to the right off balance, transferring the weight onto the right leg which quickly lowers as the straight left leg is raised to high second position (fig. 230 and 231).

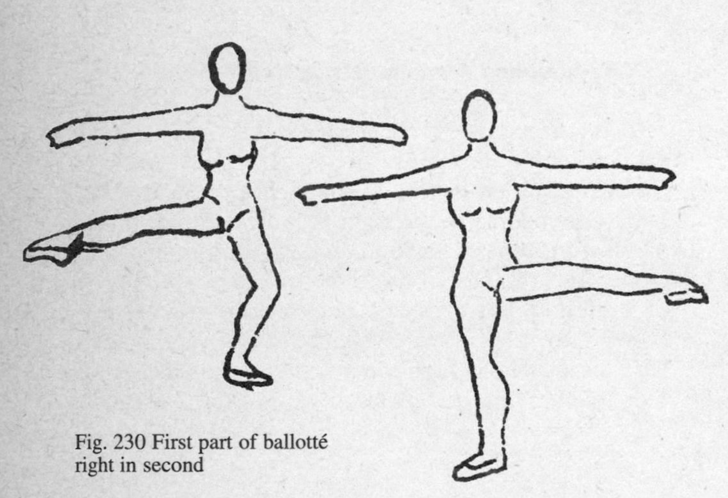

Fig. 230 First part of ballotté right in second

Fig. 231 After ballotté in second

5. Ballotté in second with the left leg

Demi-plié on the right leg and take the body to the left transferring the weight onto the left leg, as the straight right leg is raised to high second position (fig. 232 and 233).

6. Relevé in high second position

Hold the straight right leg firmly in second; small demi-plié and strong relevé onto half or full pointe of the left foot.

The arms remain in second.

Fig. 232 First part of ballotté left in second

Fig. 233 End of ballotté in second

7. Close in fifth, right foot front

Lower the left heel. Lower the right leg, straight, and close into fifth front, turning the body to face the left diagonal.

Lower the arms to position de repos.

SECOND PART

1. Plié

Full plié once again, evenly on both feet.

The right arm remains in position de repos, the left opens to demi-seconde (fig. 224).

2. Tire-bouchon turn en dehors to the right

Commence rising, closing the left arm, with energy, to position de repos giving the body impetus for two turns en dehors to the right on the left half pointe; immediately, the right foot draws up bringing the heel in front of the left cou de pied; as the left leg gradually straightens during the two turns, the pointe of the right foot brushes the other leg, gradually rising until

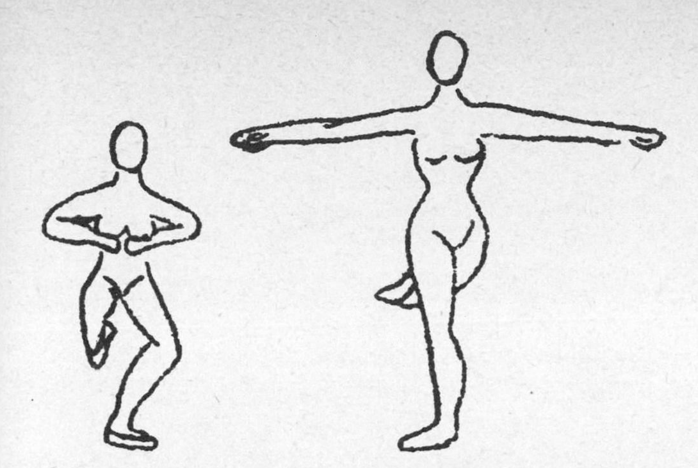

Fig. 234 First part of ballotté to fourth front with right leg

Fig. 235 End of ballotté to fourth front right; left leg fourth back

the end of the turns when the thigh is well turned out in high second, and the pointe of the foot touches the completely straight left knee (fig. 228).

3. Développé with the right leg to fourth front

After the turns, the right leg is ready to extend, with développé, to fourth front.
The arms are taken to first.

4. Ballotté to fourth front with the right leg

Small demi-plié on the left leg and take the body forward off balance, transferring the weight forward (fig. 234) onto the right leg which quickly lowers as the left leg is raised to high fourth back.
The arms open to second (fig. 235).

5. Raccourci and développé with the left leg to second

Immediately raccourci of the left leg and, with développé, extend to high second.
The arms remain in second.

6. Double rond de jambe en l'air with the left leg

Double rond de jambe en l'air en dedans with the left leg in high second.
The arms are still in second (fig. 236).

7. Fouetté with the left leg for enveloppé turn to the right

After the double rond de jambe en l'air, lower the left leg, straight, with a strong fouetté giving the body impetus for enveloppé turn en dedans to the right with the foot sur le cou de pied.
After the turn, one petit battement sur le cou de pied, with the left foot.
The arms lower with energy into position de repos, helping the impetus (fig. 237).

8. Développé to second with the left leg

After petit battement, développé to second with the left leg.
The arms, passing through first, open to second.

Fig. 236 Double rond de jambe en l'air with the left leg

Fig. 237 Fouetté with the left and enveloppé turn to the right

9. Relevé with the left leg in high second

With the left leg in high second, small demi-plié on the right and strong relevé onto half or full pointe of the right foot.
The arms remain in second.

10. Lower the right leg and close behind in fifth

Lower the right heel; lower the straight left leg, closing into fifth back.
The body turns towards the left diagonal.
The arms lower to position de repos.

1. Plié

Full plié for the third time, evenly on both legs.
The right arm remains in position de repos, the left opens to demi-seconde (fig. 224).

2. Tire-bouchon turn en dehors

Commence rising, closing the left arm with energy into position de repos, giving the body impetus for two turns en dehors to the right on the left half pointe; immediately, the right foot draws up bringing the heel onto the left cou de pied. As the left leg gradually straightens during the two turns, the pointe of the right foot brushes the other leg, gradually rising until the end of the turns when the thigh is well turned out in high second, and the pointe of the foot touches the completely straight left knee (fig. 228).

3. Développé with the right leg to fourth back

After the turns, the right leg is ready to extend with développé to high fourth back.
The arms, passing through first, open to second; then lower through position de repos to rise once more to first (fig. 238).

4. Attitude croisée right

Make a quarter turn to the right on the whole foot, pivoting on the left leg; the back, right leg curves into attitude.
The right arm is raised to fifth, the left lowers to demi-seconde (fig. 239).

5. Relevé in attitude right

Still in attitude right, demi-plié on the left leg and strong relevé onto half or full pointe of the left foot.

6. Fifth arabesque croisée

Lower the left heel. Demi-plié on the left leg, extending the right leg back into arabesque.
The right arm lowers straight, forward. The left is brought forward also, underneath the right and parallel to it.
The pose is fifth arabesque croisée (fig. 240).

Fig. 238 After the turn, développé to fourth back

Fig. 239 Attitude croisée right

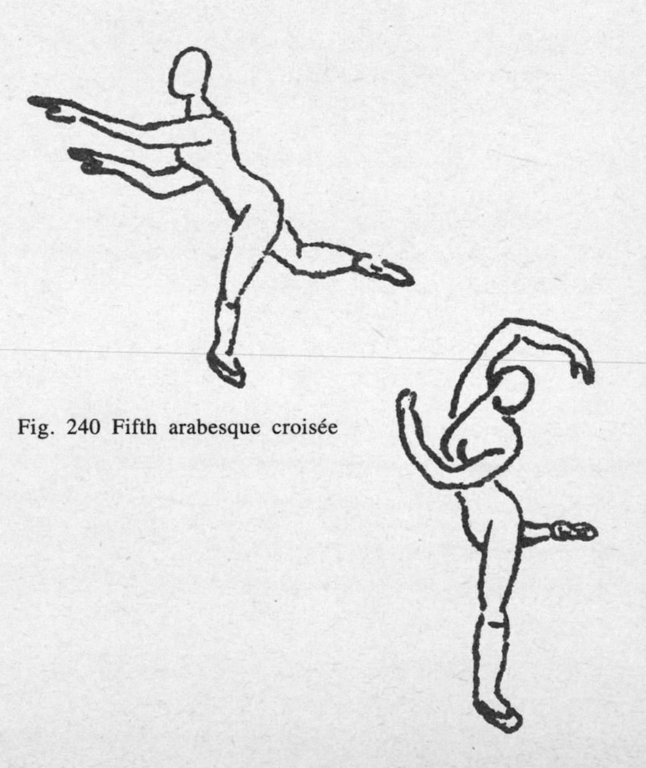

Fig. 240 Fifth arabesque croisée

Fig. 241 Renversé turn to the right

7. Position facing front with the right foot in raccourci

Straighten the left leg. Turn the body to the front; then bend the right leg and quickly extend it to fourth front at half height.

The arms lower and open to demi-seconde.

8. Renversé turn to the right et pas de bourrée

The right leg is in fourth front at half height; with a strong rond de jambe en dehors, the right leg gives the body impetus to turn right on the half pointe of the left foot.

The right arm, from behind, rises to fifth and passing through first, lowers into position de repos (the arm movement is executed, with energy, in one temps of music); the left arm closes strongly into first and lowers into position de repos.

The torso arches strongly back until it almost completely loses equilibrium. In order to recover its equilibrium, end the renversé turn with pas de bourrée finishing with the right foot front (fig. 241).

9. Glissé the right leg to fourth front

Glissé, sliding the right leg to fourth front taking the weight over the front foot. The left leg is in fourth back, pointed on the floor.

The arms are raised in attitude position, left arm in fifth.

10. Balancé to fourth back (grande préparation for pirouette)

Demi-plié on both legs, transfer the weight over the left leg in fourth back; the right remains pointed to fourth front.

At the same time, the arms perform a circular port de bras: the left lowers and opens into second, while the right is raised into fifth and lowers to first. The arms are now in low fourth left.

The heel of the right foot lowers and the weight is evenly distributed over both legs which are in a small demi-plié in fourth position.

11. Enveloppé turn to the right on the right leg

Enveloppé movement with the left leg, giving the body impetus to turn right. At the same time, the right arm lowers into position de repos; the left also goes to position de repos but with energy to give more impetus for the execution of the enveloppé turn (fig. 242).

12. Ending pose in effacé to finish

After the turn, take the whole weight onto the left leg; the right extends to fourth front, pointed on the floor.

The body arches slightly back, in alignment with the right leg.

The left arm is raised to fifth and the right goes into demi-seconde (fig. 243).

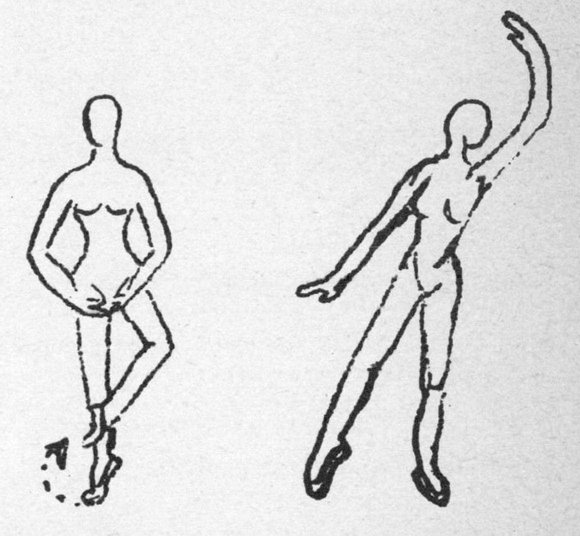

Fig. 242 Enveloppé turn to the right

Fig. 243 Final ending pose

Bring the body upright, slide the right foot into fifth front and lower the arms to position de repos.

Battement tendu with the back foot and close the left foot in fifth front.

Repeat the entire exercise immediately with the left leg.

EXERCISE 7

PAS DE CHACONNE CECCHETTI

(Score no. 7, 3rd Part)

It is well known that balance and suppleness are two basic components in dance training. Therefore, the reader should not be surprised to see constantly repeated in these pages the way in which every exercise, with new and different criteria, is designed to strengthen and stabilize the body during the various qualities of dance movements.

A pupil who does not achieve complete mastery of balance or easy suppleness of movement by practicing with perseverence, tenacity and serious application, can never become a good dancer.

In this adagio, created by Maestro Enrico Cecchetti, there is also a new way to practice balancing by continually transferring the weight alternately from one leg to another by means of various ballottés.

These movements also require the limbs to be very supple and accustomed to moving lightly.

This deliberately short adagio, ends with quite a difficult compound pirouette.

It has been inserted with the purpose of training the pupil to regulate his energy so that he will arrive at the end of the exercise without his muscles being overtired, enabling him to perform the complex pirouette correctly.

EXERCISE

Preparation

Stand in the centre of the room with the feet in fifth position, right foot front. Arms in position de repos.

1. Plié

Full plié equally on both feet.

The right arm remains in position de repos, the left opens to demi-seconde (fig. 224).

2. Tire-bouchon turn en dehors to the right

Commence rising, closing the left arm with energy into position de repos giving the body impetus for two turns en dehors to the right on the left half pointe; immediately, the right foot draws up placing the heel in front of the left cou de pied; as the left leg gradually straightens during the two turns, the pointe of the right foot brushes the other leg, gradually rising (fig. 225); at the end of the turns, the thigh is well turned out in high second and the pointe of the foot touches the completely straight left knee (fig. 228).

3. Développé with the right leg to second

After the turns, the right foot is in position for développé, extending to high second position.

The arms, passing through first, open to second.

4. First ballotté to second with the right leg

Small demi-plié on the left leg and take the body to the right off balance, transferring the weight onto the straight right leg which quickly lowers, as the left leg is raised, fully stretched, to high second position.

The arms remain in second (figs. 230 and 231).

5. Second ballotté to second with the left leg

Small demi-plié on the right leg and throw the body to the left off balance, transferring the weight onto the straight left leg which quickly lowers, as the right leg is raised, fully stretched, to high second position.

The arms are still in second (figs. 232 and 233).

6. Third ballotté to second with the right leg

This is the same as no. 4, that is:

Small demi-plié on the left leg and transfer the weight to the right, onto the straight right leg which quickly lowers, as the left leg is raised, fully stretched, to high second position.

The arms are still in second (figs. 230 and 231).

7. Turn en dedans to the right on the right leg

From second position, enveloppé with the left leg giving the body impetus to turn en dedans to the right on the half pointe of the right foot.

The arms lower to position de repos the left moving more strongly to give more impetus (fig. 242).

8. First arabesque ouverte to the right

After the turn, développé the left leg to fourth back. The body turns to the right.

The arms are raised to first; then the right arm extends forward, a little above shoulder height; the left lowers and is taken back, stretched, slightly below shoulder level, in alignment with the right (fig. 244).

Fig. 244 First arabesque ouverte

Fig. 245 Third arabesque ouverte

9. Third arabesque ouverte to the right

Still in first arabesque, the left arm lowers and rises in front, below and parallel to the right (fig. 245).

10. Ballotté to fourth back with the left leg

Turn the body to face front and open the arms to second position.

Demi-plié on the right leg and taking the body backwards off balance, transfer the weight onto the straight left leg which quickly lowers as the right leg is raised to fourth front.

The arms remain in second.

11. Attitude ouverte right turned to face left

The right foot passes through raccourci; développé to fourth back and bend the leg into attitude position.

The right arm is raised to fifth and the left lowers to demi-seconde.

The body faces slightly to the left (fig. 246).

12. Relevé in attitude position, arms in fifth

Raise the left arm; the arms are now in fifth en couronne.

Small demi-plié on the left leg and strong relevé onto half or full pointe of the left foot.

Ending: extend the right leg, lower and close it behind into fifth lowering the left heel and turning the body to face front.

The arms lower to position de repos.

13. Grande préparation in second with pirouette en dehors

Grande préparation in second to turn en dehors to the left (Volume 2, Book Four, Part One, Group 4), placing the feet firmly in second position, the weight evenly on both feet.

The lumbar region is held firmly and tensed.

The arms, in low fourth right, give the impetus (fig. 247).

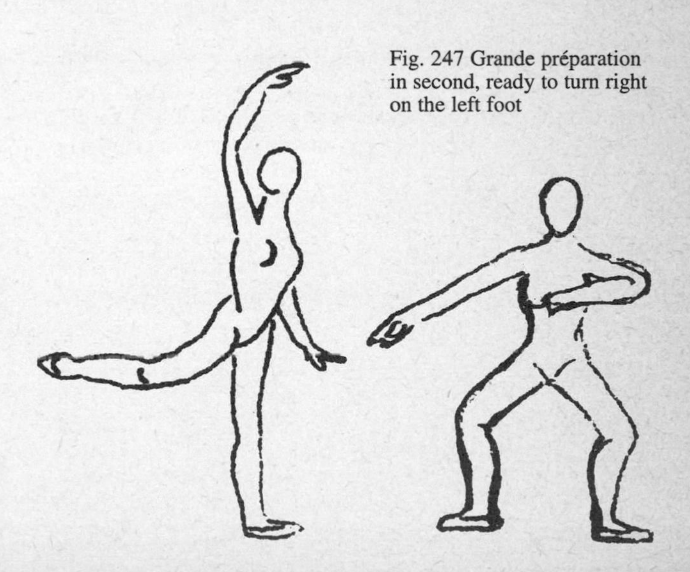

Fig. 247 Grande préparation in second, ready to turn right on the left foot

Fig. 246 Attitude right ouverte

Fig. 248 Turns en dehors to the left with the leg in second, with "snatching" movement

Fig. 249 Continue turning "filé," en dehors to the left with the foot at the cou de pied.

14. Three turns to the left with the left leg in second and then with the foot at the cou de pied

Make three "snatched" turns to the left on the half or full pointe of the right leg with the left leg in high second (fig. 248).

After each turn, the heel of the right foot lowers, rising immediately onto half or full pointe at the beginning of the new turn; the impetus comes from the movement of the left leg, extended in second position, moving like a fly-wheel.

The arms open to second and remain in this position throughout the three turns (fig. 248).

After the three snatched turns, the knee of the leg in second bends, drawing in the foot with energy, placing the heel onto the cou de pied of the right foot, giving the body, already turning freely, even more impetus for three rapid, continuous ("filés") turns to the left.

The arms are raised to fifth en couronne (fig. 249).

The pirouette ends brusquely with échappé, springing into fourth, right foot front.

The arms open to first, palms of the hands facing up.

Repeat the whole exercise immediately with the left foot.

EXERCISE 8

DÉVELOPPÉ FOUETTÉ CECCHETTI

(Score no. 8, 3rd Part)

Développé-fouetté Cecchetti is made up of a continuous succession of expressions, movements and poses. The rapid development from one pose to another allows the pupil only a very short time to prepare the body for the movement immediately following. Even the mind has no time to reflect and transmit the necessary commands to the nervous system. Nevertheless, the pupil becomes used to refining the reflexes and his intuition, allowing him to continue at the command of the movements without having to think beforehand.

All this is extremely useful for those who dedicate themselves to an art where readiness of intuition and quick reflexes are always necessary. Hesitation, or even a short delay in the execution of a step can have grave consequences, to begin with, in the imperfect execution of the step itself. A certain number of fouetté turns have been inserted in this exercise to increase the difficulty. Fouetté turn, which is fast and vigorous, always ends with one leg raised. If the body is not perfectly balanced, the raised leg groping in the air is a painful spectacle to see; neither leg is free and ready for the next movement which follows without a pause.

The maestro must give a great deal of attention to this series of phases and movements, because they must always be executed immediately correctly and exactly, without time for later correction.

EXERCISE

Preparation

Stand in the centre of the room with the feet in fifth position, right foot front. Arms in position de repos. Head erect.

1. Relevé-coupé

Small demi-plié on both legs; relevé strongly onto half or full pointe.

Coupé, quickly lowering the left heel, placing the heel of the right foot in front of the left cou de pied.

The arms remain in position de repos.

2. Développé with the right leg to fourth front effacé and relevé

Turn the body to the right; ramassé des pieds and relevé extending the right leg to fourth front.

The arms are raised to first; the left continues into fifth and the right opens to demi-seconde.

The position is en effacé to the right (fig. 250). Relevé on the left pointe.

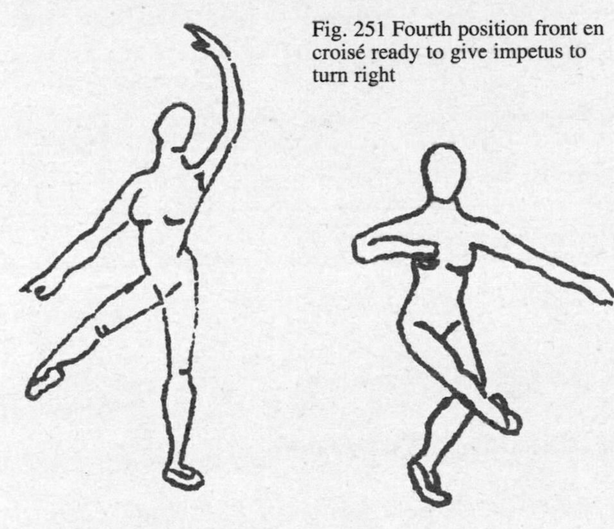

Fig. 251 Fourth position front en croisé ready to give impetus to turn right

Fig. 250 Position effacée to the right

3. Raccourci with the right – développé to fourth front croisé

Turn the body to face front. Bring the right foot to raccourci and quick développé, extending the leg to fourth front croisé with the right leg straight, slightly crossed to the left. Small demi-plié on the left, noticeably raising the heel.

The arms lower to position de repos; ramassé des bras, raise the arms to first; the left then opens to second. The arms are prepared in low fourth left (fig. 251).

4. Fouetté turn to the right ending in high second

Straighten the left leg with energy; at the same time, the right is taken vigorously to second with demi-grand rond de jambe en dehors, giving the body the impetus to turn en dehors to the right.

During the turn the right leg continues the movement, executing rond de jambe en l'air en dehors, very fast and energetically, extending to second again after the turn; the left heel lowers immediately (fouetté turn) (fig. 252).

Fig. 252 Fouetté turn to the right

Fig. 253 Pose in attitude croisée

The body remains facing front with the right leg and the arms in second position.

The right arm opens strongly to second position at the beginning of the turn to help the impetus. The arms then remain in second.

5. Raccourci with the right – développé to fourth front croisé (nos. 3 and 4 are repeated)

Repeat no. 3: bend the right leg and quick développé, extending the leg to fourth front croisé; the right leg is straight, slightly crossed to the left; small demi-plié on the left, raising the heel noticeably.

The arms lower to position de repos; ramassé de bras and raise the arms to first; the left arm opens to second (fig. 251).

6. Fouetté turn to the right ending in high second

Repeat no. 4: straighten the left leg, with energy; at the same time, the right is taken vigorously to second with demi-grand rond de jambe en dehors, giving the body the impetus to turn en dehors to the right.

During the turn, the right leg continues the movement, executing rond de jambe en l'air en dehors, very fast and energetically, extending to second once more, after the turn; the left heel lowers immediately (fouetté turn) (fig. 252).

The body remains facing front with the right leg and the arms in second position.

The right arm opens strongly to second position at the beginning of the turn to help the impetus. The arms then remain in second.

7. Fouetté – développé to fourth back – attitude croisée

After the turn, the right leg lowers with a strong fouetté, brushing the floor with the point of the foot; it rises again extending with développé to fourth back and curves into attitude. The body turns right.

The arms lower through position de repos and are raised to first; the right goes to fifth and the left opens to demi-seconde.

The body is now in the position: attitude left croisée (fig. 253).

8. Third arabesque croisée to the right

Extend the right leg to fourth back.

Extend the left arm forward slightly above shoulder height. The right lowers in front, below and parallel to the left; palms of the hands facing down.

The pose is third arabesque croisée (fig. 254).

Fig. 254 Third arabesque croisée to the right

Fig. 255 Attitude right facing front

9. Attitude right facing front

With a very small movement of the supporting left foot, turn the body to face front. The leg in fourth back curves into attitude.

The arms are taken to first, the right is raised to fifth, the left lowers to demi-seconde; the pose is attitude right, facing front (fig. 255).

10. Third arabesque ouverte to the left

Turn the body to the left. Extend the right leg to fourth back once more.

The left arm extends forward, slightly above shoulder height; the right lowers below and parallel to the left; palms facing down.

The position is third arabesque ouverte, facing left (fig. 256).

11. Ballotté to fourth back and enveloppé turn to the right

Ballotté, transferring the weight back onto the right leg which quickly lowers to fourth back.

At the same time the left leg is raised to fourth front, passing through raccourci, and extends to a position between second and fourth back.

The arms open to second.

Enveloppé with the left leg giving the body the impetus to turn en dedans to the right. The left leg remains in a low raccourci in front.

The arms lower, with energy, to position de repos helping the impetus (fig. 257).

Fig. 256 Third arabesque ouverte, facing left

Fig. 257 Enveloppé turn to the right

12. First arabesque ouverte to the right

Ending the turn slightly to the right, pass the left foot through raccourci and développé extending the left leg to high fourth back.

From position de repos, the right arm extends forward, slightly above shoulder height; the left lowers behind in line with the right, making first arabesque ouverte to the right (fig. 258).

13. Incline the torso forward in first arabesque position, then recover upright

Standing in first arabesque position, very slowly incline the torso forward, from the waist; the right arm lowers still extended, following the movement of the torso, until the hand touches the floor; the left arm is raised equally, remaining in alignment with the right arm and parallel to the fully stretched left leg which rises in equal measure (fig. 259).

Fig. 258 First arabesque ouverte to the right

Fig. 259 Incline the torso forward in first arabesque

The movement is executed at the same speed and in the same way, in reverse, bringing the torso upright, returning to first arabesque.

14. Turn to face front with the left leg in second position – fouetté

The body turns to face front; the left leg rotates into high second position.

The arms rotate into second position, then are raised to fifth (fig. 260).

Fouetté lowering the left leg and whipping the floor

with the foot, bending the knee and placing the heel behind the right cou de pied.

The arms lower to position de repos (fig. 261).

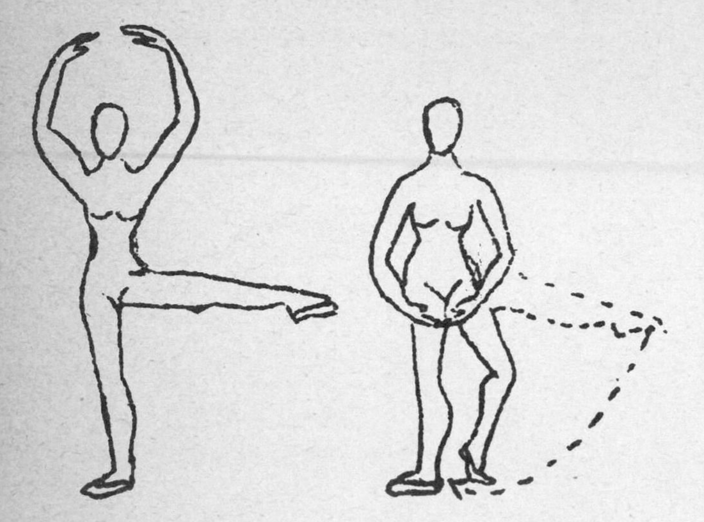

Fig. 260 Left leg in second, arms in fifth en couronne

Fig. 261 Fouetté behind the left

Fig. 262 Fifth arabesque ouverte facing right

Fig. 263 Fifth arabesque ouverte facing left

15. Développé to fourth back with the left – fifth arabesque ouverte

Développé extending the left leg to fourth back.

The arms are raised to first.

Turn the body to the right and demi-plié on the right leg.

The arms extend forward; the right above shoulder height, the left lower and parallel to the right, into fifth arabesque ouverte to the right (fig. 262).

16. Développé to fourth front with the left leg – relevé

Straighten the right leg. Turn the body to face front and bring the left foot to raccourci.

Développé, extending the left leg to fourth front.

Relevé, rising onto the half pointe of the right leg. Arms in second.

17. Ballotté to fourth front and fourth arabesque ouverte to the left

Ballotté, transferring the weight forward onto the left leg which quickly lowers in demi-plié. The right leg is extended, raised to fourth back.

The body turns to the left.

The right arm extends forward above shoulder height; the left is taken back lower, in alignment with the right, into fourth arabesque ouverte to the left (fig. 263).

18. Close in fifth, right foot front

The right leg lowers, straight, to fourth back, pointed on the floor and is held still.

The left leg gradually straightens as the body returns to face front.

The right leg, with the pointe firmly on the floor, rotates into second position, on the floor. Then, demi-battement tendu, sliding into fifth front (fig. 264).

The arms lower to position de repos.

19. Glissé with the right leg to fourth front

Small demi-plié and glissé, transferring the weight over the right leg which slides to fourth front; straighten the knees. The left leg remains extended to fourth back, pointe on the floor.

The arms are raised to half first (fig. 265).

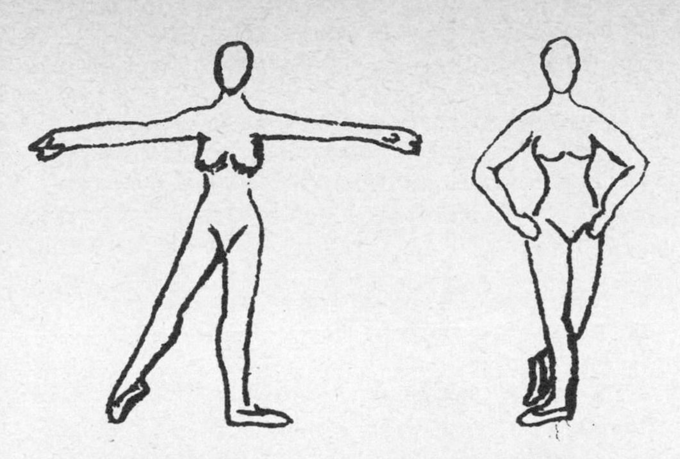

Fig. 264 Right foot in second, pointe on the floor

Fig. 265 Left foot in fourth back, pointe on the floor

20. Enveloppé turn en dedans to the right ending tipped over to the right side

Strong enveloppé with the left leg, bringing the leg into raccourci devant, giving the body the impetus to turn en dedans to the right.

The arms, from demi-seconde, close with energy into position de repos, contributing impetus (fig. 266).

After the turn, the torso tips from above the waist over the right side, while the left leg, with développé extends to high second.

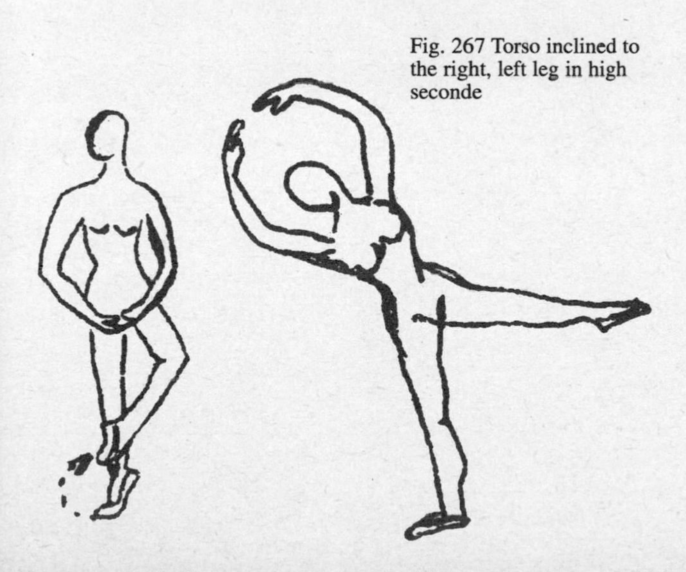

Fig. 267 Torso inclined to the right, left leg in high seconde

Fig. 266 Enveloppé turn en dedans to the right

The arms are raised to fifth (fig. 267).

Bring the body upright and lower the left leg to fifth front.

The arms lower to position de repos.

Repeat the whole exercise immediately with the left leg.

EXERCISE 9

PAS DE MASCOTTE

(Score no. 9, 3rd Part)

Like the previous exercise, this is composed of a series of continuous movements which connect a large number of poses.

The arms are very important in this exercise, continually altering their positions.

In this adagio there is a particularly sensitive movement of the arm in which the hand softly brushes the lips as the leg is thrown into jeté; this gives the movement a feeling of pleasing elegance and grace.

Also to be noted is a new, distinctive type of relevé, executed at the same time as demi-grand rond de jambe en dehors or en dedans.

As indicated above, the arm movements are particularly graceful and soft; the relevé, which is also very pleasant to see, even though it is not particularly difficult, needs to be executed very carefully and firmly so that it does not lose its own quiet elegance.

EXERCISE

Preparation

Stand in the centre of the room with the feet in fifth position, right foot front. Arms in position de repos.

1. Plié

Full plié on both feet, recover completely straightening the knees.

Begin with ramassé des bras; the arms then remain in position de repos.

2. Relevé-coupé

Demi-plié and strong relevé onto half or full pointes of both feet. The body turns slightly to the left. The head inclines slightly to the right shoulder.

Coupé, quickly lowering the left heel, placing the right heel in front of the left cou de pied. At the same time, the body returns front and with the head comes upright.

The arms remain in position de repos.

3. Développé with the right leg to fourth front

Ramassé des pieds with the right and développé to fourth front.

The arms are raised to first.

4. Relevé on the left and demi-grand rond de jambe en dehors with the right

Small demi-plié on the left leg and strong relevé onto half or full pointe of the left foot. At the same time demi-grand rond de jambe en dehors from fourth front to second with the right leg.

The arms open to second.

5. Lower the left heel and raccourci with the right foot

After the demi-grand rond de jambe, the left heel lowers and the right foot is drawn in from second to raccourci.

The arms remain in second position.

6. Développé with the right leg to fourth back

Ramassé des pieds with the right and développé, extending to fourth back.

The arms lower and with ramassé des bras, rise once more to first.

7. Relevé on the left and demi-grand rond de jambe en dedans with the right

Small demi-plié and strong relevé onto half or full pointe of the left foot. At the same time demi-grand rond de jambe en dedans from fourth back to second with the right leg.

The arms open to second.

8. Lower the left heel – raccourci and extend the right leg to fourth front croisé

After the demi-grand rond de jambe, the left heel lowers and the right leg bends; développé extending to fourth front croisé to the left. The arms close into first; the right is then raised to fifth (the arms are in fourth) (fig. 268).

9. Repeat pose no. 8

Lower the straight right leg to fourth front, pointed on the floor; slide the point along the floor, quickly draw it in and, with développé extend the leg to high fourth front croisé to the left.

At the same time, the arms lower through position de repos and rise to first, then the right continues to fifth. The arms are once more in fourth.

Returning to the pose no. 8 (fig. 268).

10. Raccourci with the right leg and extend to fourth back

The right foot draws in to raccourci; développé, extending the leg to fourth back fully stretched.

The arms lower through position de repos and are raised once more to first.

Fig. 268 Fourth front croisé, facing front

Fig. 269 First arabesque ouverte to the left

11. First arabesque ouverte to the left

The body turns to the left. The right leg is still fully stretched to fourth back.

The left arm extends forward, slightly above shoulder height, the right extends back slightly lower, in alignment with the left (fig. 269).

12. Turn to face front with the right leg in second and incline the body over the left side

Turn the body to face front; the right leg rotates into high second position.

The right arm goes to second while the left is raised to fifth; the right also rises to fifth. Incline the body over the left side (fig. 270).

Fig. 270 Torso tipped over the left side, right leg in second

Fig. 271 Jeté forward with the right leg

13. Jeté of the right leg to fourth front

Bring the torso upright and rise onto the half pointe of the left foot keeping the right leg still extended to second. Incline the torso to the right side until the body is off balance. With a jeté, quickly throw the right leg to fourth front transferring the weight onto it into a small demi-plié (slightly towards the right diagonal); the straight left leg is raised to fourth back.

The left arm lowers in second; the right arm lowers and bends; then the hand, gracefully brushing the lips with the tips of the fingers, extends forward (fig. 271).

14. Pas de bourrée commencing with the right leg

Hold this pose, taken after the jeté, for a moment (the right leg in a small demi-plié) with the left leg stretched back, the right arm extended forward and the left back.

As the right leg straightens, the left lowers behind in fifth beginning pas de bourrée that ends with the left foot back.

The arms lower through demi-seconde and close in position de repos at the end of the pas de bourrée.

15. Second arabesque with the right foot pointed on the floor to fourth back

Small demi-plié, transfer the weight onto the left leg as it slides to fourth front, diagonally right.

Straighten the knees, the right foot is pointed, on the floor, to fourth back.

The arms rise to first then the right extends forward slightly above shoulder height, the left lowers behind, slightly below and in alignment with the right (fig. 272).

16. Fourth front croisé with the right foot pointed on the floor – détourné d'Adage

Standing in second arabesque, slowly turn the body to the right (détourné d'Adage) with small movements of the left foot. The right leg, pointed on the floor, rotates without raising the pointe of the foot from the ground.

After the turn, the body faces diagonally left with the right foot pointed, à terre, to fourth front croisé.

During the détourné d'Adage, the arms move from second arabesque to low fourth left (fig. 273).

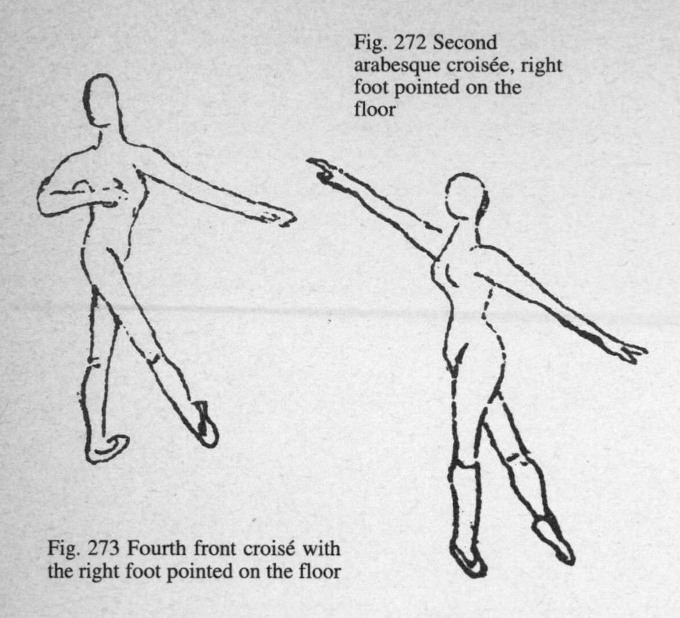

Fig. 272 Second arabesque croisée, right foot pointed on the floor

Fig. 273 Fourth front croisé with the right foot pointed on the floor

17. Jeté with the right leg and two turns in attitude to the right

Raise the straight right leg (still in fourth front croisé) to half height. Then, with a jeté sideways, throw the right leg to the right transferring the weight onto the pointe (piqué).

This movement gives the impetus for the body to turn en dedans to the right on the right pointe.

The left leg is raised in attitude position.

The right arm opens with energy, going to demi-seconde increasing the impetus; the left goes to fifth.

There should be enough force for the body to make two turns to the right on the right pointe (piqué), in attitude position (fig. 274).

18. Two enveloppé turns with the left leg en dedans to the right on the right leg

After the turns in attitude, lower the right heel, lower the left leg to fourth back; strong fouetté en dedans giving the body the impetus for two turns en dedans to the right on the right leg.

The arms lower strongly to position de repos, to give more force.

19. Tip over the right side with the left leg extended in second

After the two turns en dedans, développé extending the left leg into high second.

Raise the arms into fifth and tip the torso over the right side (fig. 275).

20. Jeté with the left leg and pas de bourrée

Bring the torso upright, rise onto the half pointe of the right foot and jeté, throwing the body off balance,

Fig. 274 Piqué turn en dedans in attitude, to the right

Fig. 275 Torso tipped over the right side; left leg in second

to the left, sharply lowering the left leg and raising the right leg back, at half height.

The right arm goes to demi-seconde, the left lowers, curves gracefully, lightly brushes the lips with the tips of the fingers, then reaches forward.

Lower the right leg to fifth back, begin pas de bourrée ending with the right foot front. After the pas de bourrée the arms close to position de repos.

21. Assemblé soutenu en dedans to the right and battement tendu with the left foot

Slight demi-plié on both legs as the left leg goes to second position, pointe on the floor. With an entwining movement, the left leg crosses over in front of the right leg, lowering the heel.

The knees straighten and the feet rise onto the half or full pointe causing the body to turn right. That is assemblé soutenu en dedans.

After the turn, lower the heels into a tight fifth, right foot front.

The arms rise through fifth before lowering to position de repos.

Battement tendu, taking the left foot to fifth front.

Repeat the whole exercise immediately on the left side.

EXERCISE 10

PAS DE CHACONNE

(Score no. 10, 3rd Part)

To understand the purpose of this exercise, which has no particular characteristics of its own, we recall all that has been said about the other adagi. The continual and methodical development of muscular sensitivity, balance, etc. and especially the constant search for various movements allow the pupil to practice for the attainment of complete freedom of movement.

All parts of the body must move independently, combining together to create the harmonious positions, static or dynamic, which make up dance.

We continue to emphasize how important it is to link the different steps together in a variety of ways so that the pupil does not become used to the same, unchanging sequence of steps.

For example, if an assemblé is always given followed by pas de bourrée and suddenly these two steps are put into reverse order, the pupil will find them difficult to execute; since he has always performed the two steps in a particular way, he will have absorbed them as if they were one complete step.

Exercise

Preparation

Stand in the centre of the room with the feet in fifth position, right foot front. Arms in position de repos.

1. Grand rond de jambe à terre en dehors with the right leg

Demi-plié on both legs and extend the right leg to fourth front, on the floor.

The arms rise to first. The head inclines over the right shoulder (fig. 276).

Grand rond de jambe à terre en dehors; the straight right leg describes a half circle from fourth front to fourth back, keeping the pointe on the floor.

The left leg remains in demi-plié.

The arms open to second during the movement. At the same time the head turns to the opposite side, inclining over the left shoulder (fig. 277).

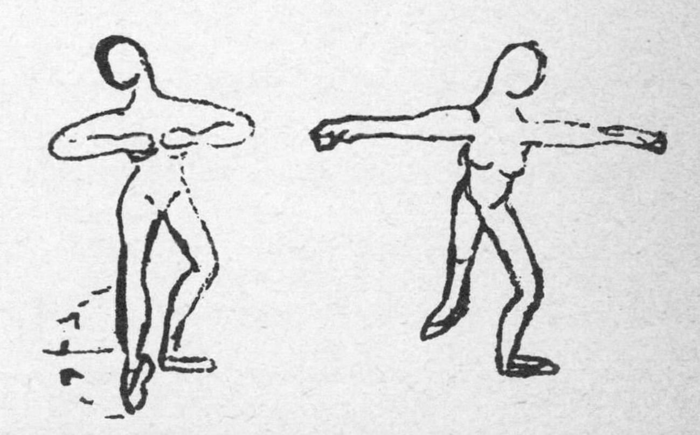

Fig. 276 Beginning of rond de jambe; leg fourth front

Fig. 277 End of rond de jambe; leg fourth back

2. Relevé and petits battements sur le cou de pied on the right

The left leg gradually straightens, while the straight right leg slides along the floor from fourth back and closes into fifth back.

The arms lower to position de repos.

Relevé rising onto the half or full pointe of the right foot; at the same time the left foot draws up to the front of the right cou de pied and, with an easy movement, executes nine petits battements sur le cou de pied ending behind.

Then both heels lower into fifth position, right foot front.

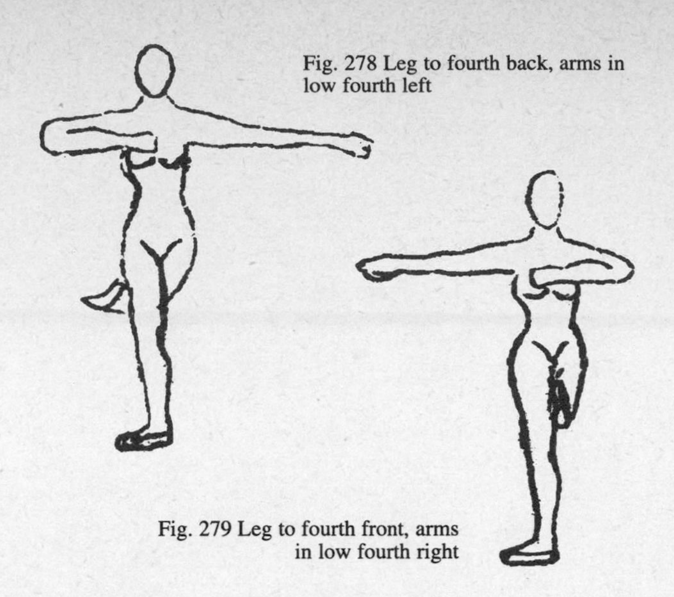

Fig. 278 Leg to fourth back, arms in low fourth left

Fig. 279 Leg to fourth front, arms in low fourth right

3. Repeat – relevé and petits battements sur le cou de pied on the right

Relevé a second time onto the half or full pointe of the right foot while the left goes behind the right cou de pied and, with an easy movement, executes 8 petits battements sur le cou de pied, ending back.

Coupé, quickly lowering the left foot to fifth back, placing the heel of the right foot in front of the left cou de pied.

The arms remain in position de repos.

4. Développé with the right leg to fourth front

Développé extending the right leg to high fourth front. The arms are taken to second.

5. Ballotté to fourth front with the right leg

Small demi-plié on the left leg and taking the body forward, transfer the weight forward onto the right leg which lowers quickly in fourth front as the straight left leg is raised to fourth back.

During the demi-plié preceding the ballotté, the right arm goes to first so that the arms are in low fourth left (fig. 278).

6. Grand rond de jambe en dedans with the left leg

Grand rond de jambe taking the left leg from fourth back to high fourth front.

Co-ordinating with the leg, the arms reverse the low fourth position: as the right arm gradually opens to second, the left arm bends into first (fig. 279).

7. Relevé with the left leg extended to fourth front

With the left leg extended to high fourth front, demi-plié and relevé onto the half or full pointe of the right foot. Then lower the heel.

The arms remain in low fourth right.

8. Ballotté in fourth front with the left; attitude with the right

Transfer the weight forward onto the left leg which quickly lowers; the right leg is raised to fourth back bending into attitude position.

The right arm is raised to fifth, the left opens to second (fig. 280).

9. Third arabesque croisée to the right

Extend the right leg to fourth back. Turn the body to the right diagonal.

The arms lower to position de repos; the torso turns to the right and the arms extend forward: the left slightly above shoulder height and the right a little lower and parallel to the left (fig. 281).

Fig. 280 Attitude right facing front

Fig. 281 Third arabesque croisée to the right

10. Tour de promenade en troisième arabesque

Standing in third arabesque, with small movements of the supporting left foot, one slow tour de promenade making one complete turn of the body to the right (fig. 281).

11. Raccourci and développé with the right leg to fourth front croisé to the left

The turn ends facing front; the right leg bends and, with développé, extends to fourth front croisé to the left.

Lower the arms to position de repos and, with ramassé des bras, raise them through first, then open the left to second. The arms are in low fourth left.

12. Jeté onto the right leg and turn en dedans to the right with the left leg in second

Jeté, transferring the weight onto the right leg which lowers, with energy, slightly to the right side; this gives the body the impetus to turn en dedans to the right with the left leg in high second position.

The right arm opens strongly to second to give the body more impetus.

The arms are in second (fig. 282).

13. Rond de jambe en l'air with the left leg and développé to fourth front

After the turn with the left leg extended in second, rond de jambe en l'air en dehors, then développé, slowly extending the leg to fourth front.

The arms close to first.

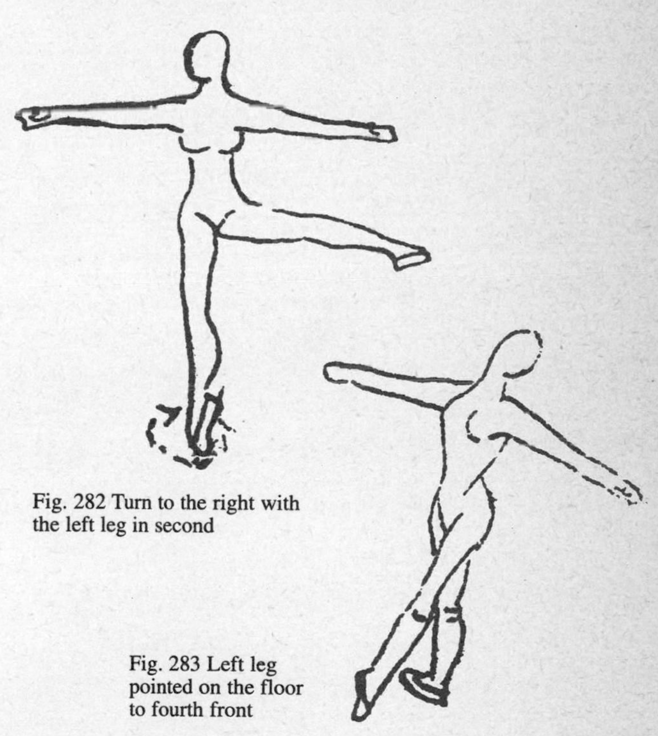

Fig. 282 Turn to the right with the left leg in second

Fig. 283 Left leg pointed on the floor to fourth front

14. Pointe the left foot to fourth front, on the floor

Lower the left leg, straight, pointed to fourth front, on the floor.

The arms open to second (fig. 283).

Fig. 284 Second arabesque ouverte to the right

Fig. 285 Movement of battement à cloche with the left

15. Left foot on the right cou de pied

Draw the left heel onto the right cou de pied.
The arms lower to position de repos.

16. Petits battements with the left foot – développé to fourth back and attitude facing front

One petit battement sur le cou de pied taking the left foot behind the right cou de pied.
Développé to extend the left leg to fourth back, bending it into attitude position.
The arms are taken to third left.

17. Second arabesque ouverte to the right

Extend the left leg to fourth back. Turn the body slightly to the right diagonal.
The left arm lowers and extends forward slightly above shoulder height, the right extends back, a little lower and in alignment with the left (fig. 284).

18. Battements à cloche with the left, closing in fifth front

Execute two battements à cloche, that is: briskly lower the left leg, fully stretched, from high fourth back, passing through first to high fourth front; continue the movement, lowering the leg again, passing through first to high fourth back; then with a similar movement take it once more to high fourth front to lower and close it in fifth front.
Co-ordinating with the first battement à cloche, the arms lower from second arabesque (left front and right back) and reverse into the opposite position: right front and left back.
The head inclines to the left shoulder (fig. 285).
The position of the arms and the head remain unchanged during the successive battements à cloche with the left leg.
Finally, when the left leg lowers to close in fifth front, the arms lower to position de repos, the head comes erect and the body turns front.
Battements à cloche are executed with a certain grace, softening the natural vigor of this movement.

Repeat the whole exercise with the left leg.

EXERCISE 11

CINQ RELEVÉS

(Score no. 11, 3rd Part)

All the adagi based on relevés, like this one, are designed to train the dancer to have a firm sense of balance especially when standing on one leg either on half or full pointe.
The relevé exercises also develop the external and internal leg muscles, particularly the tibials and flexors.
The legs and feet of a dancer must become strong and elastic like steel levers; this allows them every skill and perfect execution.

However, relevés have many purposes and uses. They strengthen the pointes, the insteps and ankles. Most of all they contribute greatly to the reinforcement of the lumbar region. This is perhaps its most important function, because the secret of balance lies in the lumbar region. A maestro who discovers a young pupil with a naturally strong back can begin hoping to form a good dancer.

Much care and perseverance are required before this quite tiring exercise, can bear fruit.

In this adagio the relevés are executed with the leg raised: to the front, at the side, to the back, and with one foot at the cou de pied of the other leg.

One relevé with the leg raised and one with the foot at the cou de pied, count as one movement only.

EXERCISE

Preparation

Stand in the centre of the room with the feet in fifth position, right foot front. Arms in position de repos.

1. Plié

Full plié with the feet tightly closed in fifth. Rise slowly until the knees are fully stretched.

The arms remain in position de repos.

2. Relevé-coupé

Small demi-plié and strong relevé onto the half pointes or full pointes of both feet. The body turns slightly to the left diagonal.

The head inclines slightly to the right shoulder.

After a short pause, the feet move alternately with pas de bourrée sur la place. Coupé, sharply lowering the left heel, placing the heel of the right foot on the left cou de pied.

At the same time, the body returns to face front and the head comes erect.

The arms are still in position de repos.

3. First relevé with the right leg in high fourth front

Ramassé des pieds with the right leg; développé to high fourth front.

Ramassé des bras and raise the arms through first to second.

Small demi-plié on the left leg in this position and strong relevé onto half pointe or full pointe (fig. 286).

Lower the left heel; lower the right leg, well stretched, to fourth front, pointed on the floor; slowly draw the right foot in placing the heel on the left cou de pied. The arms lower slowly.

4. Relevé with the right foot at the left cou de pied

Small demi-plié on the left leg, strong relevé onto half pointe or full pointe with the right foot on the left cou de pied (fig. 287).

The arms are still in position de repos.

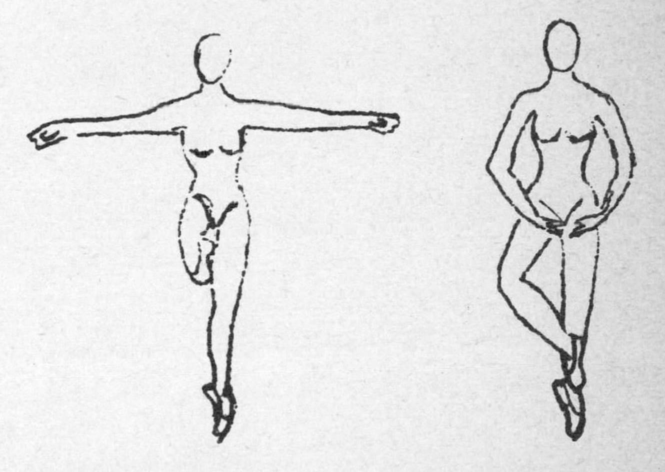

Fig. 286 First relevé with the right leg in fourth front

Fig. 287 Relevé with the right leg in front of the left cou de pied

5. Second relevé with the right leg in high second

Ramassé des pieds with the right leg and développé to high second.

Ramassé des bras and raise the arms through first to second.

Small demi-plié on the left leg in this position and relevé strongly onto half pointe or full pointe (fig. 288).

Lower the left heel, lower the right leg, well stretched, to second, pointe on the floor and slowly draw the foot in, placing the heel behind the right cou de pied.

The arms lower slowly to position de repos.

6. Relevé with the right foot at the left cou de pied

Small demi-plié on the left leg; strong relevé onto the half or full pointe with the right foot on the left cou de pied (fig. 289).

Lower the left heel.

The arms are still in position de repos.

7. Third relevé with the right leg in high fourth back

Ramassé des pieds with the right; développé, extending the leg to high fourth back.

Ramassé des bras and raise the arms through first to second.

In this position, small demi-plié on the left; strong relevé onto half or full pointe (fig. 290).

Lower the left heel, lower the right leg to fourth back, pointe on the floor; slowly draw the foot in, placing the heel behind the left cou de pied.

The arms lower slowly to position de repos.

8. Relevé with the right foot at the left cou de pied

With the right foot behind the left cou de pied, small demi-plié on the left leg; strong relevé onto half pointe or full pointe (fig. 289).

Lower the left heel.

The arms are still in position de repos.

9. Fourth relevé with the right leg in high second

Ramassé des pieds with the right leg and développé to high second.

Ramassé des bras and raise the arms through first to second.

Small demi-plié on the left leg; strong relevé rising onto half pointe or full pointe (fig. 288).

Lower the left heel; lower the fully stretched right leg to second, pointe on the floor; slowly draw the foot in, placing the heel in front of the left cou de pied.

The arms lower slowly to position de repos.

10. Relevé with the right foot at the left cou de pied

Small demi-plié and strong relevé, rising onto half pointe or full pointe with the right foot at the left cou de pied (fig. 287).

The arms are still in position de repos.

11. Fifth relevé with the leg in high fourth front

Ramassé des pieds with the right leg and développé to high fourth front.

Ramassé des bras and raise the arms through first to second.

Small demi-plié on the left leg in this position; strong relevé onto half pointe or full pointe (fig. 286).

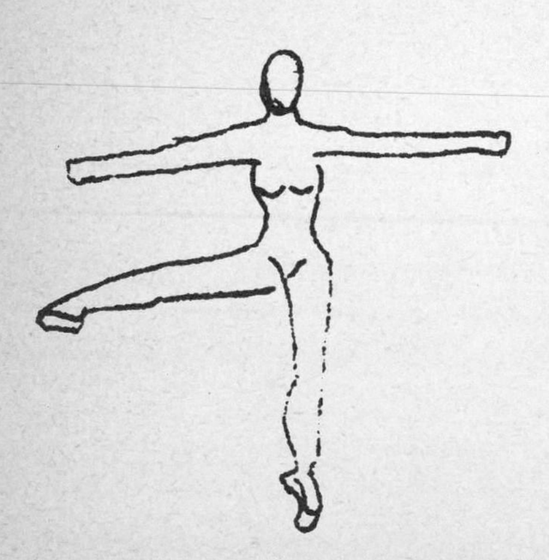

Fig. 288 Second relevé with the right leg in high second

Fig. 289 Relevé with the right foot at the cou de pied

Fig. 290 Third relevé with the right leg in high fourth back

With a quicker movement, lower the left heel as the right leg lowers, drawing in the foot placing the heel in front of the left cou de pied.

The arms, coordinating with the movement of the legs, lower to position de repos (fig. 287).

12. Relevé and battement dégagé into second with the right leg – close

The right foot is on the left cou de pied; small demi-plié on the left (fast), straighten the leg and relevé strongly onto half pointe or full pointe.

During the relevé, battement dégagé extending the right leg to demi-seconde straightening the knee closing quickly behind into fifth.

The left heel lowers and the feet close tightly into fifth, left foot front.

The arms, coordinating with the battement dégagé, open to demi-seconde, then lower to position de repos.

Repeat the whole exercise immediately with the left leg.

EXERCISE 12

FIRST AND SECOND ARABESQUE

(Score no. 12, 3rd Part)

Arabesque: the mind immediately turns to precious engravings by Florentine artists, or the abundantly elegant scrolls of the Renaissance period, or perhaps to delicate embroidery or fabulous drawings in the Moorish style.

In fact, *arabesques* are a series of poses of sublime grace and harmony. They are amongst the most beautiful, most delicately elegant and the most characteristic. Obviously then, particular attention has been given to these in the adagi of this method. In fact, this exercise and the following, are dedicated completely to studying these poses. They are gradually formed based upon ever more complex and difficult movements.

The difficulties this adagio presents must be completely concealed so that the marvelous harmony of these poses is not disturbed. They should always give the impression that their composition has been inspired from within; that they are formed by the spirit and executed without the help of any material force.

Achieving an almost perfect execution, without any anxiety, wins admiring approval for the dancer from the enthusiastic spectator. But to reach that level, the pupil must dedicate his heart and soul, not only his muscles.

We will now make look at some details necessary for the preparation of the study of this Adagio.

To begin with, remember that arabesque is never taken facing the front because its line runs lengthways (longitudinal) and would not be seen by the audience. Therefore, it is taken in a slightly diagonal direction which is the best position to show off every nuance of this attractive and graceful pose.

We also recall that in this method the wishes and creative taste of Maestro Enrico Cecchetti are carefully observed; he always emphasized that these arabesqes should be executed with the torso well erect. Other schools have preferred to retain the traditional method of arabesque with the torso inclined forward. We are reminded, therefore, of a practical answer that the Maestro E. Cecchetti would give to those who asked his opinion in reference to this.

He would say, 'Given that the position of the body is always more graceful when not distorted from its natural position, try standing in an arabesque with the torso inclined forward. Now lower the arms and the leg: how do you feel standing with the legs together and the body bent over like a bow? Try the arabesque with the torso upright and continue the experiment: you will find yourself in an upright and perfectly natural position!'

Arabesques taken in this way are one of the prerogatives of this method; today they are still called "Arabesques Cecchetti."

There are five basic arabesques; these can be taken ouverte or croisée. In this way, the creative taste of the maestro can fashion imaginative poses just by changing the positions of the arms. We will call the attention of the reader to this when describing the following adagio.

In this adagio we examine the first and the second arabesque, both ouverte and croisée.

Exercise

Preparation

Stand in the centre of the room with the feet in fifth position, right foot front. The arms in position de repos.

1. Balancé to fourth front and to fourth back

Small demi-plié on both legs extending the right leg to fourth front; transfer the weight onto the right and straighten the knees; the left heel is raised, the left foot remains pointed on the floor to fourth back.

The arms open slightly to demi-seconde (fig. 291).

Continue the balancé movement; small demi-plié lowering the left heel and transferring the weight onto the left leg. Straighten the knees and raise the right heel; the right foot remains pointed on the floor to fourth front.

The arms are raised to half first, slightly open (fig. 292).

Slide the pointe along the floor drawing the right foot, in placing the heel in front of the left cou de pied.

The arms return to position de repos.

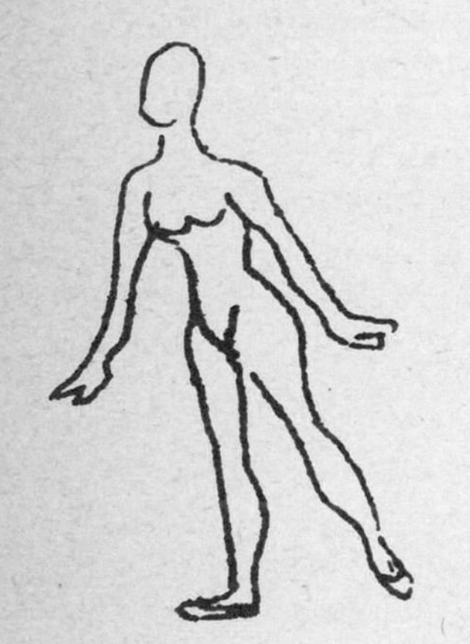

Fig. 291 Balancé to fourth front

Fig. 292 Balancé to fourth back

2. First arabesque ouverte to the left

The body turns slightly to the left diagonal; petit battement sur le cou de pied with the right, taking the right foot behind; développé extending the leg to fourth back.

Ramassé des bras and open the arms; the left raised forward above shoulder level and the right lowered behind and in alignment with the left.

3. Tour de promenade in first arabesque

With small movements of the supporting left foot, very slowly make one tour de promenade in first arabesque en dehors to the left; the turn ends returning to the point of departure.

4. In first arabesque, incline and recover the torso

Still in first arabesque, slowly incline the torso forward from the waist; the left arm (which remains in first arabesque) lowers, following the movement of the torso until it touches the floor with the tips of the fingers; the right is raised in equal measure, still remaining in alignment with the left arm and parallel to the right leg; this is raised, also in equal measure, still fully stretched (fig. 293).

At the same speed, execute the movement in reverse; the torso recovers to an upright position into the normal first arabesque.

5. Fouetté with the right leg and enveloppé turn to the left

Strong fouetté bringing the right foot front, brushing underneath the tips of the toes along the floor.

This gives the body the impetus for one enveloppé turn to the left on the left half pointe.

The arms go to position de repos (fig. 294).

6. After the turn, développé with the right leg to second

End the enveloppé turn facing front. Developpé extending the right leg to high second.

The arms, passing through first, open to second.

7. First arabesque to the left (for the second time)

Holding the arms firmly and the right leg in second, turn the body to the left. Automatically, the arms and the leg turn into first arabesque ouverte to the left.

8. Fouetté with the right leg and enveloppé turn to the left (for the second time)

The right leg executes a second fouetté à terre, giving the body impetus for enveloppé turn to the left, exactly as explained in no. 5.

Arms in position de repos.

9. After the turn, développé with the right leg to second

End the turn facing front; développé extending the right leg to high second (exactly as explained in no. 6).

The arms, passing through first, open to second.

Fig. 293 Inclining the torso in first arabesque to the left

Fig. 294 Enveloppé turn to the left on half pointe

10. Demi-grand rond de jambe with the right leg and second arabesque croisée to the right

Demi-grand rond de jambe with the right leg, from the second to fourth back; the torso turns right from the waist up.

The right arm, straight, extends forward above shoulder height, the left extends behind below and in alignment with the right.

The pose is second arabesque croisée (fig. 295).

11. Relevé in second arabesque croisée to the right – turn the body to face front

Small demi-plié on the left leg and strong relevé rising onto half pointe or full pointe of the left foot; lower the heel. The body turns to the front with the right leg in fourth back.

The arms are taken to second.

12. Ballotté to fourth back with the right leg and enveloppé turn to the right on the left leg

Ballotté, transferring the weight back onto the right leg which quickly lowers in fourth back as the straight

Fig. 295 Second arabesque croisée to the right

Fig. 296 Enveloppé turn to the right on the half pointe

Fig. 297 First arabesque ouverte to the right

Fig. 298 Second arabesque ouverte to the right

left leg is raised to high fourth front. Raccourci of the left foot and extend the leg to second.

With a strong enveloppé movement, the left foot is taken in front, giving the body the impetus to turn to the right on the half pointe of the right foot.

The arms, from the second, go strongly to position de repos; this movement increases the impetus (fig. 296).

13. First arabesque ouverte to the right

End the enveloppé turn facing the right wall; développé extending the left leg to fourth back.

The arms go to first arabesque: right arm straight in front, the left back (fig. 297).

14. Second arabesque ouverte to the right

Standing with the left leg in high fourth back, reverse the position of the arms, that is: extend the left arm forward above shoulder height; the right back, lower and in alignment with the left (fig. 298).

15. Développé to fourth front with the left – détourné d'Adage to the right – first arabesque croisée to the left

Turn the torso to the left from the waist up.

The arms open to second.

Raccourci of the left leg and développé to fourth front.

Execute détourné d'Adage to the right: turn the torso slowly to the right; still remaining firmly in fourth front, the left leg rotates; after the torso has made one half turn, the leg will automatically be in fourth back.

Then, with small movements of the supporting right foot, continue turning until the body faces the left wall.

During the last half turn, the arms move slowly into first arabesque croisée: the right extended forward towards the left wall, the left back towards the right wall (fig. 299).

16. Demi-tour de promenade to the right – first arabesque ouverte to the right

Standing in first arabesque croisée to the left; small movements of the right supporting foot, executing demi-tour de promenade; the body makes one half turn en dehors to the right, ending facing the right wall in first arabesque ouverte to the right: remaining in this position, the arabesque is now literally reversed, from first arabesque croisée to the left, to first arabesque ouverte to the right.

17. Turn front and développé to fourth front

Turn the torso to the front from the waist up. The left leg rotates into second position. The arms turn into second.

Raccourci of the left leg and extend to fourth front.

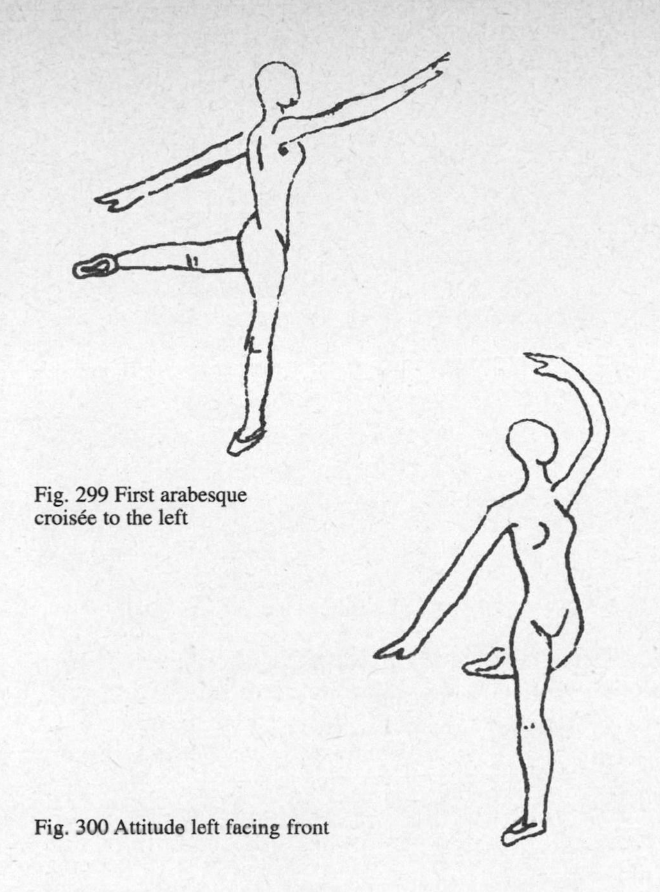

Fig. 299 First arabesque croisée to the left

Fig. 300 Attitude left facing front

18. Ballotté – pas de bourrée – attitude left

Ballotté, taking the weight forward onto the left leg which lowers sharply in fourth front as the right leg is raised behind. Continuing the movement, lower the right leg immediately into pas de bourrée to the side ending in fifth with the right foot front.

Small demi-plié on both legs, glissade sliding the right foot to fourth front.

Straighten the right leg and raise the left leg to attitude.

The left arm is raised to fifth and the right to demi-seconde (fig. 300).

19. Grande préparation in fourth for turns en dedans

Grande préparation in fourth: small demi-plié on the right leg and lower the left leg to fourth back, transferring the weight onto the left leg; the right leg is pointed, on the floor, to fourth front (fig. 301).

Circular port de bras lowering the left arm to second; the right is raised through fifth to lower in first (the arms are in low fourth position left).

As soon as the arms are in low fourth left, lower the right heel and centre the weight over both legs; demi-plié in fourth (fig. 302).

20. Enveloppé turn en dedans to the right and final pose effacée to the right

From this position, enveloppé with the left leg, giving the body impetus to turn to the right on the right leg.

During the turn the left leg will remain in front of the cou de pied.

The arms, with a vigorous movement, are taken to position de repos, helping notably with the impetus.

After the turn, lower the left leg taking the weight onto it as the right leg extends to fourth front, pointe on the floor.

The left arm is raised to fifth, the right to demi-seconde.

The body inclines to the left side (the position is effacé) exactly the same as the position in which the grande préparation in fourth for turns en dedans commences (fig. 301).

Repeat the whole exercise with the left leg.

EXERCISE 13

THIRD, FOURTH AND FIFTH ARABESQUE

(Score no. 13, 3rd Part)

There is little to say about this exercise that has not already been indicated. This is a supplement to exercise no. 12 in which the first and second arabesque are examined. In the same way, this adagio concentrates on the third, fourth and fifth arabesque. Again, care must be taken to avoid executing arabesques facing directly front.

As we have already indicated, in this exercise, as well as the classic arabesques, established through unchangeable rules of technique, we will see the addition of two poses (figs. 271 and 276) derived from arabesque which are most charming and typical of the Cecchetti Method.

The last movement, in which the arms lower to position de repos, is particularly charming and elegant, ending with the fingers entwined and the palms of the hands facing down.

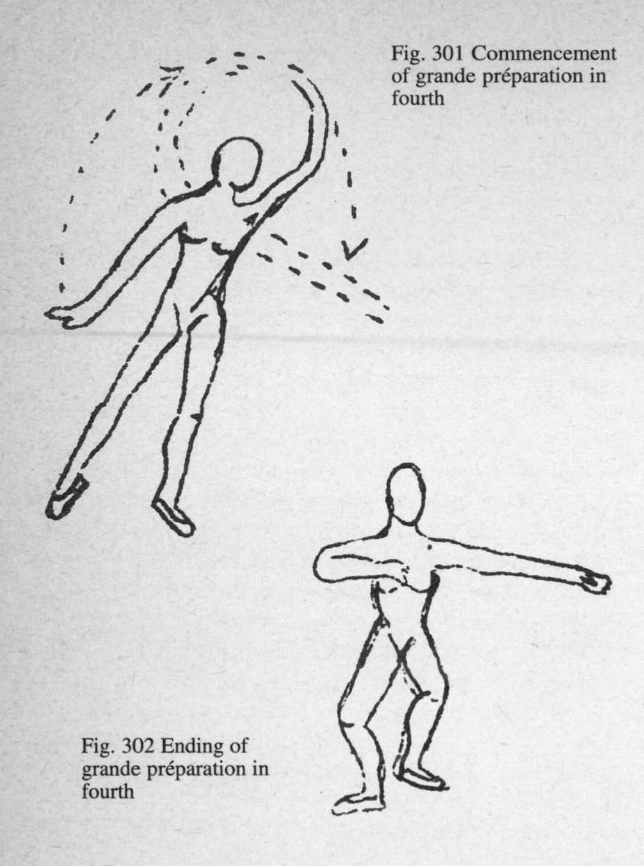

Fig. 301 Commencement of grande préparation in fourth

Fig. 302 Ending of grande préparation in fourth

EXERCISE

Preparation

Stand in the centre of the room with the feet in fifth position, right foot front. The arms in position de repos.

1. Relevé-coupé

Small demi-plié and relevé onto the half or full pointes.

Quickly lower the left heel; the right heel is placed in front of the left cou de pied.

The arms remain in position de repos.

2. Développé to fourth front with the right leg

Ramassé des pieds, raising the right leg; développé, extending the leg to high fourth front.

The right arm is raised to fifth and the left to second; the arms are in third right (fig. 303).

3. Ballotté to fourth front and third arabesque ouverte to the right

Small demi-plié on the left leg; ballotté, transferring the weight forward onto the straight right leg which lowers, as the left is raised, fully stretched, to high fourth back.

The right arm extends forward above shoulder height; the left is taken forward, straight, below and parallel to the right.

The body turns diagonally right (fig. 304).

Fig. 303 Right leg in fourth front, arms in third right

Fig. 304 Third arabesque ouverte to the right

4. Cecchetti pose to the right

Remaining in third arabesque, the right arm is drawn in; the fingers are placed on the chin, barely touching, while the elbow rests on the back of the left hand; the left elbow is drawn in, very close to the breast.

The head inclines to the right (fig. 305).

5. Third arabesque ouverte to the right – turn to the front with the left leg in second – relevé

Return into third arabesque ouverte to the right (fig. 304).

Turn the torso left to face front. The left leg rotates until it is extended to high second position.

The arms open to second.

Still in this position, relevé rising onto half pointe or full pointe of the right foot.

6. Jeté with the left leg – pas de bourrée (ending with the right foot in fourth front)

Jeté, transferring the weight onto the left leg which is thrown towards the left diagonal; as the leg lowers, the right leg is raised behind.

Pas de bourrée ending with the weight over the right leg in fourth front; the left leg remains pointed, on the floor, to fourth back.

During the jeté, the left hand brushes the lips and the arm lowers to demi-seconde (fig. 306).

At the end of pas de bourrée, the arms are taken to position de repos.

Fig. 305 Cecchetti pose to the right

Fig. 306 Jeté onto the left leg and first movement of pas de bourrée

7. Développé to fourth back with the left leg – third arabesque croisée to the left

Développé extending the left leg to high fourth back, turning the body to the left.

The right arm extends forward to above shoulder height; the left is brought forward below and parallel to the right. The pose is third arabesque croisée to the left (fig. 307).

8. Enveloppé turn to the right ending with the left leg in second and tipped over the right side

Open the arms to second. The left leg comes in with an energetic enveloppé, giving the body impetus to turn en dedans to the right on the half pointe of the right foot.

At the same time the arms lower to position de repos with a strong movement, contributing notably to the impetus.

After the turn, which ends facing front, the left leg extends, well stretched, to second.

The arms are raised to fifth.

Incline the body, from the waist up, over the right side. The arms and the left leg follow the movement naturally (fig. 308); the body recovers upright; the left leg lowers, fully stretched, to fourth front.

The arms are taken to position de repos.

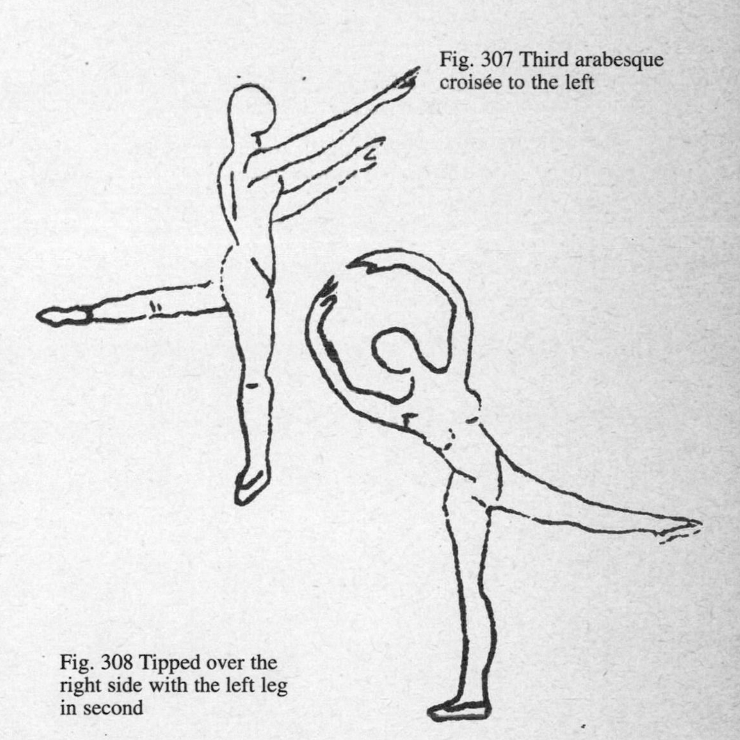

Fig. 307 Third arabesque croisée to the left

Fig. 308 Tipped over the right side with the left leg in second

9. Relevé on both feet and turn in a circle to the left

Small demi-plié and relevé onto the half pointes or full pointes of both feet.

The left arm is raised to fifth and the right to demi-seconde.

The head inclines to the left shoulder; with tiny steps on the pointes (pas de bourrée marché sur les pointes) make a small circle with the diameter of about one yard (1 meter), turning to the left.

After the turn, coupé and lower the right heel; placing the left heel in front of the right cou de pied.

10. Développé to fourth front with the left leg – ballotté – fourth arabesque ouverte

Développé extending the left leg to high fourth front.

The arms, passing through first, are taken to second.

Small demi-plié on the right leg, ballotté, transferring the weight forward and to the left, onto the left leg which lowers as the right is raised, well stretched, to high fourth back.

The right arm extends forward above shoulder height; the left is taken back lower, in alignment with the right.

The left leg is in demi-plié completing the position, fourth arabesque ouverte to the left (fig. 309).

Fig. 309 Fourth arabesque ouverte to the left

Fig. 310 Cecchetti pose no. 2 to the left

11. Cecchetti pose no. 2 to the left

Straighten the left knee. Turn the torso to the right from above the waist; the arms open to second. From this position the arms lower and are raised to first but very displaced, towards the left. Join the hands as if in prayer and bend the arms, so that the hands brush the left cheek very softly.

The head inclines slightly to the left (fig. 310).

12. Fifth arabesque ouverte to the left

Extend the arms forward, the left above shoulder height and the right below and parallel to the left.

Demi-plié on the left leg, completing the pose, fifth arabesque ouverte to the left (fig. 311).

13. First arabesque ouverte to the left and tour de promenade to the left

Straighten the left knee. Take the right arm back in line with the left, making the pose first arabesque ouverte to the left (fig. 312).

In this position, gradually move the left foot, making one tour de promenade very slowly to the left, returning to the point of departure.

14. Grand rond de jambe en dedans with the right leg – ending

Turn the body to the front from the waist up, with the right leg still in fourth back.

The arms move into second position.

Grand rond de jambe en dedans taking the right leg from fourth back to fourth front; then, with a soft movement, slowly lower the straight leg to fourth front, pointe on the floor; close in fifth front.

Co-ordinating with the movement of the leg, the arms lower softly to position de repos; bend the elbows slightly, raise the forearms, turn the palms of the hands to face the floor; join the hands, intertwining the fingers. Extend the elbows, once more, and stretch the arms towards the floor.

In this position, battement tendu taking the left foot to fifth front.

Repeat the whole exercise immediately with the left leg.

Fig. 311 Fifth arabesque ouverte to the left

Fig. 312 First arabesque ouverte to the left

EXERCISE 14

GRAND ROND DE JAMBE EN TOURNANT AVEC JETÉ

(Score no. 14, 3rd Part)

There is nothing remarkable about this adagio.

Its sole purpose is to continue training each part of the body, increasing stability and precision.

This exercise, in keeping with the spirit and principles of these adagi, is based on all manner and variety of movements with varying degrees of difficulty; this allows the pupil to practice certain poses.

The grand jeté in this exercise must be executed carefully; from fourth position back, with jeté, the leg is thrown to fourth front passing through raccourci.

EXERCISE

Preparation

Stand in the centre of the room with the feet in fifth position, right foot front. Arms in position de repos.

1. Plié

Full plié evenly on both legs.

The right arm remains in position de repos, the left opens to demi-seconde (fig. 313).

2. Tire-bouchon turn en dehors to the right

Commence rising; close the left arm, with energy, to position de repos giving the body impetus to turn en dehors to the right on the half pointe of the left foot.

Immediately, the right foot draws up, placing the heel in front of the left cou de pied; as the left leg gradually straightens during the turn, the right pointe brushes along the left leg until, at the end of the turn, the right thigh is fully turned out in high second and the pointe of the right foot touches the knee of the fully stretched left leg (fig. 314).

3. Développé to fourth front with the right leg

After the turn, développé extending the right leg to high fourth front.

The arms are raised to first.

4. Demi-grand rond de jambe en dehors with the right leg, turn to the right and développé to second

Demi-grand rond de jambe en dehors with the right leg, first slowly and then with energy, to give the body impetus to turn en dehors to the right.

Fig. 313 Plié and preparation for turning right

Fig. 314 Tire-bouchon turn en dehors to the right

At the end of demi-grand rond de jambe, the right leg is in high second position; raccourci and remain in this position throughout the turn.

The arms, coordinating with the above movement, open into second and lower strongly to position de repos contributing impetus (fig. 315).

After the turn, développé quickly, extending the right leg to high second.

The arms open to second (fig. 316).

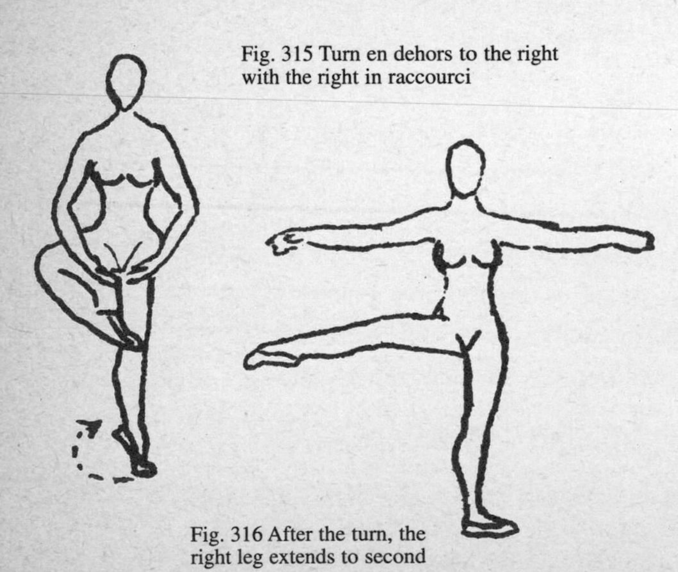

Fig. 315 Turn en dehors to the right with the right in raccourci

Fig. 316 After the turn, the right leg extends to second

5. Two ballottés in second with the right leg and the left leg

1st ballotté – Small demi-plié on left leg; ballotté (fig. 317), transferring the weight to the right side onto the right leg which lowers as the straight left leg is raised to high second.

The arms remain in second.

2nd ballotté – Small demi-plié on the right leg; with a second ballotté (fig. 318) transfer the weight to the left, onto the left leg which lowers as the straight right leg is raised to high second.

The arms are still in second.

Fig. 317 Ballotté in second with the right leg to the right

Fig. 318 Ballotté in second with the left leg to the left

6. Effacé position to the right with the right leg – fourth front on the floor and fourth back

Keeping the right leg firmly extended to second, turn the torso, from the waist up, towards the right diagonal so that the right leg ends extended to fourth front.

The left arm is raised to fifth and the right lowers to demi-seconde: effacé position (fig. 319). Lower the straight right leg to fourth front, pointed on the floor; pass through first to fourth back, at half height.

The arms are taken to first.

7. Développé and grand jeté to fourth front in attitude

Raccourci of the right leg (fig. 320); développé, and grand jeté, taking the weight onto the right leg which is thrown to fourth front, still straight, ending with the left leg raised to attitude.

The left arm rises to fifth; the right opens to demi-seconde (fig. 321).

Fig. 319 Effacé position right

Fig. 320 Jeté with the right to fourth front

Fig. 321 After jeté, attitude ouverte left

8. Développé to fourth front croisé to the right – jeté, turn in arabesque

Raccourci with the left leg and développé extending the leg to fourth front croisé to the right.

Arms third right.

Jeté to the left side: step onto the left foot giving the body impetus for one turn to the left in first arabesque (the right leg extended behind, at half height).

Then: lower and close the right foot in fifth back.

The arms lower to position de repos.

9. Développé to second in écarté

Développé extending the right leg to high second. The body faces the left diagonal. The right leg, extended in second remains pointed towards the right diagonal.

The arms are raised to third right (fig. 322).

10. Jeté, pas de bourrée, second arabesque pointe on the floor

Jeté to the side onto the straight right leg, followed by pas de bourrée left. On the last temps, demi-plié and glissé, sliding the left leg to fourth front (diagonally right).

Slowly straighten the knees taking the weight onto the left leg; the right remains pointed, on the floor, to fourth back.

The arms lower and then rise and are taken into second arabesque croisée: right front, left back (fig. 323).

11. Piqué turn en dehors in first arabesque

Slightly raise the right leg and, step onto it with energy, giving the body the impetus to make two turns en dehors to the right in first arabesque ending to the right (left leg well raised behind).

Arms in first arabesque: right front, left back.

Fig. 322 Écarté position, diagonally right with the left leg

Fig. 323 After glissé forward with the right, second arabesque croisée right, pointe on the floor

12. Pas de bourrée turning and turn en dehors in attitude

Lower the left leg and pas de bourrée turning to the right.

On completing pas de bourrée, immediately raise the right leg to fourth front at half height; grand rond de jambe en dehors giving the body the impetus to turn en dehors to the right on the left pointe in attitude right.

During pas de bourrée turning, the arms lower to position de repos; then they are raised to attitude right.

13. Raccourci with the right leg and développé in fourth front

Raccourci with the right leg; développé slowly, extending the leg to fourth front.

The arms lower through position de repos and are raised to second.

14. Ballotté to fourth front

Slowly execute ballotté to fourth front, lowering the right leg to the floor and raising the straight left leg to high fourth back.

The arms remain in second.

15. Raccourci and développé with the left leg to second – rond de jambe en l'air and développé to fourth front

Raccourci of the left leg; extend the leg to high second. Rond de jambe en l'air en dehors; développé, extending the leg to high fourth front.

The arms remain in second.

16. Lower the left leg and close in fifth, relevé and final pose

Slowly lower the left leg and close in fifth front.

Relevé onto the pointes of both feet; quickly lower the left heel as the right foot draws up, placing the heel behind the cou de pied of the left leg.

Battement dégagé opening the right leg to second at half height (fig. 324); sharply bend the knee placing the pointe of the foot, on the floor, behind and touching the left leg.

The body turns slightly to the right; the hands are joined as if in prayer and are taken up, to the left. The head, inclining left, softly rests the cheek on the back of the right hand (fig. 325).

Repeat the whole exercise to the left.

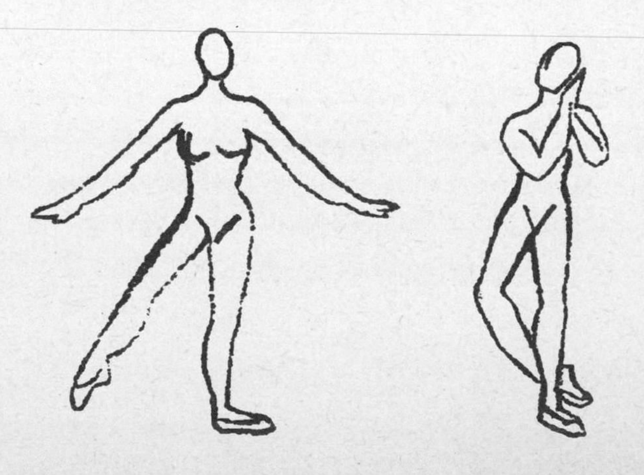

Fig. 324 Battement dégagé right

Fig. 325 Final pose

EXERCISE 15

FOUETTÉ BALLOTTÉ

(Score no. 15, 3rd Part)

This exercise, which has some important characteristics, is divided into two parts.

The first part is slow and smooth, while the second part is bright and energetic.

The complete exercise is very long and quite tiring; the pupil must distribute his energy so that when he reaches the end of the adagio, he will still be perfectly able to overcome the final difficulties.

We draw attention to a particular variation of ballotté, executed in an incomplete manner. The part which has been removed is later replaced, after a relevé. This step has been named demi-ballotté to distinguish it from the real ballotté.

This adagio is very important and useful because of the continual and varied movements of the arms which are the most difficult part of its execution.

The study of the positions and movements of the arms is one of the most refined parts of dance training. Unfortunately, this is too often neglected, causing the pupils to have an intolerable, incomplete and deficient technique, from the start. Frequently, a dancer demonstrates excellent qualities and general preparation, but a shamefully insufficient technique of the arms.

The graceful changes of the head and shoulders, which in certain poses and movements give a poetic charm to a position, are directly linked to the movements of the arms; so the very important role of the arms in dance can be clearly seen.

EXERCISE

FIRST PART
FOUETTÉ BALLOTÉ EN FACE

Preparation

Stand in the centre of the room with the feet in fifth position, right foot front. Arms in position de repos.

1. Relevé-coupé

Small demi-plié and relevé onto half or full pointes.

The body turns slightly to the left, the head inclines to the right shoulder.

The left arm is raised to fifth, and the right to demi-seconde.

After a short pause, move the arms with a circular port de bras: the left arm, passing through second, lowers to position de repos; the right arm follows the left, rising to fifth, and through first, lowers to position de repos to join the left.

Then, slightly turn the torso to the right, from the waist up; passing the left arm through first, raising it once more to fifth, opening to second again; the right, still following, rises to second.

End the circular port de bras with the arms in second; coupé, sharply lowering the left heel, placing the heel of the right foot in front of the left cou de pied.

The left arm curves into first; the arms are in low fourth right.

Fig. 326 Développé with the right leg to fourth front, relevé onto pointe

Fig. 327 Demi-grand rond de jambe taking the right leg to second

2. Développé with the right leg to fourth front – relevé and demi-grand rond de jambe en dehors

Ramassé des pieds and développé extending the right leg to fourth front.

The arms remain in low fourth right.

Small demi-plié on the left leg and relevé onto half pointe or full pointe of the right foot.

The left arm is raised to fifth (fig. 326).

At the same time, demi-grand rond de jambe en dehors taking the right leg to second; lower the left heel.

The right arm is raised to fifth and the left lowers to second (fig. 327).

In other words, at the beginning of the movement the arms are in third left and at the end they are in third right.

3. Tour de promenade with the right leg extended in second, then in attitude

Execute small movements of the left foot with the right leg in second and the arms third right; make one tour de promenade to the left.

After the turn, demi-grand rond de jambe en dehors taking the right leg to fourth back curving it into attitude. The pose is attitude right.

Lower the left arm through position de repos to first; at the same time lowering the right arm slowly to first (both arms are now in first). Continue the movement, raising the left arm to fifth as the right opens to second (the position third right is reversed to become third left).

4. Fourth arabesque ouverte to the left

Demi-plié on the left and extend the right leg to fourth back; the torso, from the waist up, turns slightly to the left.

The right arm lowers and is extended forward, above shoulder height; the left extends back, lower and in alignment with the right (fig. 328).

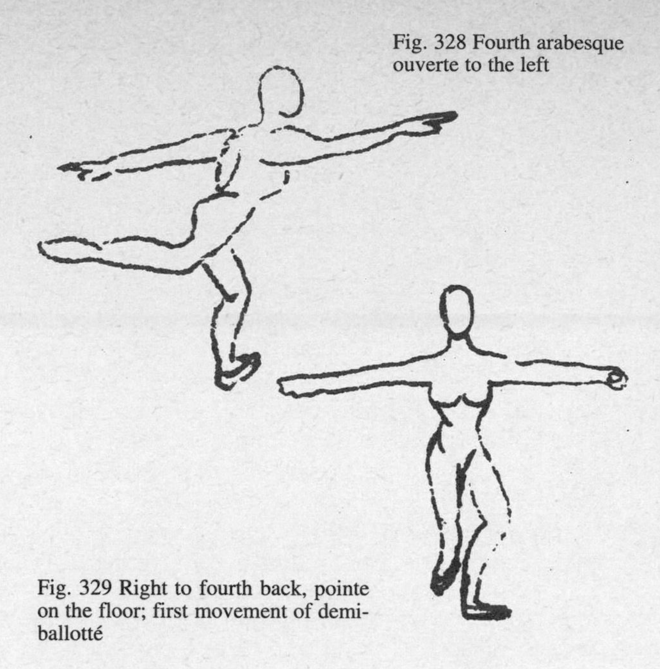

Fig. 328 Fourth arabesque ouverte to the left

Fig. 329 Right to fourth back, pointe on the floor; first movement of demi-ballotté

5. Demi-ballotté with the right leg (relevé-coupé with the left)

Turn the torso front, opening the arms to second.

Demi-ballotté: lower the straight right leg to fourth back, pointe on the floor (fig. 329); slowly straighten the left leg, sliding the right pointe along the floor, gradually closing the foot in fifth back with the leg still stretched (the arms gradually lower to position de repos).

Immediately, slow demi-plié and strong relevé onto half or full pointes. Demi-ballotté with coupé, lowering the right heel as the left foot draws in, placing the heel in front of the right cou de pied.

The arms remain in position de repos.

6. Développé with the left leg to fourth front into pose effacée

Turn the body diagonally left. Ramassé des pieds and développé the left leg to fourth front.

The arms are raised to first; then the right goes to fifth and the left opens to demi-seconde (fig. 330).

7. Demi-ballotté with the left leg (relevé-coupé with the right)

The body returns front. The arms are taken to second.

Demi-ballotté: lower the straight left leg to fourth front, pointe on the floor; at the same time, small demi-plié on the right (fig. 331). Slowly straighten the right knee, sliding the pointe of the left foot along the floor, gradually closing the foot in fifth front with the leg still stretched (the arms lower to position de repos coordinating with the movement).

Immediately, demi-plié and relevé onto half pointes or full pointes. After demi-ballotté coupé, lower the left heel as the right foot draws in placing the heel behind the left cou de pied.

The arms remain in position de repos.

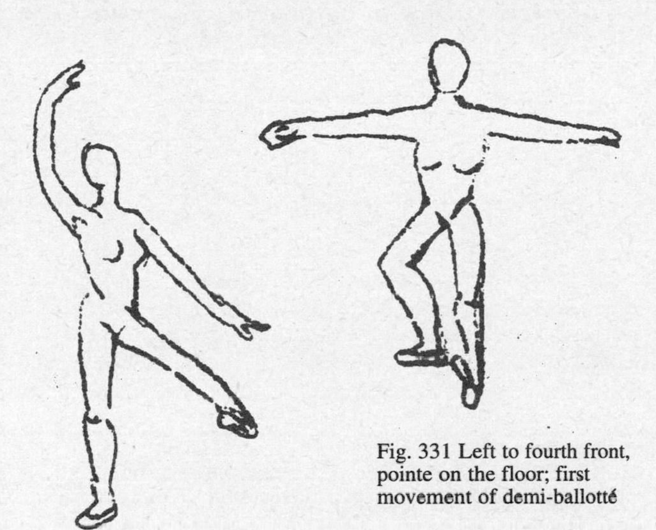

Fig. 330 Position effacée left

Fig. 331 Left to fourth front, pointe on the floor; first movement of demi-ballotté

Fig. 332 Right foot in raccourci

Fig. 333 Original pose, right leg in fourth back

8. Raccourci with the right – développé to fourth back – original pose

Ramassé des pieds and raise the right foot to raccourci.

The arms pass through first to fifth (fig. 332).

Développé, extending the right leg to fourth back.

The arms extend and lower, slightly forward; the palms of the hands turn to face front and downwards, making an original pose (fig. 333).

9. Fifth arabesque ouverte to the left

Turn the torso slightly to the left; demi-plié on the left leg keeping the right, fully stretched, to fourth back.

The left arm extends forward above shoulder height; the right is taken forward, below and parallel to the left.

10. Demi-ballotté with the right leg (relevé-coupé with the left)

Turn the torso to the front opening the arms to second.

Demi-ballotté lowering the straight right leg to fourth back, pointed on the floor. Slowly straighten the left knee, sliding the right pointe along the floor, with the leg still straight, until the foot gradually closes into fifth back.

At the same time, the arms lower to position de repos.

Slow demi-plié and strong relevé onto half or full pointes. Sharply lower the right heel as the left foot draws in placing the heel in front of the right cou de pied.

The arms remain in position de repos.

11. Développé with the left leg to fourth front – relevé and demi-grand rond de jambe en dehors

Ramassé des pieds and développé, extending the left leg to fourth front.

The arms are taken to low fourth right.

Small demi-plié on the right leg and strong relevé onto half pointe or full pointe of the right foot (the right arm is raised to fifth); at the same time, demi-grand rond de jambe taking the left leg to second. The right heel lowers.

The left arm is raised to fifth and the right lowers to second.

At the beginning of the movement the arms are taken to third right and they will end, in third left.

12. Demi-grand rond de jambe en dehors with the left leg – demi-ballotté (relevé-coupé with the right foot)

Demi-grand rond de jambe en dehors taking the left leg to fourth back.

The left arm lowers to second; both arms are now in second.

Small demi-plié on the right leg and demi-ballotté, lowering the straight left leg to fourth back, pointe on the floor.

Slowly straighten the right knee sliding the pointe of the left foot along the floor, with the leg still straight, gradually closing into fifth back.

The arms, coordinating with this movement, lower to position de repos.

Small demi-plié and strong relevé rising onto the half pointes or full pointes of both feet. Coupé, sharply lowering the left heel, placing the right heel in front of the left cou de pied.

The arms remain in position de repos.

END OF THE FIRST PART

SECOND PART
FOUETTÉ BALLOTTÉ EN TOURNANT

1. Développé with the right leg to fourth front

Continue from the last position of the first part. Ramassé des pieds and développé, extending the right leg to fourth front.

The arms go to first (fig. 334).

2. Relevé and demi-grand rond de jambe en dehors with the right leg

Small demi-plié on the left leg; strong relevé rising onto half pointe or full pointe of the left foot; at the same time, demi-grand rond de jambe taking the right leg to second.

The arms open to second; then the right is raised to fifth; the arms are third right (fig. 335).

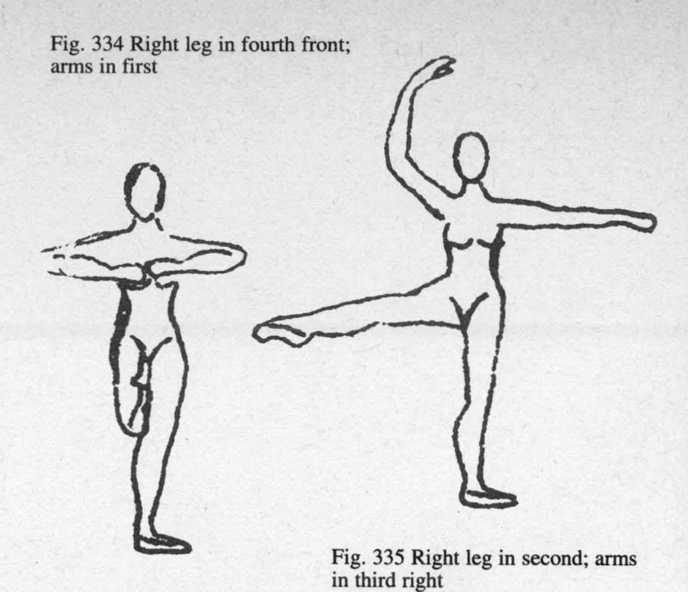

Fig. 334 Right leg in fourth front; arms in first

Fig. 335 Right leg in second; arms in third right

3. Demi-grand rond de jambe en dehors with the right leg and attitude

Demi-grand rond de jambe en dehors taking the right leg to fourth back and curving it into attitude.

The arms remain in third right.

4. Second arabesque croisée to the right

Turn the body to the right. The leg extends to fourth back.

The right arm extends forward to above shoulder height; the left extends back lower and in alignment with the right (fig. 336).

5. Développé with the right leg to fourth front – effacé position

Raccourci with the right leg; développé, extending the leg to fourth front.

The right arm lowers to demi-seconde, completing the position effacé to the right (fig. 337).

6. Turn en dehors to the right

Small demi-plié on the left leg and relevé strongly, rising onto half pointe; rond de jambe, with energy,

Fig. 336 Second arabesque croisée to the right

Fig. 337 Effacé position to the right

Fig. 338 Turn en dehors to the right with the right foot at raccourci

Fig. 339 Fourth arabesque ouverte to the right

taking the right leg to fourth back and into raccourci giving the body impetus to turn en dehors to the right.

The arms lower with energy, to position de repos, contributing impetus (fig. 338).

7. Développé to fourth front – ballotté – fourth arabesque ouverte

After the turn, développé extending the right leg to fourth front. Rise onto half pointe; ballotté, transferring the weight forward onto the right leg which lowers quickly in demi-plié, as the left is raised, extended to fourth back.

The arms are raised to first; during the ballotté, the left arm extends forward above shoulder height and the right is taken back lower, and in line with the left.

The pose is fourth arabesque ouverte (fig. 339).

8. Turn en dehors to the left in attitude

Relevé quickly, rising onto the half pointe of the right foot as the left leg, in fourth back, curves strongly into attitude.

These movements must be executed with great energy in order to give the body impetus to turn en dehors to the left.

The arms rise vigorously to fifth (fig. 340); just before the end of the turn, the right arm lowers to demi-seconde. The turn ends in attitude position (fig. 341).

9. Third arabesque ouverte to the right

Lower the right heel turning the body to the right. The left leg extends to fourth back.

The arms lower through second, softly rising forward once more: the right above shoulder height, the left below and parallel to the right, completing the position, third arabesque ouverte to the right.

10. Ballotté fouetté with the right leg – enveloppé turn ending in attitude

Small demi-plié on the right leg; ballotté, taking the weight back onto the left leg which quickly lowers as the straight right is raised to high fourth front; raccourci and extend to high second.

Fig. 340 Turn en dehors to the left with the left leg in attitude; arms in fifth

Fig. 341 End of turn to the left in position of attitude left

Fouetté, lowering the right leg, with energy, brushing the floor underneath the toes and, continuing the movement, enveloppé bringing the foot in front of raccourci, giving the body impetus to turn en dedans to the left.

Halfway through the turn, the right leg is taken from raccourci front, back into attitude.

The arms open to second, lower through position de repos and, with energy, are raised to fifth.

11. Demi-ballotté with the right leg (relevé-coupé with the left)

After the turn, lower the left heel with a slight plié. Demi-ballotté, lowering the right leg to fourth back, pointed on the floor. Straighten the left knee while the right foot slides along the floor, gradually closing into fifth back.

The arms lower through second and gradually close to position de repos.

Small demi-plié and strong relevé, rising onto the half pointes or full pointes of both feet.

Sharply lower the right heel placing the left heel in front of the right cou de pied.

The arms remain in position de repos.

12. Développé with the left leg to fourth front – grand rond de jambe en dehors – ending

Développé extending the left leg to fourth front. The arms rise to first.

Grand rond de jambe en dehors taking the left leg to fourth back.

The arms open to second.

Demi-plié on the right sliding the left foot along the floor, until it gradually closes in fifth back.

The arms lower to position de repos.

Relevé, rising onto the half pointes or full pointes of both feet.

Lower the heels with a small demi-plié and, one grand changement and one entrechat quatre.

Repeat the whole exercise with the left leg.

EXERCISE 16

GLISSADE – JETÉ – FOUETTÉ

(Score no. 16, 3rd Part)

In this exercise, we have movements which are alternately fast and slow. This accustoms the pupil to sending his muscles the amount of energy required for movements of different qualities.

The muscles are never forced more than is necessary when executing certain movements; in this way the dancer is not needlessly overtired. When he has complete control of all his muscles, he will have made great progress in his training. Only by regulating energy without wasting it, will the dancer have the stamina to arrive at the end of a long, involved exercise, still fresh and in excellent condition.

Recently, the dancer-sportsman has become a frequent sight; he ends his acrobatics with loose hair, perspiring face and body, heaving breast – all testimony to his exertions; this is artistic affectation, hoping to invite sympathy and admiration.

But this is not Dance.

On the contrary, the dancer must always be very careful to hide his fatigue. The audience must be made to believe that almost unnatural beings live and act on stage, that their leaps and turns are due to an imponderable, divine gift which has allowed them to defeat all the laws of gravity.

EXERCISE

Preparation

Stand in the centre of the room with the feet in fifth position, right foot front. Arms in position de repos.

1. Chassé to fourth front and two balancés, backwards and forwards

Small demi-plié and transfer the weight over the right leg as it slides to fourth front; straighten the knees, the left foot remains pointed on the floor, to fourth back.

The arms are taken to half first.

The head turns right (fig. 342).

Balancé back: with the feet remaining in fourth, demi-plié on both legs, lowering the left heel; the weight is taken back onto the left leg. The knees straighten and the right foot remains pointed on the floor, to fourth front.

The arms open to demi-seconde.

The head turns left (fig. 343).

Balancé en avant: with the feet firmly in fourth, demi-plié on both legs, lowering the right heel; the weight is transferred forward onto the right leg. The knees straighten and the left leg remains pointed on the floor, to fourth back.

The arms are raised to first at half height.

The head turns right (fig. 342).

Slide the left foot into fifth back.

The head comes erect.

2. Two glissades to the right with the right leg – jeté with the left and coupé with the right

Two petites glissades with the right leg to the right (closing fifth back and fifth front).

Jeté to second with the left leg (the right foot is raised behind).

Coupé and step sharply onto the right foot placing the heel of the left foot in front of the right cou de pied.

The arms remain in position de repos during the glissades and open to demi-seconde during the jeté, returning to position de repos.

The head turns left for the first glissade, for the second glissade, it turns right.

3. Développé with the left leg into fourth front croisé

Développé extending the left leg to high fourth front.

With small movements of the right foot, turn the body slightly to the right. The position becomes: quatrième en avant croisée, to the right.

The arms rise to first; then the right goes to fifth, and the left to demi-seconde (fig. 344).

Fig. 344 Quatrième en avant croisée to the right

Fig. 342 With the feet in fourth, balancé forward

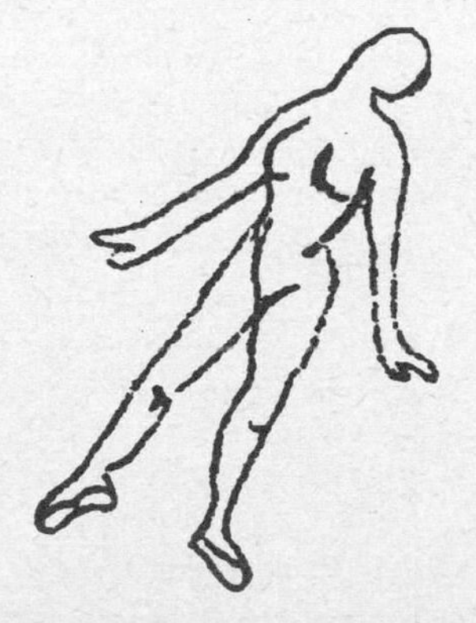

Fig. 343 With the feet in fourth, balancé back

Fig. 345 Twisting into renversé turn to the left

4. Détourné d'Adage to the right ending in attitude left facing front

With small movements of the supporting leg, slowly turn the body to the right with détourné d'Adage: during the turn of the body, the left leg which is in fourth front, remains in this position, rotating gradually until it is in fourth back; then it curves into attitude.

After the détourné d'Adage, the body will be attitude left, facing front. The arms synchronise with the body as it turns; the right arm lowers to demi-seconde, the left is raised to fifth completing the position, attitude left.

5. Slowly arch back twisting into renversé left

Standing in attitude left, facing front; slowly arch the torso back bending as far as possible over the right side.

The left arm remains in fifth and follows the movement of the torso. The right gradually curves into first (fig. 345).

The movement is similar to renversé turn, but without the turn.

Just as slowly, the torso recovers to the upright position; the left foot gradually passes through raccourci and extends quickly to high second.

The arms coordinate with the movement of the leg, passing together through first position and opening strongly to second.

6. Rond de jambe en l'air – enveloppé turn en dedans to the right continued and ended in attitude left

Double rond de jambe en l'air en dedans followed by an energetic movement giving the impetus for two enveloppé turns to the right.

During the first turn the left foot remains in raccourci devant; in the second turn, the left leg passes back into attitude.

In the first temps, the arms lower vigorously to position de repos, contributing more impetus; as the left leg goes into attitude during the second turn, the arms are raised through first; the left arm continues to fifth, the right opens to demi-seconde.

7. Fouetté – développé the left leg to fourth back – first arabesque

Lower the left leg, straight; fouetté behind brushing the foot along the floor underneath the toes, bending the knee; at the same time turning the body to the right. Continue the movement, bringing the left foot to raccourci; développé extending the leg to fourth back.

The arms lower and are raised once more: the right extends forward above shoulder height, the left extends back lower and in alignment with the right to complete the position of first arabesque ouverte to the right.

8. Renversé turn to the left with pas de bourrée détourné – battement tendu in second

Renversé turn to the left: push the left leg back and curve it; at the same time, incline the torso strongly over the right side and arch backwards. This twisting movement gives the body the impetus to turn left. When coming off balance, lower the left leg and end the movement with pas de bourrée détourné to the left closing in fifth, right foot front (fig. 345).

As the turn commences, the left arm rises, from behind, into fifth; the right bends strongly into first.

Fig. 346 Battement tendu of the right leg to second

Fig. 347 Inclining the torso over the left side

Continuing the movement, the left lowers to first to join the right; together they move into position de repos.

Battement tendu, opening the right foot to second.

The arms remain in position de repos (fig. 346).

9. Développé with the right leg to second and tip the torso over the left side

Développé with the right leg to high second; the torso, from the waist up, gradually inclines over the left side.

The arms pass through first to fifth.

The head turns left (fig. 347).

The torso, gradually recovers to the upright position; the straight right leg lowers to hip height, following the movement of the torso.

The arms open gradually, lowering to demi-seconde.

10. Pas de bourrée right – battement tendu into second – échappé sur les pointes in fourth – half turn to the right sur les pointes

The torso comes erect, the right leg continues to lower until it closes behind in fifth with a small demi-plié on the left leg; straightening the knee, rise onto the half pointes of both feet. This movement commences the first part of pas de bourrée which ends with the right foot in fifth front.

Battement tendu, taking the left foot to fifth front.

Échappé to fourth onto the pointes, very crossed to the right diagonal, left foot front.

The arms are raised to low fourth right.

The head turns to the left shoulder (fig. 348).

Still in fourth position on the pointes, make a very sharp half turn to the right towards the left diagonal.

The arms reverse the low fourth so that they are in low fourth left.

The head turns to the right shoulder (fig. 349).

Repeat the exercise with the left leg.

EXERCISE 17

GLISSADE CECCHETTI

(Score no. 17, 3rd Part)

Most of the following exercises continue to practice, in various arrangements, the movements and levels previously described.

By varying the difficulty in the execution of the exercise, the pupil can complete his training.

Years of work and effort have gone into perfecting all the movements; these have been studied individually and each one is there for a specific reason. These are the strengths which have made the Cecchetti Method insuperable and the part of the adagi is one of the masterpieces of this School. The greatness of the Maestro is seen in the Adagio section; it is principally through this that Pavlova, Karsavina, Preobrajenskaja and all the great dancers of previous generations were created.

EXERCISE

Preparation

Stand in the centre of the room with the feet in fifth position, right foot front. Arms in position de repos.

1. Glissade to second with the right leg and jeté sideways to the right in first arabesque

Glissade with the right leg to second, closing the left behind in fifth. The arms open slightly and then return to position de repos.

The head inclines left.

Jeté springing sideways, throwing the right leg to second; at the same time, the left leg is raised to fourth back and the body turns to the right.

The right arm extends forward above shoulder height; the left extends back, lower and in alignment with the right.

Alighting, the position is first arabesque ouverte to the right, standing on the right leg.

2. Enveloppé turn continued in first arabesque

Turn the body to the front. The arms go to second.

Enveloppé with the left leg; the rond de jambe

movement gives the body the impetus to turn en dedans to the right.

The arms are lowered with energy into position de repos contributing more force to the turn.

After the first turn in the position described above, without a pause, the turn continues in first arabesque. In order to take this position, the left foot, from raccourci front, extends to fourth back with développé, as the body continues turning.

The right arm is forward, above shoulder height and the left back, lower and in alignment with the right.

Fig. 348 Échappé in fourth sur les pointes; ready to turn right

Fig. 349 Standing on the full pointes in fourth after the turn to the right

N.B. We repeat: the two turns must be done consecutively ("filés"), without a pause; one in enveloppé position, and the other in first arabesque. The complete turn ends in first arabesque ouverte to the right (fig. 350).

3. "Cecchetti" reposing position

From first arabesque, facing right, the torso turns to the front and the arms are brought into second; the left leg remains in fourth back.

Lower the arms and raise them again to first. Then, the right arm draws in; the fingers are placed on the right cheek and the elbow rests on the back of the left hand; the left arm is bent, crossed underneath and close to the breast.

The head turns left (fig. 351).

4. First arabesque ouverte to the right

Turn the torso to the right; extend the right arm forward and the left back, once more taking the pose: first arabesque ouverte to the right (fig. 350).

5. Facing front with the left leg in high second

Turn the torso front once more, bringing the arms to second.

The left leg stays in fourth back, then rotates until it is in high second position.

6. Développé with the left leg to fourth front

Bring the left foot to raccourci and développé to fourth front.

The arms are lowered through position de repos and raised to first.

7. Fouetté turn to the left

Small demi-plié on the right leg.

The right arm opens to second (the arms are in low fourth right).

Strong relevé onto the half pointe or full pointe of the right foot and execute one fouetté turning left: very energetically, take the left leg to second giving the body the impetus to turn en dehors to the left. During the turn, the left leg executes grand rond de jambe en l'air en dehors extending strongly, once more, to second at the end of the turn; the right heel lowers sharply.

8. Attitude with the arms in fifth en couronne

After the fouetté turned with the left leg extended in second, demi-grand rond de jambe immediately, taking the leg to fourth back and curve it in to attitude.

The arms are raised into fifth en couronne.

Fig. 350 First arabesque open to the right after the complex turn

Fig. 351 "Cecchetti" reposing position to the right

9. Third arabesque croisée to the left

Turn the body to the left. Extend the left leg to fourth back and lower the arms; the right above the left which is parallel (palms of the hands facing down).

10. First arabesque croisée – détourné d'Adage to the left, left leg passes to fourth front

The left arm extends behind, lower and in line with the right, completing the position: first arabesque croisée to the left. Détourné d'Adage, slowly turning the body to the left (fig. 352). The left leg remains extended to fourth back; as the body turns, it rotates into fourth front (fig. 353).

The arms are taken to second.

11. Ballotté – fourth arabesque ouverte to the left – pas de bourrée

The left leg is in high fourth front; rise onto the right half pointe and, ballotté (slightly towards left), transferring the weight onto the left leg which lowers quickly in demi-plié, as the straight right leg is raised to fourth back.

The right arm is taken forward above shoulder height and the left back lower and in line with the right.

The position is: fourth arabesque ouverte to the left.

Straighten the left leg; the right lowers into fifth back into the first part of pas de bourrée; rise onto the half pointes and end the pas de bourrée to the left with the right foot front.

12. Grande préparation to second for pirouette and two turns en dehors to the right

Grande préparation to second for pirouette with the right leg.

The arms end their movement in low fourth left.

Two or more turns en dehors to the right with the right foot on the front of the left cou de pied.

Échappé sharply to fourth, left foot front, to end the pirouette.

During the turn, the arms are in position de repos; they end in first position, slightly bent with the palms facing up.

Repeat the whole exercise with the left leg.

EXERCISE 18

DEMI-ROND DE JAMBE

(Score no. 18, 3rd Part)

The only observation to be made in this exercise is the execution, in two parts, of grand rond de jambe en dehors. Throughout the movement of the working leg, the supporting leg bends and straightens twice: once as the leg passes from fourth front to second, and the second time when the leg passes from second to fourth back.

EXERCISE

Preparation

Stand in the centre of the room with the feet in fifth position, right foot front. Arms in position de repos.

Fig. 352 Beginning détourné d'Adage in first arabesque croisée to the left

Fig. 353 Détourné d'Adage to the left ends with the left to fourth front with the body to the right

1. Plié – relevé-coupé

Full plié and recover, completely straightening the knees.

Demi-plié and relevé onto half or full pointes of both feet.

The body turns slightly to the left; the head inclines right.

After a short pause, move the feet with pas de bourrée sur la place; coupé, sharply lowering the left heel placing the heel of the right foot in front of the left cou de pied.

The arms are in position de repos.

2. Développé with the right leg to fourth front and demi-rond de jambe

Développé the right leg to fourth front.

The arms are raised to first.

Demi-plié on the left leg (fig. 354); slowly straighten the knee as the right leg is taken to second with demi-rond de jambe en dehors.

The arms open to second (fig. 355).

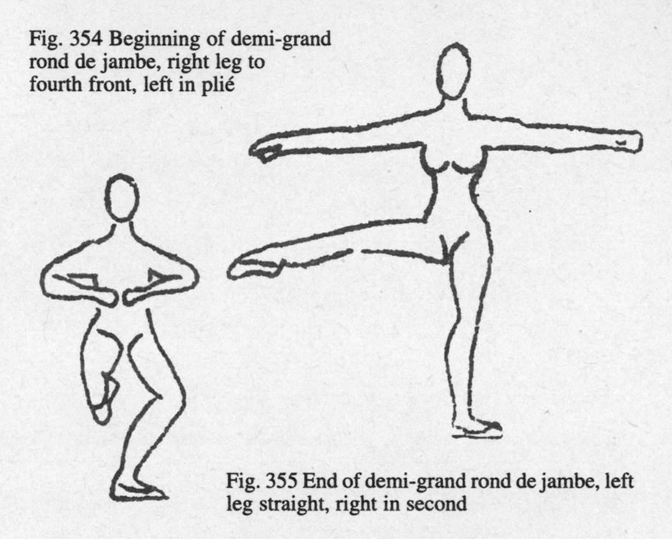

Fig. 354 Beginning of demi-grand rond de jambe, right leg to fourth front, left in plié

Fig. 355 End of demi-grand rond de jambe, left leg straight, right in second

3. Demi-grand rond de jambe en dehors from second to fourth back with the right leg

Demi-plié on the left leg (fig. 356) and straighten slowly as the right leg is taken from second to fourth back with one more demi-grand rond de jambe.

The arms remain in second (fig. 357).

4. Grand rond de jambe en dedans with the right leg, raccourci with the right and développé to fourth back

One complete slow grand rond de jambe en dedans taking the right leg from fourth back to fourth front; raccourci and développé, extending the right leg once more to fourth back.

The arms lower through position de repos and rise once more, to open again to second.

5. Grand rond de jambe en dedans with the right leg

Full grand rond de jambe en dedans taking the right leg, once more, to fourth front.

The arms remain in second.

Fig. 356 Beginning of demi-grand rond de jambe, right leg in second, left in plié

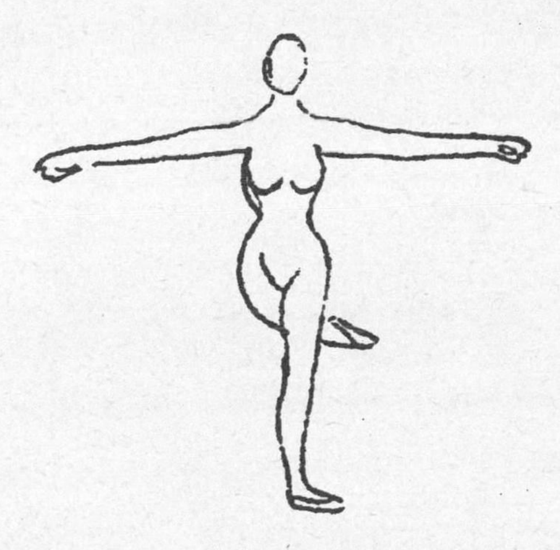

Fig. 357 End of demi-grand rond de jambe, right to fourth back, left leg straight

6. Renversé turn to the right followed by pas de bourrée

Small demi-plié on the left leg and straighten it with energy; at the same time, strong grand rond de jambe en dehors with the right leg, giving the body the impetus for renversé turn to the right.

As the torso twists, the right arm rises from behind,

Fig. 358 Renversé turn to the right

passes through fifth, and lowers to first; it is joined by the left arm which had bent vigorously into first, and together they go to position de repos (fig. 358).

After the renversé turn, pas de bourrée to recover balance; close in fifth, left foot front.

The arms open and close once more into position de repos.

Repeat the whole exercise with the left.

EXERCISE 19

COUPÉ – FOUETTÉ SIMPLE

(Score no. 19, 3rd Part)

The peculiarity of this exercise, which makes it slightly different from the others, is the continuous, fast execution of the various movements, while maintaining the smoothness of the adagio rhythm.

The exercise has a musical accompaniment which suits each movement perfectly.

EXERCISE

Preparation

Stand in the centre of the room with the feet in fifth position, right foot front. Arms in position de repos.

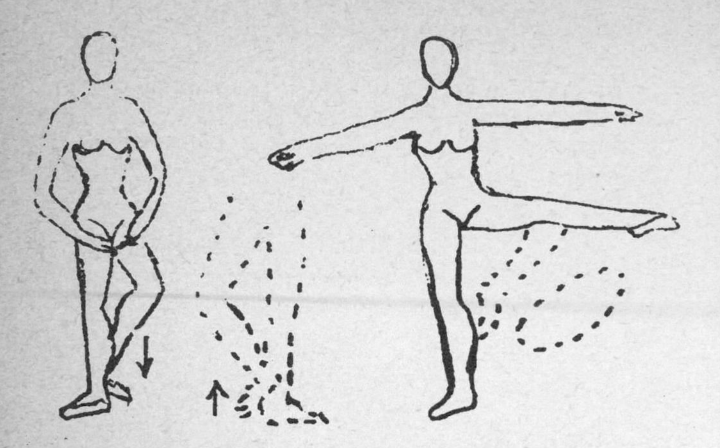

Fig. 359 Coupé behind with the left foot

Fig. 360 Left leg stretched in second and double rond de jambe en l'air

1. Coupé with the left foot

Small demi-plié on both legs. Slightly raise the left foot behind; lower the left foot sharply, straightening the knee; placing the right heel in front of the left cou de pied.

The arms remain in position de repos (fig. 359).

2. Développé with the right leg to fourth front

Ramassé des pied, and développé, extending the right leg to fourth front.

The arms are raised to first.

3. Ballotté to fourth front with the right leg

Slight plié on the left leg; ballotté transferring the weight forward onto the straight right leg as the left leg is raised, fully stretched, to fourth back.

4. Raccourci with the left leg and extend the leg to second – two ronds de jambe en l'air with the left leg

Immediately, bring the left foot to raccourci, extend to second and execute two quick ronds de jambe en l'air en dehors ending in second (fig. 360).

The arms open to second, then lower through position de repos and rise once more through first to second.

5. Fouetté and enveloppé turn to the right – extend to second and close in fifth

Immediately, with an energetic fouetté, the left leg lowers in front; the underside of the toes brush the floor, giving the body the impetus for enveloppé turn to the right.

The arms are lowered strongly to position de repos, contributing more energy.

After the turn, the left leg extends to second.

The arms pass through first, coordinating with the movement of the leg, and open to second.

Without a pause, the straight left leg lowers to fifth back.

The arms lower to position de repos.

6. Coupé with the right foot

Small demi-plié on both legs. Slightly raise the right foot in front; sharply lower the right foot straightening the knee, placing the left heel behind the right cou de pied.

The arms remain in position de repos.

7. Développé with the left leg to fourth back and ballotté to fourth back

Ramassé des pieds and développé, extending the left leg to fourth back.

The arms are raised to first.

Small demi-plié on the right; ballotté throwing the leg backwards off balance transfer the weight onto the straight left leg as the right is raised to high fourth front.

The arms open to second.

8. Raccourci and extend the right leg to second – two ronds de jambe en l'air

From fourth position front, raccourci and extend the right leg to high second. Execute two rapid ronds de jambe en l'air en dehors, ending in second.

The arms lower through position de repos, raised through first to open once more in second.

9. Fouetté and enveloppé turn to the left – extend to second

Immediately, with an energetic fouetté, lower the straight right leg; the underside of the toes brush the floor, giving the body impetus for enveloppé turn en dedans to the left.

The arms lower strongly into position de repos contributing more force.

After the turn, the right leg extends to second.

The arms pass through first, coordinating with the movement of the leg, and open to second.

10. Relevé and close the right leg into fifth back

With the right leg extended to high second, small plié on the left and relevé onto the half pointe or full pointe of the left foot.

Lower the left heel as the straight right leg lowers into fifth back.

The arms lower to position de repos.

Repeat the whole exercise with the left leg.

EXERCISE 20

GRAND FOUETTÉ À L'ARABESQUE

(Score no. 20, 3rd Part)

In this adagio, movements which have already been described are repeated in alternate and different ways.

This exercise is executed with the right leg and repeated immediately on the left leg, concluding with a single coda.

EXERCISE

Preparation

Stand in the centre of the room with the feet in fifth position, right foot front. Arms in position de repos.

1. Plié

Full plié and recover slowly, straightening the knees completely.

2. Relevé-coupé with the left foot

Relevé onto half or full pointes of both feet. The body turns a little to the left diagonal.

The head inclines slightly to the right.

After a short pause, the feet move with pas de bourrée sur la place.

Coupé, sharply lowering the left heel placing right heel in front of the left cou de pied.

The arms remain in position de repos.

3. Développé with the right leg to fourth front

Ramassé des pieds with the right; développé, extending the right leg to high fourth front.

The arms are raised to first.

4. Grand rond de jambe en dehors – raccourci and développé with the right leg

Small plié on the left; grand rond de jambe en dehors slowly straightening the left leg; the right leg moves from high fourth front passes through second to high fourth back.

The arms open to second.

Raccourci and développé with the right leg to high second.

The arms remain in second.

5. Fouetté and enveloppé turn with the right leg – fourth position front croisé with the right leg

Fouetté, strongly lowering the straight right leg in front; the underside of the toes brush the floor giving the body impetus for enveloppé turn en dedans to the left.

The arms lower strongly to position de repos contributing more impetus.

End the turn facing the left diagonal; développé extending the right leg to fourth front, ending in the pose quatrième en avant croisée to the left.

The arms are raised through first, then the left goes to fifth and the right opens to demi-seconde (fig. 361).

6. Détourné d'Adage to the left – first arabesque croisée

With small movements of the supporting left foot, turn the body slowly with détourné d'Adage to the left

Fig. 361 Fourth front croisé to the right

Fig. 362 After the détourné d'Adage, first arabesque croisée to the right

until it faces the right wall; the right leg rotates, remaining extended and pointed to the left wall.

The left arm lowers and extends forward above shoulder height; the right remains back, lower and in line with the left. The pose is first arabesque croisée to the right (fig. 362).

7. Demi-grand rond de jambe en dedans with the right leg – fouetté and enveloppé turn to the left

Slow demi-grand rond de jambe taking the right leg from fourth back to second.

The arms go to second.

With an energetic fouetté, the right foot lowers in front; the underside of the toes brush the floor, giving the body impetus for enveloppé turn en dedans to the left.

The arms lower and close strongly into position de repos, contributing to the impetus.

8. Développé with the right leg to fourth back and grand rond de jambe en dedans

After the turn, raccourci of the right leg and développé, extending the leg to fourth back.

The arms are raised to first.

Grand rond de jambe en dedans taking the right leg slowly from fourth back, through second to fourth front.

The arms open to second.

9. Lower the right leg to fourth front and grand rond de jambe à terre en dehors

Slowly lower the right leg to fourth front, pointed on the floor; demi-plié on the left leg.

The arms rise through first; the left opens to second (low fourth left).

The head inclines to the right shoulder.

Grand rond de jambe à terre en dehors, keeping the pointe on the floor, taking the right leg to fourth back.

At the same time, the left arm curves slowly into first and the right opens to second.

The head turns to the left shoulder.

Slowly straighten the left knee while the right foot, sliding the pointe along the floor, closes behind in fifth.

The arms lower to position de repos.

10. Relevé and lower the heels

Small demi-plié and relevé, rising onto half pointes or full pointes.

Lower the heels, relaxing the knees.

The arms remain in position de repos.

N.B. Repeat the whole exercise from no. 1 to no. 10 with the left leg; then continue with the coda which concludes and completes the whole exercise.

CODA

Preparation

After the exercise has been executed with the left leg also, the feet are in fifth, right foot front. The arms in position de repos.

1. Fourth position of the feet, left foot behind, pointed on the floor

Small demi-plié and transfer the weight over the right leg as it slides to fourth front; at the same time the knees straighten once more so that the straight left leg remains pointed to fourth back, on the floor (fig. 363).

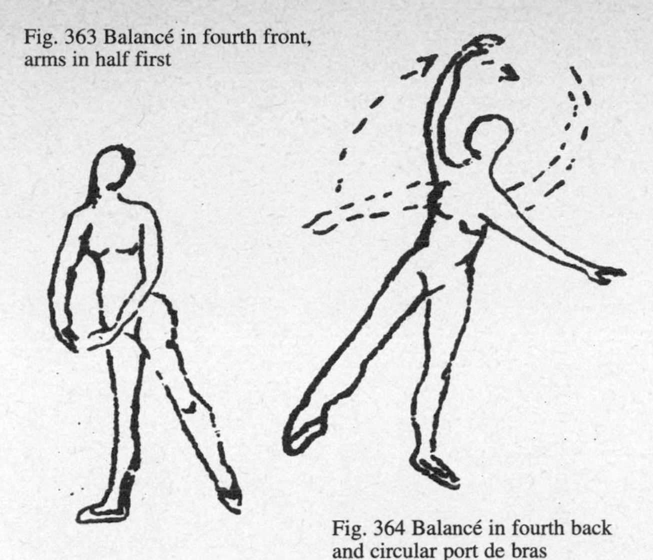

Fig. 363 Balancé in fourth front, arms in half first

Fig. 364 Balancé in fourth back and circular port de bras

The arms are raised to half first.

Make the same movement in reverse, with a swaying movement, taking the weight onto the back left leg. The straight right leg remains pointed to fourth front, on the floor.

At the same time, the arms execute a circular port de bras: the left arm rises to fifth and the right to demi-seconde. Then the left lowers to demi-seconde and the right rises to fifth (fig. 364).

Sharply lower the right heel; demi-plié with the feet in fourth and the weight evenly over both legs.

The right arm lowers to first. The arms are in low fourth left.

2. Enveloppé turn to the right

Quick movement en dedans with the left leg; this gives the body the impetus for enveloppé turn en dedans to the right on the half pointe of the right foot; the heel of the left foot is in front of the left cou de pied.

The arms go strongly to position de repos, contributing to the impetus.

3. Glissé with the left to fourth front – enveloppé turn en dedans to the left continued into and ending in attitude

After the enveloppé turn en dedans to the right, lower the left foot in fifth front. Small demi-plié and transfer the weight onto the left leg as it slides, with glissé to fourth front; at the same time, the knees straighten once more, leaving the right foot pointed to fourth back, on the floor (fig. 365).

The arms open to demi-seconde.

With an energetic enveloppé movement, the right foot goes to raccourci front, giving the body impetus for enveloppé turn en dedans to the left on the half pointe of the left foot.

During the turn, the right foot passes through raccourci to attitude position.

As the turn commences, the arms close strongly into position de repos; during the turn, the right arm is raised to fifth, the left goes to demi-seconde; the position is attitude right (fig. 366).

4. Développé with the right leg to second

After the turn in attitude, raccourci of the right leg and développé, extending the leg to second.

The arms lower to position de repos, pass through first and open to second.

Fig. 365 Balancé in fourth front, arms in half first

Fig. 366 Double turn en dedans to the left, passing to attitude right

5. Relevé – lower the right leg into fifth front

Relevé onto the half pointe of the left foot with the right leg in high second. Slowly lower the straight right leg to fifth front and slowly lower the left heel.

The arms lower gradually to position de repos.

EXERCISE 21

HUIT RELEVÉS

(Score no. 21, 3rd Part)

This exercise completes the study of relevés in the Adagio section.

We see the importance of relevés when we recall just how extensively they have been described in adagi no. 1 (Trois Relevés), and no. 2 (Cinq Relevés).

This adagio combines the relevé movement with the eight basic poses in dance (Book 3, Part 1). These develop slowly throughout the exercise so that they can be executed exactly and with perfect placing.

The direction of each position must be taken with great attention, especially certain poses which have been named according to their direction.

EXERCISE

Preparation

Stand in the centre of the room with the feet in fifth position, right foot front. Arms in position de repos.

1. First relevé: développé to croisé en avant

Turn the body diagonally left. Ramassé des pieds and développé extending the right leg to fourth front.

The torso from the waist up turns front; the body inclines slightly back; the head turns slightly to the right shoulder.

The arms are raised to first; the left continues to fifth and the right opens to second (the arms are now in third left).

Relevé in this pose, croisé en avant, rising onto half pointe or full pointe of the left foot (fig. 367).

Lower the left heel, slowly lower the right leg to fourth front, pointe on the floor; draw the foot in gradually, sliding the pointe along the floor placing the heel onto the left cou de pied.

The arms lower to position de repos (fig. 368).

Fig. 367 First relevé in the position croisée en avant

Fig. 368 Facing front with the right foot on the left cou de pied

2. Second relevé: développé to écarté

Turn the body to the left diagonal. Ramassé des pieds, développé extending the right leg to high second.

The head turns right.

The arms are raised to first; then the right continues into fifth and the left opens to second (the arms are third left).

Relevé in the pose écartée, rising onto half pointe or full pointe of the left foot (fig. 369).

Then, lower the left heel and slowly lower the right leg to second, pointed on the floor. Draw the foot in gradually, sliding the pointe along the floor placing the heel in front of the left cou de pied.

The arms lower to position de repos (fig. 368).

3. Third relevé: développé in position en quatrième en avant

The body faces front. Ramassé des pieds, développé extending the right leg to high fourth front.

The arms are raised through first and open to second.

Relevé in the pose en quatrième en avant, rising onto half pointe or full pointe of the left foot (fig. 370).

Lower the left heel and lower the right leg to fourth front, pointe on the floor. Draw the foot in gradually, sliding the pointe along the floor and placing the heel in front of the left cou de pied.

The arms lower to position de repos (fig. 368).

4. Fourth relevé: développé to effacé

Turn the body to the right diagonal. Ramassé des pieds, développé, extending the right leg into fourth front.

The head turns to the left.

The arms are raised to first, then the left continues into fifth and the right to second (a little low); the arms are third left.

Relevé onto half pointe or full pointe of the left foot in effacé position (fig. 371).

Lower the left heel and slowly lower the right leg to fourth front, pointe on the floor. Draw the foot in gradually, sliding the pointe along the floor, placing the heel in front of the left cou de pied.

The arms lower to position de repos (fig. 368).

5. Fifth relevé: développé à la seconde

The body faces front. Ramassé des pieds, développé extending the right leg to high second.

Fig. 369 Second relevé in the position écartée

Fig. 370 Third relevé in the position en quatrième en avant

The arms are raised through first to second.

Relevé onto half pointe or full pointe of the left foot in the pose à la seconde (fig. 372).

Lower the left heel and slowly lower the right leg to second, pointed on the floor. Draw the foot in gradually, sliding the pointe along the floor, placing the heel behind the left cou de pied.

The arms lower to position de repos.

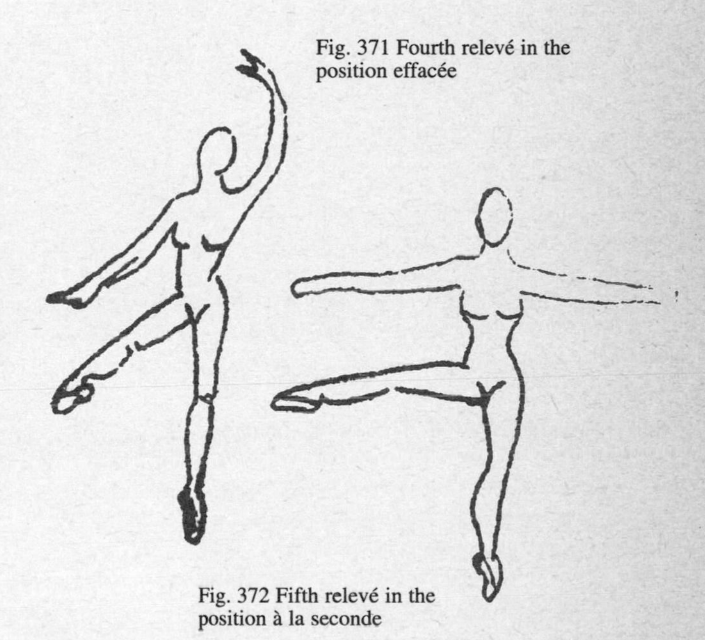

Fig. 371 Fourth relevé in the position effacée

Fig. 372 Fifth relevé in the position à la seconde

6. Sixth relevé: développé to épaulé position

Turn the body to face the left wall. Ramassé des pieds, développé extending the right leg to high fourth back.

The head turns to the right shoulder.

The right arm is raised straight forward above shoulder height, the left is raised behind, lower and in line with the right.

Relevé in the pose épaulée, on half pointe or full pointe of the left foot (fig. 373).

Lower the left heel and slowly lower the right leg to fourth back, pointed on the floor. Draw the foot in gradually, sliding the pointe along the floor, placing the heel behind the left cou de pied.

The arms lower to position de repos.

7. Seventh relevé: développé à la quatrième en arrière

The body faces front. Ramassé des pieds, développé extending the right leg to high fourth back.

The arms are raised through first to second.

Relevé in the pose à la quatrième en arrière, on half pointe or full pointe of the left foot (fig. 374).

Lower the left heel and slowly lower the right leg to fourth back, pointe on the floor. Draw the foot in gradually, sliding the pointe along the floor, placing the heel behind the left cou de pied.

The arms lower to position de repos.

Fig. 373 Sixth relevé in the position épaulée

Fig. 374 Seventh relevé à la quatrième en arrière

8. Eighth relevé: développé to croisé en arrière

Turn the body to the right diagonal. Ramassé des pieds, développé extending the right leg to fourth back.

Turn the torso slightly to the front, from the waist up, inclining a little to the right.

The head inclines slightly right.

The arms are raised to first, then the left continues to fifth and the right opens and lowers to demi-seconde.

Relevé in the pose croisée en arrière, on half pointe or full pointe of the left foot (fig. 375).

Lower the left heel remaining in the pose croisée en arrière.

N.B. The eighth relevé is executed faster, in one bar only.

9. Ending movement

Still in the pose croisée en arriére, slowly incline the torso over the right side; the right leg curves in behind until it almost touches the head.

Coordinating with this movement, the left arm lowers and bends into first; the right is raised to fifth (fig. 376).

The body gradually returns to the upright position; the right leg lowers into fifth back; the arms lower to position de repos.

Repeat the whole exercise with the left leg.

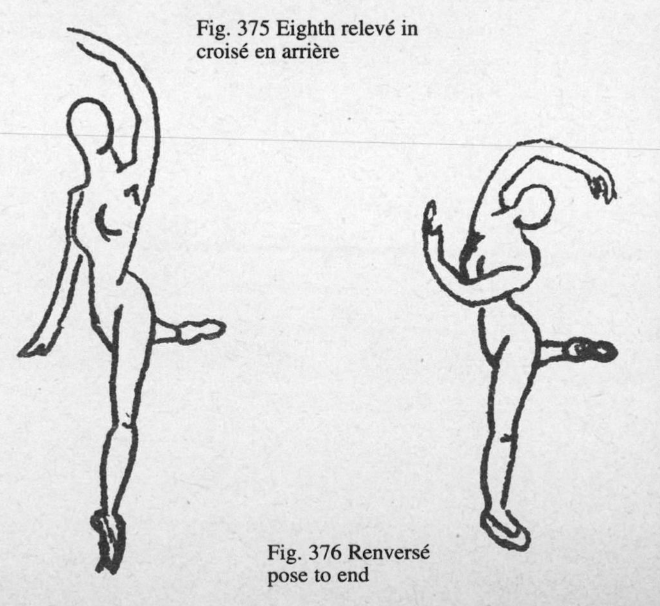

Fig. 375 Eighth relevé in croisé en arrière

Fig. 376 Renversé pose to end

EXERCISE 22

GRAND ROND DE JAMBE EN TOURNANT AVEC RELEVÉ

(Score no. 22, 3rd Part)

In this exercise, grand rond de jambe is once more examined; every possible way of executing this movement is found here linked together in continuous succession.

The exercise ends with two consecutive turns in second and attitude, finishing in fourth arabesque. As these pirouettes are quite difficult, they require a great deal of practice. Performed in this way, they are very effective, with a certain elegance, and are very pleasant to see.

EXERCISE

Preparation

Stand in the centre of the room with the feet in fifth position, right foot front. Arms in position de repos.

1. Plié

Full plié, evenly balanced on both feet.

The right arm remains in position de repos, the left opens to demi-seconde (fig. 377).

Fig. 377 Plié and preparation to turn en dehors to the right

Fig. 378 Tire-bouchon turn to the right

2. Tire-bouchon turn en dehors to the right

Commence rising; close the left arm, with energy, to position de repos giving the body impetus to turn en dehors to the right on the half pointe of the left foot. Immediately, the right foot draws up, placing the heel in front of the left cou de pied; as the left leg gradually straightens during the turn, the right pointe brushes along the left leg until, at the end of the turn, the right thigh is fully turned out in high second and the pointe of the right foot touches the knee of the fully stretched left leg.

The arms are in position de repos (fig. 378).

3. Développé to fourth front and grand rond de jambe en dehors

After the turn, développé extending the right leg to fourth front.

The arms are raised to first.

Small demi-plié on left leg; grand rond de jambe en dehors taking the fully stretched right leg to fourth back.

The left leg straightens as the right leg passes through second.

The arms open to second.

The right leg continues the movement bringing the foot through raccourci to développé, extending the leg to fourth front.

The arms lower through position de repos and rise to first.

4. Relevé and demi-rond de jambe en dehors with the right

Small demi-plié on the left leg and relevé, rising onto half pointe or full pointe of the left foot; at the same time, demi-grand rond de jambe en dehors taking the right leg, fully stretched, from fourth front to second position.

The left heel lowers.

5. Développé with the right leg to fourth back

Raccourci of the right leg and développé, extending the right leg to fourth back.

The arms pass through position de repos to first.

6. Relevé and demi-grand rond de jambe en dedans with the right

Small demi-plié on the left leg and relevé, rising onto half pointe or full pointe; at the same time, demi-grand rond de jambe taking the right leg, fully stretched, from fourth back to second. The left heel lowers.

The arms open to second.

7. Développé with the right leg to fourth front

Raccourci of the right leg and développé, extending the leg to fourth front.

The arms lower through position de repos and rise to first.

8. Turn en dehors to the right with the right leg extended in second

Small demi-plié on the left leg and relevé, rising onto half pointe or full pointe of the left foot. At the same time, strong demi-grand rond de jambe en dehors taking the right leg from fourth front to second giving the body impetus to turn en dehors to the right with the leg extended in second.

The arms open to second, coordinating with the legs, effectively contributing impetus (fig. 379).

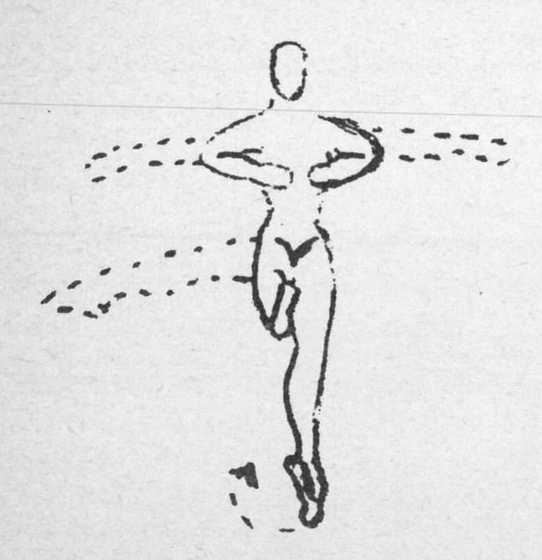

Fig. 379 The right leg to fourth front, demi-rond de jambe and turn to the right with the right leg in second

9. Quick développé to fourth front with the right leg

After the turn in second, lower the left heel; with a quick movement, raccourci of the right leg and développé extending the right leg to fourth front.

The right arm curves into first; the left is in second, taken slightly back (fig. 380).

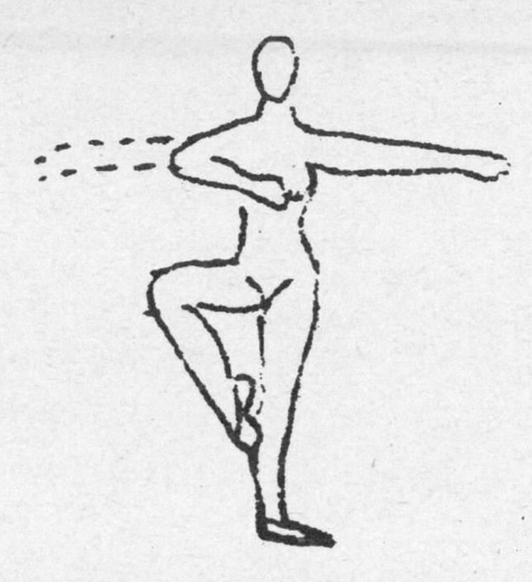

Fig. 380 Right foot to raccourci, extend to fourth front

10. Turn en dehors to the right in attitude

Small demi-plié on the left leg and relevé, rising onto half pointe or full pointe of the left foot; with an energetic grand rond de jambe en dehors the right is taken from fourth front to fourth back and curved into attitude, giving the body impetus to turn en dehors to the right.

The right arm opens strongly through second into fifth; the left, to help the impetus, is taken forward and, passing through position de repos, rises again in demi-seconde.

The turn is in attitude (fig. 381).

11. End in fourth arabesque croisée to the right

End the turn on the right diagonal sharply lowering the left heel with an immediate stop in demi-plié; the right leg extends to fourth back.

The right arm lowers forward, above shoulder height, the left extends back, lower and in line with the right completing the position fourth arabesque croisée to the right (fig. 382).

Fig. 381 Right leg to fourth front and turn to the right in attitude

Fig. 382 The turn ends in fourth arabesque croisée

12. Feet in fifth, left foot front

Turn the body front. Straighten the left knee and lower the right leg into fifth back.
The arms lower to position de repos.

Repeat the whole exercise with the left leg.

EXERCISE 23

PAS DE L'ALLIANCE

(Score no. 23, 3rd Part)

This adagio was composed in London in 1918. Its name was given by Maestro Enrico Cecchetti in homage to the nations who, together with his homeland, fought in the Great War.

Many years later when I began working on this book, and in agreement with my father, music in a more suitable rhythm was chosen for this adagio. Certain modifications were made to the exercise, created in a moment of euphoria, in order to adapt it for teaching purposes.

EXERCISE

Preparation

Stand in the centre of the room with the feet in fifth position, right foot front. Arms in position de repos.

1. Balancé in second with the right leg to the right

In a lively manner, open the right leg to second, pointe on the floor; lower the right heel and transfer the weight onto the right leg, at the same time raising the left heel. Sliding the pointe along the floor, close the left foot in fifth back with demi-plié.
The arms open slightly and close again in position de repos.
The body inclines slightly to the right side.
The head turns and inclines right (figs. 383 and 384).

2. Balancé in second with the left leg to the left

Still in a lively manner, and without a pause, open the left leg to second, pointe on the floor; lower the left heel and transfer the weight onto the left leg. At the same time, the heel of the right foot is raised; then, sliding the pointe along the floor, the right leg closes in fifth front with demi-plié.
The arms open a little and close again to position de repos.
The body inclines slightly to the left side.
The head is inclined and turned left.

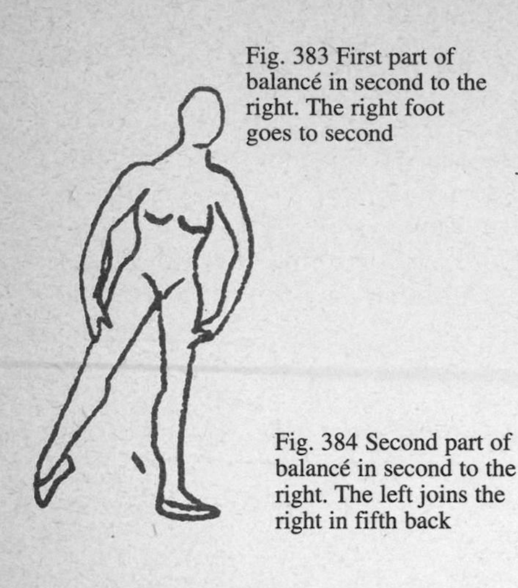

Fig. 383 First part of balancé in second to the right. The right foot goes to second

Fig. 384 Second part of balancé in second to the right. The left joins the right in fifth back

3. Développé – jeté with the right leg and pas de bourrée

Small développé, diagonally right, with the right leg; jeté transferring the weight slightly forward onto the right leg followed immediately by pas de bourrée to the right, ending in fifth, left foot front.

The left arm is taken to demi-seconde, the right is raised through first and the hand taken to the mouth; during the jeté it opens and lowers as if throwing a kiss. Both arms close to position de repos (fig. 385).

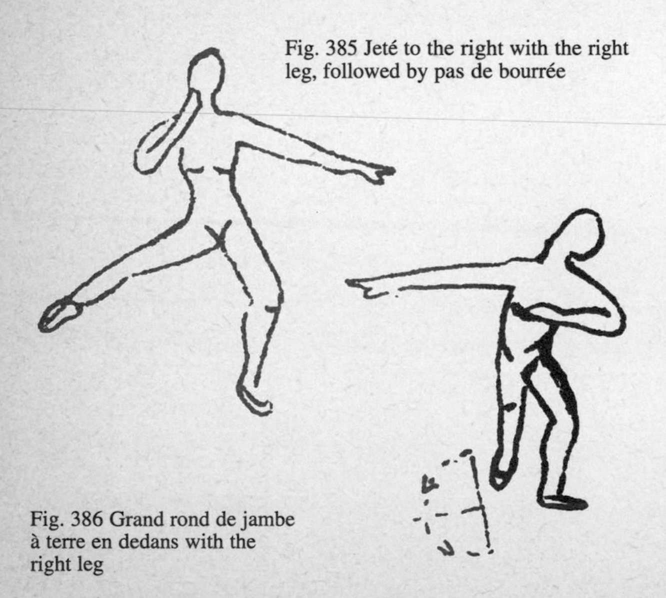

Fig. 385 Jeté to the right with the right leg, followed by pas de bourrée

Fig. 386 Grand rond de jambe à terre en dedans with the right leg

4. Grand rond de jambe à terre en dedans with the right

Demi-plié, extend and reach the right leg to fourth back, pointe on the floor; grand rond de jambe à terre, en dedans, taking the leg to fourth front.

As the movement commences, the arms are taken to low fourth right (fig. 386).

The torso inclines slightly over the left side.

The head inclines left.

During rond de jambe, the right leg moves from fourth back to fourth front; the arms reverse positions from low fourth right to low fourth left, coordinating with the movement of the leg.

The torso gradually inclines over the right side.

The head inclines right.

5. Relevé – pas de bourrée sur la place – coupé

Slowly straighten the left leg; the pointe of the right foot slides along the floor and closes in fifth front.

Relevé, rising onto the pointes, facing the left diagonal.

The arms lower to position de repos; the head turns and inclines over the right shoulder.

Small pas de bourrée sur la place.

Coupé, sharply lowering the right heel placing the left heel on the right cou de pied.

6. Développé to second – slow enveloppé turn ending in attitude

Développé extending the left leg to high second.

The arms are taken to second.

Bring the left foot in strongly, giving the body the impetus for one slow enveloppé turn en dedans to the right; the left foot passes through raccourci to fourth back, ending the turn in attitude.

The arms lower through position de repos; then the left is raised to fifth, the right opens to demi-seconde.

7. Développé with the left leg to second – tipped over

Raccourci of the left leg and développé slowly extending the leg to high second; the torso, following the movement of the leg, slowly tips over to the right, inclining over the right side.

The arms are taken to second and rise gradually to fifth (fig. 387).

Fig. 387 Tipped over the right side, left leg in second

Fig. 388 First arabesque ouverte to the right

8. First arabesque ouverte to the right – relevé – closing into fifth

Turn sharply to the side to face the right wall; the body returns upright.

The right arm extends forward above shoulder height; the left extends back below and in line with, the right.

The position is: first arabesque ouverte to the right (fig. 388).

Relevé in this position onto the right pointe. Lower the left leg to fifth back turning the body front.

The arms lower to position de repos.

9. Développé with the left leg to fourth back – turn en dedans in second and in first arabesque

Développé extending the left leg to high fourth back.

The arms are taken to low fourth left.

Strong demi-grand rond de jambe en dedans, giving the body impetus to turn en dedans to the right with the left leg in high second.

The arms are in second.

After the first turn in second, the pirouette continues, sharply taking the position of first arabesque. End the turns facing left, still in the same position; this is now first arabesque croisée to the left (fig. 389).

10. Position en croisé en avant to the right with the left leg

Standing in first arabesque croisée to the left, sharply turn the body to the left, to face the right wall. During the movement, the left leg remains in the same direction; as the body turns, the leg rotates from fourth back automatically into fourth front.

The right arm rises to fifth, the left is taken to demi-seconde. The pose is en croisé en avant to the right; left leg in high fourth front (fig. 390).

The right arm lowers to second, the left is taken to first (low fourth right).

Fig. 389 First arabesque croisée to the left; execute half turn to the left

Fig. 390 After the half turn, the pose is en croisé en avant to the right, left leg in fourth

11. Jeté, turn in first arabesque, pas de bourrée turning left – renversé turn

Jeté throwing the left leg vigorously to the left giving the body impetus to turn left in first arabesque.

After the turn, lower the right leg; cross the right foot over the left into pas de bourrée turning left.

Raise the left leg to fourth front; grand rond de jambe en dehors giving the body impetus to make one renversé turn, to the left.

The arms open to demi-seconde during jeté; they pass through position de repos, rising to fifth and opening during the renversé turn.

12. Battement tendu – développé to fourth front

Battement tendu to second with the right leg.

Ramassé des pieds, développé extending the right leg to high fourth front.

The arms are raised to first.

13. Grand rond de jambe – tour de promenade – attitude

Slow grand rond de jambe en dehors with the straight right leg.

At the same time, turn the body to the right making one slow tour de promenade to the right. The turn ends taking the body to face front in attitude position.

The arms gradually open to second, then the right rises to fifth.

14. Demi-ballotté – relevé-coupé

Extend the straight right leg to fourth back, on the floor; demi-plié on the left.

Straighten the left knee; the right pointe slides along the floor and closes into fifth back.

Relevé, rising onto the full pointes of both feet.

Coupé, sharply lowering the right heel placing the left heel in front of the right cou de pied.

The arms are taken through second and lower to position de repos.

15. Développé to fourth front

Ramassé des pieds, développé extending the left leg to high fourth front.

The arms are taken to second.

Fig. 391 The right leg extends, the left lowers and closes in fifth front

Fig. 392 On pointes in final pose

16. Ending in fifth and relevé

Slow demi-plié on the right; straighten the right as the straight left leg gradually lowers and, sliding the pointe along the floor, closes into fifth front (fig. 391).

The arms lower slowly to position de repos.

Relevé sharply onto full pointes, turning the body to the right diagonal; the left shoulder goes forward and the head turns to the left shoulder.

During the relevé, the arms rise sharply, extended with the hands turned outwards and the palms facing down (fig. 392).

Repeat the whole exercise with the left leg.

EXERCISE 24

DEMI-CONTRETEMPS D'ADAGE

(Score no. 24, 3rd Part)

Last of the adagi in this method, it takes its name from the first movement of the exercise. This concludes the study of all the adagio movements up until now, analyzed and examined in every way possible.

EXERCISE

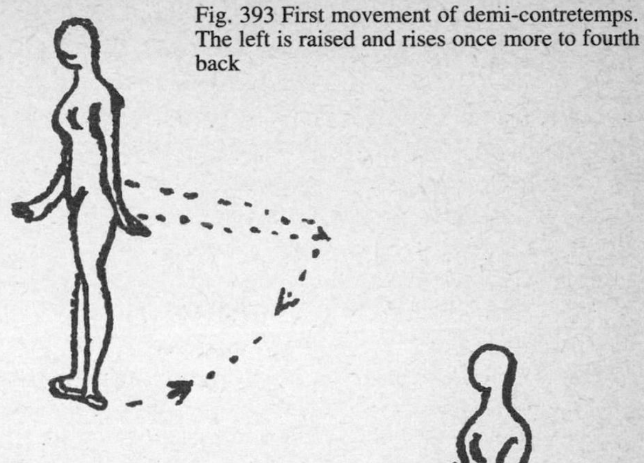

Fig. 393 First movement of demi-contretemps. The left is raised and rises once more to fourth back

Preparation

Stand in the centre of the room with the feet in fifth position, right foot front. Arms in position de repos.

1. Demi-contretemps d'Adage with the left leg

Rise onto half pointe of both feet, knees fully stretched.

Raise the left leg straight to fourth back at half height; lower the leg until it beats and bounces off the calf of the right leg and returns immediately to high fourth back (fig. 393).

Open the arms slightly to demi-seconde.

From fourth back, the left leg lowers, passing through first to fourth front, on the floor; at the same time, lower the right heel and demi-plié.

The arms close into position de repos (fig. 394).

Transfer the weight onto the left leg and straighten the knees. The right foot remains pointed to fourth back, on the floor. Close the right foot into fifth back.

The arms lower to position de repos.

Fig. 394 Second movement of demi-contrtemps. The left passes through first to fourth front

2. Relevé-coupé

Relevé, rising onto half pointes or full pointes. Coupé, sharply lowering the left heel placing the right heel behind the left cou de pied.

The arms are lowered to position de repos.

3. Développé to second – rond de jambe en l'air and attitude with the right leg

Facing front, développé extending the right leg to high second; two ronds de jambe en l'air en dehors. Begin a third continued into développé taking the right leg to fourth back, curving into attitude.

The arms are raised through first and open to second; the right is raised to fifth completing the position, attitude right.

4. Demi-ballotté with the right leg

Demi-plié on the left leg; the right lowers to fourth back, pointe on the floor.

Slowly straighten the left leg; the straight right leg, brushing the pointe along the floor, closes into fifth back.

The arms lower to position de repos.

Relevé rising onto half pointes or full pointes; coupé, sharply lowering the right heel, placing the left heel in front of the right cou de pied.

5. Petits battements sur le cou de pied with the left – extend the left leg and bring it once more in front of the right

Execute several rapid petits battements sur le cou de pied, with the left foot; extend the left leg to second, at half height and bring it in again, replacing the heel in front of the right cou de pied.

The arms open slightly as the left leg extends to second, closing immediately to position de repos.

6. Two développés slightly faster with the left leg to second and to fourth front

Développé extending the left leg to high second. The arms are raised through first to second.

Lower the straight left leg to second, pointe on the

floor; draw the foot in and développé once more; this time the leg extends to high fourth front.

The arms are taken to fourth left (fig. 395).

Lower the left leg, straight, to fourth front, pointe on the floor; sliding the foot along the floor, close in fifth front.

The arms lower into position de repos.

7. Relevé sur les pointes and make a small circle turning to the left

Relevé, rising onto the pointes; with quite fast, petits pas de bourré marchés, move in a small circle to the left; the radius of the circle is around 2 feet (about 75 cm) (fig. 396).

The arms are raised to first; the left continues to fifth, the right opens to second. During the turn the arms make a circular port de bras; they finish in position de repos.

8. Demi-contretemps d'Adage with the right leg

Rise onto half pointes of both feet, legs fully stretched. Raise the straight right leg to fourth back at half height; lower the leg until it beats and bounces off the calf of the left leg, returning immediately to high fourth back.

Open the arms a little to demi-seconde.

From fourth back, the right leg lowers, passing through first to fourth front, on the floor.

At the same time, lower the left heel and demi-plié on both legs.

The arms close to position de repos.

Transfer the weight onto the right leg and straighten the knees; the left foot remains pointed to fourth back, on the floor then closes into fifth back.

The arms are raised through low first and open to demi-seconde.

9. Enveloppé turn en dedans to the right ending in attitude

With an enveloppé movement, raccourci devant of the left leg, giving the body impetus to turn en dedans to the right; before the end of the turn, the left foot passes through raccourci to fourth back in attitude.

The arms close strongly to position de repos; the left arm is raised to fifth, the right to demi-seconde to complete the attitude position.

10. Grand rond de jambe en dedans with the left leg

Grand rond de jambe en dedans taking the left leg to fourth front.

The arms open to second.

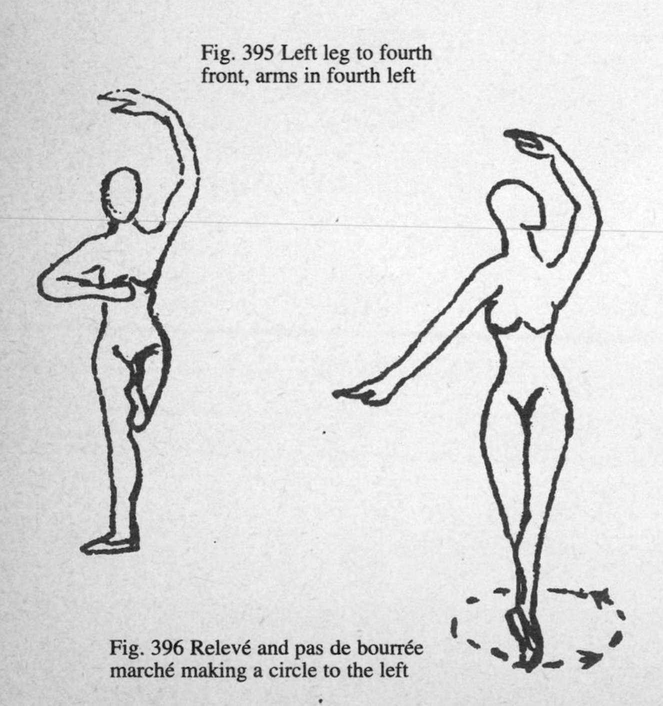

Fig. 395 Left leg to fourth front, arms in fourth left

Fig. 396 Relevé and pas de bourrée marché making a circle to the left

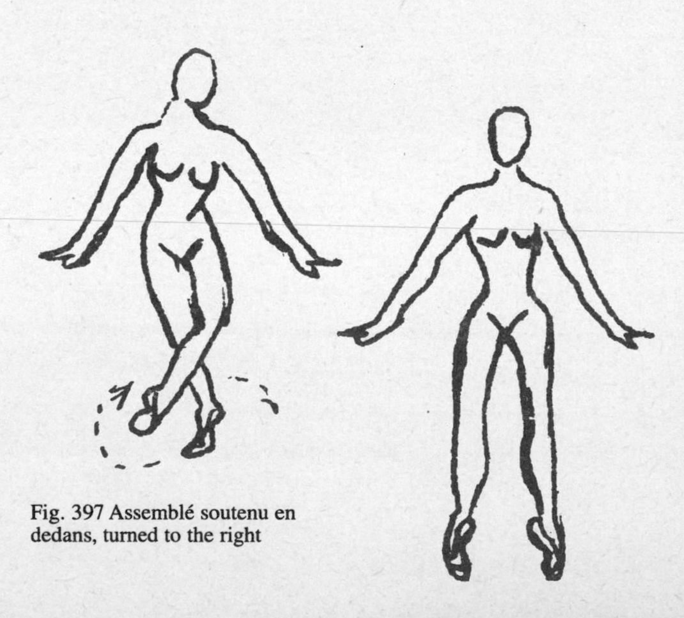

Fig. 397 Assemblé soutenu en dedans, turned to the right

Fig. 398 Échappé in second sur les pointes

11. Détourné d'Adage ending in first arabesque croisée

Without a pause, détourné d'Adage turning to the right; the left leg remains pointed in the same direction. As the body turns, the leg rotates. After the first half turn, the leg is in fourth back and remains in this position until the end of the movement.

During the turn, the right arm extends forward above shoulder height and the left is taken back, below and in line with the right, completing the position of first arabesque.

Continue to turn in first arabesque until the body faces the left wall; the position is now first arabesque croisée to the left.

12. Assemblé soutenu en dedans – échappé in second – relevé sur les pointes

The left leg begins rond de jambe en dedans, into assemblé soutenu en dedans turning to the right on full pointes. After the turn, lower the heels with the feet tightly closed in fifth, right foot front.

The arms rise through fifth and lower to position de repos (fig. 397).

Fast échappé to second on pointes and close in fifth, left foot front (fig. 398).

The arms open a little to demi-seconde and return to position de repos.

Relevé, immediately rising onto both pointes.

The arms are raised to fifth.

Lower the heels, feet in fifth, left foot front.

Lower the arms into position de repos.

Repeat the whole exercise with the left leg.